VOICES FROM
BRITAIN

VOICES FROM
BRITAIN

BROADCASTS FROM THE BBC 1939 – 1945

EDITED AND COMPILED BY

HENNING KRABBE

FONTHILL

Ariel between Wisdom and Gaiety. A sculpture by Eric Gill on Broadcasting House.

Frontispiece: Winston Churchill with Neville Chamberlain, early 1940.

Fonthill Media Limited
Fonthill Media LLC
www.fonthillmedia.com
office@fonthillmedia.com

First published in the United Kingdom 1947

British Library Cataloguing in Publication Data:
A catalogue record for this book is available from the British Library

ISBN 978-1-78155-174-5

Typeset in 10pt on 13pt Sabon LT Std
Printed and bound in England

Contents

Foreword to the 2013 Edition

Henning Krabbe was a Danish radio journalist who escaped to London where he broadcast to the Danish resistance from the BBC. After the war was over he took it upon himself to produce this edited edition of some of the most famous speeches. In this book is contained a complete history of the Second World War which being for oral transmission enjoys immediacy, vibrancy and passion. The BBC was an important organ in the body of resistance to Hitler all over Europe. These speeches embody a minute proportion of wartime output, but demonstrate the spirit of the time in a manner which no written histories can equal. This work was first published in 1947. This 2013 edition contains minor amendments, but essentially the speeches themselves are untouched. The original book had a handful of illustrations, extra photographs have been added to this new edition.

A German bomber over the Surrey Docks, London, September 1940.

Prelude

On 30 January 1933, Adolf Hitler became Chancellor of the German Reich. A revolution, utterly ruthless and oppressive, but of terrific power, swept Germany. In 1935 Hitler repudiated the military clauses in the Versailles Treaty and announced the reintroduction of conscription in Germany. In March, 1936, he occupied the Rhineland and started rearming on a gigantic scale. In the Spanish Civil War, begun in July, 1936, the new weapons were tried out. On 12 March 1938, Germany invaded Austria.

An immense enthusiasm filled the German people. Hitler had thrown off the yoke of the Versailles Treaty, and by the gigantic armament programme he had given work to every German. He had made National-Socialist Germany the greatest military power in Europe. Germany behind Hitler was marching towards world domination.

The first great European war crisis arose over Czechoslovakia, and it came to a head in September, 1938, the long-planned date when Germany would be ready for war. Neither England nor France were prepared, and on 15 September 1938 the British Prime Minister, Neville Chamberlain, flew to Berchtesgaden. Hitler's terms for the surrender of the Sudeten districts in Czechoslovakia had been accepted by the Czech Government under heavy pressure, when Chamberlain flew again to Germany and found that Hitler had increased his demands. It was on his return from Godesberg, at a time when war seemed inevitable, that Chamberlain, on 27 September, broadcast to the Empire, a speech which also marks the beginning of the European Service of the BBC.

NEVILLE CHAMBERLAIN TO THE EMPIRE

Broadcast to the British Empire, September 27 1938

Tomorrow Parliament is going to meet and I shall be making a full statement of the events which have led up to the present anxious and critical situation. An earlier statement would not have been possible when I was flying backwards and forwards across Europe, and the position was changing from hour to hour, but today there is a lull for a brief time, and I want to say a few words to you, men and women of Britain and the Empire, and, perhaps, to others as well.

First of all I must say something to those who have written to my wife or myself in these last few weeks, to tell us of their gratitude for my efforts and to assure us of their prayers for my success. Most of these letters have come from women — mothers or sisters of our own countrymen; but there are countless others besides, from France, from Belgium, from Italy, even from Germany; and it has been heart-breaking to read of the growing anxiety they reveal and their intense relief when they thought, too soon, that the danger of war was past. If I felt my responsibility heavy before, to read such letters has made it seem almost overwhelming. How horrible-fantastic-incredible it is that we should be digging trenches and trying on gasmasks here because of a quarrel in a far-away country between people of whom we know nothing. It seems still more impossible that a quarrel which has already been settled in principle should be the subject of war. I can well understand the reasons why the Czech Government have felt unable to accept the terms which have been put before them in the German Memorandum, yet I believe, after my talks with Herr Hitler, that if only time were allowed it ought to be possible for the arrangements for transferring the territory that the Czech Government has agreed to give to Germany to be settled by agreement under conditions which would assure fair treatment to the population concerned.

You know already that I have done all that one man can do to compose this quarrel. After my visits to Germany I have realised vividly how Herr Hitler feels that he must champion other Germans, and his indignation that grievances have not been met before this. He told me privately — and last night repeated publicly — that after this Sudeten German question is settled, that is the end of Germany's territorial claims in Europe.

After my first visit to Berchtesgaden I did get the assent of the Czech Government to proposals which gave the substance of what Herr Hitler wanted, and I was taken completely by surprise when I got back to Germany and found that he insisted that the territory should be handed over to him immediately, and immediately occupied by German troops, without previous arrangements for safeguarding the people within the territory who were not Germans or did not want to join the German Reich. I must say that I find this attitude unreasonable. If it arises out of any doubts that Herr Hitler feels about the intentions of the

Czech Government to carry out their promises and hand over the territory, I have offered on behalf of the British Government to guarantee their words, and I am sure the value of our promise will not be underrated anywhere.

I shall not give up the hope of a peaceful solution, or abandon my efforts for peace as long as any chance for peace remains. I would not hesitate to pay even a third visit to Germany if I thought it would do any good; but at this moment I see nothing further that I can usefully do in the way of mediation.

Do not be alarmed if you hear of men being called up to man the anti-aircraft defences, or ships; these are only precautionary measures such as a government must take in times like these, but they do not necessarily mean that we have determined on war, or that war is imminent. However much we may sympathise with a small nation confronted by a big and powerful neighbour, we cannot in all circumstances undertake to involve the whole British Empire in war simply on her account. If we have to fight, it must be on larger issues than that. I am myself a man of peace to the depths of my soul; armed conflict between nations is a nightmare to me. But if I were convinced that any nation had made up its mind to dominate the world by fear of its force I should feel that it must be resisted. Under such a domination life for people who believe in liberty would not be worth living. But war is a fearful thing, and we must be very clear before we embark on it that it is really the great issues that are at stake, and that the call to risk everything in their defence, when all the consequences are weighed, is irresistible.

For the present I ask you to wait as calmly as you can for the events of the next few days. As long as war has not begun there is always hope that it may be prevented. And you know that I am going to work for peace to the last moment.

. . . . .

Neville Chamberlain British ambassador Nevile Henderson, German foreign minister Joachim von Ribbentrop and Adolf Hitler, Munich, 15 September 1938.

On 29 September Chamberlain and Daladier met Hitler and Mussolini at Munich. Neither Czechoslovakia nor Russia took part in the Conference. The agreement reached meant the virtual dismemberment of Czechoslovakia, but so great was the relief of the British people that war had been avoided, that Chamberlain, on his return, was received with an enthusiasm such as had never been accorded to any British Prime Minister. Few saw the position in its true light. Among the voices who spoke against him was that of a man who was to play a decisive part in the history of the war. Winston Churchill's great speech in Parliament on 5 October was a denunciation, not only of the Munich Agreement, but of the policy which Britain had been pursuing for a number of years.

CHURCHILL ON THE MUNICH AGREEMENT

House of Commons, October 5 1938

I will begin by saying what everybody would like to ignore or forget but which must nevertheless be stated, namely, that we have sustained a total and unmitigated defeat, and that France has suffered even more than we have. The utmost my right hon. Friend the Prime Minister has been able to secure by all his immense exertions, by all the great efforts and mobilisation which took place in this country, and by all the anguish and strain through which we have passed in this country, the utmost he has been able to gain for Czechoslovakia in the matters which were in dispute has been that the German dictator, instead of snatching the victuals from the table, has been content to have them served to him course by course.

We really must not waste time after all this long debate upon the difference between the positions reached at Berchtesgaden, at Godesberg and at Munich. They can be very simply epitomised, if the House will permit me to vary the metaphor. £1 was demanded at the pistol's point. When it was given, £2 were demanded at the pistol's point. Finally, the dictator consented to take £1 17s. 6d. and the rest in promises of goodwill for the future.

I will say this, that I believe the Czechs, left to themselves and told they were going to get no help from the Western Powers, would have been able to make better terms than they have got after all this tremendous perturbation; they could hardly have had worse.

All is over. Silent, mournful, abandoned, broken, Czechoslovakia recedes into the darkness. She has suffered in every respect by her association with the Western democracies and with the League of Nations, of which she has always been an obedient servant.

I venture to think that in the future the Czechoslovak State cannot be maintained as an independent entity. I think you will find that in a period of

Oulton Torchbearers FC

Fixtures 2016/17

September
Sat 3rd	A Christchurch FC
TBC	A Destiny FC (KO TBC)
Sat 10th	H Bradford Gateway FC
Sat 17th	A New Life Hull FC
Sat 24th	A Holbeck FC

October
Sat 1st	*FA CHALLENGE CUP (KO 2PM)*
Sat 8th	A Mowbray CCFC
Sat 15th	A AFC Huddersfield
Sat 29th	A York Elim FC

November
Sat 5th	A Acomb Gateway United FC
Sat 12th	A Working Wonders FC
Sat 19th	H Destiny FC
Sat 26th	H Christchurch FC

January
Sat 7th	A Bowling Eagles FC
Sat 14th	H St Pauls Pilgrims FC
Sat 21st	H Mowbray CCFC
Sat 28th	H AFC Huddersfield

February
Sat 4th	*YCFL CUP*
Sat 11th	A St Pauls Pilgrims FC
Sat 18th	H York Elim FC
Sat 25th	H Acomb Gateway United FC

March
Sat 4th	*YCFL CUP*
Sat 11th	H Working Wonders FC
Sat 18th	A Bradford Gateway
Sat 25th	*YCFL CUP*

April
Sat 1st	H New Life Hull FC
Sat 8th	H Bowling Eagles FC

May
Sat 5th	*YCFL Trophy Final*
Sat 12th	*YCFL Cup Final*

Kick off times 10:30am (unless stated)
Cup Matches in italics more details TBC

time which may be measured by years, but may be measured only by months, Czechoslovakia will be engulfed in the Nazi régime. But we cannot consider the abandonment and ruin of Czechoslovakia in the light only of what happened only last month. It is the most grievous consequence of what we have done and what we have left undone in the last five years—five years of futile good intentions, five years of eager search for the line of least resistance, five years of uninterrupted retreat of British power, five years of neglect of our air defences. Those are the features which I stand here to expose and which marked an improvident stewardship for which Great Britain and France have dearly to pay. We have been reduced in those five years from a position of security so overwhelming and so unchallengeable that we never cared to think about it. We have been reduced from a position where the very word "war" was considered one which could be used only by persons qualifying for a lunatic asylum. We have been reduced from a position of safety and power—power to do good, power to be generous to a beaten foe, power to make terms with Germany, power to give her proper redress for her grievances, power to stop her arming if we chose, power to take any step in strength or mercy or justice which we thought right—reduced in five years from a position safe and unchallenged to where we stand now.

When I think of the fair hopes of a long peace which still lay before Europe at the beginning of 1933 when Herr Hitler first obtained power, and of all the opportunities of arresting the growth of the Nazi power which have been thrown away, when I think of the immense combinations and resources which have been neglected or squandered, I cannot believe that a parallel exists in the whole course of history. So far as this country is concerned the responsibility must rest with those who have had the undisputed control of our political affairs.

They neither prevented Germany from rearming, nor did they rearm ourselves in time. They quarrelled with Italy without saving Ethiopia. They exploited and discredited the vast institution of the League of Nations and they neglected to make alliances and combinations which might have repaired previous errors.

We are in the presence of a disaster of the first magnitude which has befallen Great Britain and France. Do not let us blind ourselves to that. The system of alliances in Central Europe upon which France has relied for her safety has been swept away.

But it is not a question only of losing influence in Europe. It goes far deeper than that. You have to consider the character of the Nazi movement and the rule which it implies. The Prime Minister desires to see cordial relations between this country and Germany. But never will you have friendship with the present German Government. There can never be friendship between the British democracy and the Nazi power, that power which spurns Christian ethics, which cheers its onward course by a barbarous paganism, which vaunts the spirit of aggression and conquest, which derives strength and perverted pleasure from persecution, and uses, as we have seen, with pitiless brutality the threat of murderous force. That power cannot ever be the trusted friend of the British democracy.

What I find unendurable is the sense of our country falling into the power, into the orbit and influence of Nazi Germany, and of our existence becoming dependent on their goodwill or pleasure. It is to prevent that that I have tried my best to urge the maintenance of every bulwark of defence—first, the timely creation of an Air Force superior to anything within striking distance of our shores; secondly, the gathering together of the collective strength of many nations; and thirdly, the making of alliances and military conventions, all within the Covenant, in order to gather together forces at any rate to restrain the onward movement of this power. It has all been in vain. Every position has been successively undermined and abandoned on specious and plausible excuses.

An effort at rearmament, the like of which has not been seen, ought to be made forthwith, and all the resources of this country and all its united strength should be bent to that task. If one tithe of the cheers lavished on this transaction of Czechoslovakia had been given to the small band of Members, who were endeavouring to get timely rearmament set in motion, we should not now be in the position in which we are. I remember for two years having to face, not only the Government's deprecation, but their stern disapproval.

I do not grudge our loyal, brave people, who were ready to do their duty no matter what the cost, who never flinched under the strain of last week—I

Adolf Hitler in his element, 1938.

do not grudge them the natural, spontaneous outburst of joy and relief when they learned that the hard ordeal would no longer be required of them at the moment; but they should know the truth. They should know that there has been gross neglect and deficiency in our defences; they should know that we have sustained a defeat without a war, the consequences of which will travel far with us along our road; they should know that we have passed an awful milestone in our history, when the whole equilibrium of Europe has been deranged, and that the terrible words have for the time being been pronounced against the Western democracies: "Thou art weighed in the balance and found wanting." And do not suppose that this is the end. This is only the beginning of the reckoning. This is only the first sip, the first foretaste of a bitter cup which will be proffered to us year by year unless by a supreme recovery of moral health and martial vigour, we arise again and take our stand for freedom as in the olden time.

. . . . .

On 15 March 1939, Hitler tore up the Munich Agreement and made an end of Czechoslovakia.

The invasion of Prague was later described by an eyewitness.

THE INVASION OF PRAGUE

Peter Smollett, Home Service, March 14 1941

On the night of March 14 1939, between nine and ten o'clock, I was sitting in the news room of a Prague paper waiting for my calls to London to come through. Calls and telegrams began to come in from other parts of Bohemia. "Riots in Brno ... Nazis are beating up Czechs and Jews," a provincial correspondent had just phoned through from the south. Another message from the north read: "German armoured cars have crossed the border and are tearing through Moravska Ostrava."

Under our windows, German students, recently arrived from the Reich as tourists were strutting about, giving the Nazi salute and terrorising Czechs in the heart of their own capital.

Just then London came through and I told them what I had heard. The sub-editor cut me short and said: "No more scare stuff tonight, they won't believe a word of it here. They say Munich settled the whole dirty business and Hitler promised Chamberlain personally to leave Czechoslovakia alone." I wondered. Perhaps they had better information in London after all.

At eleven the Foreign Editor took me aside and said, "Things look very bad. The Nazis are broadcasting atrocity stories now. They say German students are being murdered in the streets of Prague. I think they are preparing to march in to 'protect their blood brothers.' You'd better go out and see for yourself. Apart from a few hooligans molesting Jews in the cafés everything is quiet."

I went home to bed. At 4.20 the 'phone rang. A broken voice came through. It said: "Listen, they will be here in the morning. Hitler has got to work on Hacha and made him sign away the Republic. I was just on to the Broadcasting Station. They are going to announce it at five. They have told the people to maintain law and order when the German tanks drive in ... They'll cross the border at Melnik at six. Our troops will be confined to barracks and must surrender their arms before midday. I'll try to make for Poland. Perhaps you can send some money to me in Warsaw. It's all over."

Well, so it was true after all. It had to be. This man who had rung me had never given a wrong story to a paper in his life. I sent a flash to London, dressed, and went downstairs.

The charwomen were scrubbing the floor in the hall, the chairs stood upside down on the tables and the night porter was adding up some figures. The place was chilly and full of dismal smells.

I felt sick. I told the lift-boy the news, and he searched my face to make sure I wasn't drunk. Then he said, "But . . . you have guaranteed to protect us after we gave in at Munich. Surely you will declare war now."

I didn't answer. I rang a few Czech friends and one or two anti-Nazi refugees to warn them they had better hide. I knew they were bound to be on the Gestapo black list.

Dawn broke at seven, and workers and office girls could be seen hurrying to their jobs. Snow was falling now and some of the people were laughing as they slogged along.

I ordered breakfast and sat in the restaurant waiting for another personal call to London.

The big ground-floor windows gave you a full view of St. Wenceslas Square, the Piccadilly Circus of Prague. Suddenly the loud-speakers began to blare out warnings to the public. These loud-speakers had been rigged up in the streets a few months ago when the city was celebrating the hundredth anniversary of the Czech Youth Movement. Now they admonished the nation to mourn in silence. They repeated the familiar interval signal and again and again said: "Citizens, remain calm, there is nothing you can do. Don't resist the German troops." It was eerie. I went up to my room. My balcony looked out on to the Square. So I took up my position to watch the saddest spectacle of my life:

An endless column of open cars, dirty grey juggernauts, mud-splashed, with frozen snow clotted on the windscreens, robot-like figures of men sitting in them with empty faces of stone under grey steel helmets and goggles, light machine guns held between their knees, pointing upward towards the roof tops and windows and sideways at the crowds which lined the streets. Little motor-cycles dashing ahead to clear the path and here and there a tank, an armoured car, a lorry with infantry. Suddenly the whole column stopped. Just a couple of hundred yards up the road a tank had come stuck. It had not broken down; it had had to stop. For between it and the other cars the people had suddenly surged forward and formed a barricade of human bodies, civilians in black coats and yellow macintoshes, men and women, even children. There they stood, solidly facing the German tank, holding up the invader—even if only for a moment. There they stood, holding each other by the hand and sang the "Hroma Peklo," the age-old song of Slav defiance, hummed in secret by the Czechs while they lived under the tyranny of the Habsburgs.

> Thunder and hell, your rage is in vain,
> The Slav tongue shall live—our name will remain.

> So long as our hearts for the nation will beat,
> We don't care how many Germans we meet.

> Even if they're as numerous as devils in hell,
> God will protect us.

They cried it into the faces of the conquerors. "Thunder and hell, your rage is in vain," the refrain rose up from the streets—and the low grey clouds poured snow down on to the square of St. Wenceslas. The commanding officer of the German tank column called for the police. The Czech police had to push back the Czech people, and the loud-speakers cried: "Citizens, remain calm, avoid bloodshed." The women shouted at the Germans: "Clear out, you swine, this is our country; we'll kick you out before you know it." The police struggled with the crowd; some of them tore off their uniforms and joined the people. But the people were unarmed.

The tanks pushed on. In the centre of the square they crossed over from the left to the right side of the road and drove on in the same direction, thus proving even in this small detail that Prague was now part of Germany, where traffic runs on the right side of the road.

Half an hour later the Horst Wessel song was sung in the streets of Prague. There was nothing more to see—I had seen enough ...

. . . . .

The last months before the outbreak of the European war were marked by rapid manoeuvring for position, by new aggression and by desperate attempts to preserve the peace. Fascist Italy, which had conquered Abyssinia, and established the Franco régime in Spain, now invaded Albania. Britain, who had been unable to save Czechoslovakia, gave unilateral guarantees to Poland, to Rumania, to Greece, without having secured an agreement with Russia. The all-important Anglo-Russian military talks in Moscow, in the summer, failed, not only because of twenty years of hostility and distrust, but because the Allies were unwilling to grant the requests which Russia deemed indispensable for her defence: the occupation of the three small Baltic States and of bases in Finland. Further, Poland refused to let Russian soldiers fight on Polish soil.

On 22 August the German Foreign Minister, von Ribbentrop, went to Moscow to sign a Non-Aggression Pact between Germany and Soviet Russia.

The way was open for Hitler. Always profuse in assurances, he declared: "We have decided to conclude a pact which excludes the use of force by either side for all eternity. It is a final decision. Russia and Germany fought one another in the world war, and both were losers by that. This will not happen again."

The German-Russian Non-Aggression Pact was Russia's Munich. It gave her 22 months' respite; after that she had to bear alone, for nearly three years, the onslaught of the German armies on the Continent.

On 1 September Germany invaded Poland without a declaration of war. On 3 September Britain presented a two-hour ultimatum to Germany, expiring at 11 a.m. That day England and France declared war on Germany.

Of all the nations who became involved in the war against the Axis powers only England and France did not wait till they were attacked, but took up arms against Hitler's Germany.

CHAPTER I

The Beginning

September, 1939—May, 1940

At 11.15 on Sunday morning, 3 September 1939, the Prime Minister, Neville Chamberlain, broadcast to the British people.

BRITAIN'S DECLARATION OF WAR

Broadcast to the British Empire, September 3 1939

I am speaking to you from the Cabinet Room at 10 Downing Street. This morning the British Ambassador in Berlin handed the German Government a final Note stating that, unless we heard from them by 11 o'clock that they were prepared at once to withdraw their troops from Poland, a state of war would exist between us. I have to tell you now that no such undertaking has been received, and that consequently this country is at war with Germany.

You can imagine what a bitter blow it is to me that all my long struggle to win peace has failed. Yet I cannot believe that there is anything more or anything different that I could have done and that would have been more successful.

Up to the very last it would have been quite possible to have arranged a peaceful and honourable settlement between Germany and Poland, but Hitler would not have it. He had evidently made up his mind to attack Poland whatever happened, and although he now says he put forward reasonable proposals which were rejected by the Poles, that is not a true statement.

The proposals were never shown to the Poles, nor to us, and, though they were announced in a German broadcast on Thursday night, Hitler did not wait to hear comments on them, but ordered his troops to cross the Polish frontier. His action shows convincingly that there is no chance of expecting that this man will ever give up his practice of using force to gain his will. He can only be stopped by force.

Neville Chamberlain broadcasting to the Nation, Sunday 3 September 1939.

We and France are today, in fulfilment of our obligation, going to the aid of Poland, who is so bravely resisting this wicked and unprovoked attack on her people. We have a clear conscience. We have done all that any country could do to establish peace. The situation in which no word given by Germany's ruler could be trusted, and no people or country could feel themselves safe, has become intolerable. And now that we have resolved to finish it, I know that you will all play your part with calmness and courage. At such a moment as this the assurances of support that we have received from the Empire are a source of profound encouragement to us.

Now may God bless you all. May He defend the right. It is the evil things that we shall be fighting against—brute force, bad faith, injustice, oppression and persecution—and against them I am certain that the right will prevail.

. . . . .

In the evening, H.M. King George VI spoke to the British Empire from Buckingham Palace.

THE KING TO HIS PEOPLES

Broadcast to the British Empire, September 3 1939

In this grave hour, perhaps the most fateful in our history, I send to every household of my peoples, both at home and overseas, this message, spoken with the same depth of feeling for each one of you as if I were able to cross your threshold and speak to you myself.

For the second time in the lives of most of us we are at war. Over and over again we have tried to find a peaceful way out of the differences between ourselves and those who are now our enemies. But it has been in vain. We have been forced into a conflict. For we are called, with our allies, to meet the challenge of a principle which, if it were to prevail, would be fatal to any civilised order in the world.

It is the principle which permits a State, in the selfish pursuit of power, to disregard its treaties and its solemn pledges; which sanctions the use of force, or threat of force, against the sovereignty and independence of other States. Such a principle, stripped of all disguise, is surely the mere primitive doctrine that might is right; and if this principle were established throughout the world, the freedom of our own country and the whole British Commonwealth of Nations would be in danger. But far more than this—the peoples of the world would be kept in the bondage of fear, and all hopes of settled peace and of the security of justice and liberty among nations would be ended.

This is the ultimate issue which confronts us. For the sake of all that we ourselves hold dear, and of the world's order and peace, it is unthinkable that we should refuse to meet the challenge.

It is to this high purpose that I now call my people at home and my peoples across the seas, who will make our cause their own. I ask them to stand calm, firm, and united in this time of trial. The task will be hard. There may be dark days ahead, and war can no longer be confined to the battlefield. But we can only do the right as we see the right, and reverently commit our cause to God. If one and all we keep resolutely faithful to it, ready for whatever service or sacrifice it may demand, then, with God's help, we shall prevail.

May He bless and keep us all.

. . . . .

The entry into the war of the peoples of the British Commonwealth was described in a radio chronicle.

THE EMPIRE'S ANSWER

Home Service, October 6 1939

At the moment when the people of Britain heard their Prime Minister telling them they were at war with Germany, his voice was heard in all parts of the British world. Britain had accepted the Nazi challenge. The Empire's answer was swift as the news flashed around the world.

The declaration sped to the Mediterranean from the fortress of Gibraltar in the west, to the island of Cyprus in the east. Malta wears a peaceful air. In the grand harbour of Valetta, gaily painted boats sail to and fro. But behind rises the capital, guarded by its many forts. Malta is ready.

Down to the glittering Atlantic flew the news, to the Gambia, Sierra Leone, and the Gold Coast. The Governor of the Gold Coast had ordered mobilisation. Within a day and a night all territorial troops had reported for duty.

The news flashed to Nigeria, to St. Helena, lonely Ascension Island and to weather-beaten Tristan da Cunha, the most isolated outpost in the world. Then to South Africa.

At Table Bay is heard the noise of riveters and hammers as the labourers work at full pressure to complete Cape Town's six-million pound harbour, planned for the eventuality of the closing of the Mediterranean. To all its people the message of war brings home the urgent importance of the responsibility that lies upon South Africa to man her coast defences, and to keep open the vital trade routes to the Eastern Seas.

South Africa is at war!

On 7 September, the Prime Minister, General Smuts, addressed the House of Assembly: "The House, which was free to have decided otherwise, takes a stand for the defence of freedom and the destruction of Hitlerism and all it implies. The aim of the Union is to assist in the destruction of a system which is seeking to impose on the world a domination of violence and force.

Beyond the meadows of the dairy country, the orchards and the veld. beyond Basutoland, Bechuanaland, Swaziland, is Southern Rhodesia, the land of the lion and the waterfalls.

When Great Britain went to war on September 3, Rhodesia also went to war.

Northward now past North Rhodesia, past the great lakes of Nyasaland, Tanganyika, and Uganda into Kenya. That same weekend hundreds of husbands and sons are trekking into Nairobi from far up country. Their womenfolk take over control of the firms.

British Somaliland is ready. The people of Mauritius, Zanzibar, Seychelles, lovely islands of the Indian Ocean, are quiet, loyal and prepared.

India, September 3. His Excellency the Viceroy broadcast to the Indian people: "In a cause such as this I am confident that the whole-hearted sympathy and support of all this great country, whether British India or the Indian States, will be forthcoming without distinction of classes, creed, race, or political party. I am confident that, on a day on which all that is most precious and most significant in the civilisation of the modern world stands in peril, India will make a contribution on the side of human freedom as against the rule of force and will play a part worthy of her place among the great nations and historic civilisations of the world."

India is awake and armed. Far beyond her own coasts, her troops are on guard with her friends and allies at Aden, Suez and Singapore, entries to the ocean of Eastern Africa, Arabia and Australia, as well as of India.

The fighting men of the Punjab and Rajput lands are ready. Over two hundred of the great Princes of India have offered their men, their money and their swords. From the Himalayas to the sea India is awake.

Eastward to Burma, to the rich plains and the golden pagodas. From Burma southward to the tea plantations of Ceylon, across the sunstricken Indian Ocean, through the hazardous Straits of

Malacca along the coast of Malaya, to the capital of the Straits Settlements and one of the keypoints of defence in the East, the stronghold of Singapore. Radio carried the news through city streets and sultans' palaces, lonely rubber estates and tin mines throughout the peninsula.

Eastward of Singapore is the South China Sea, whose waves beat against the shores of the once-wild lands of Sarawak and North Borneo, and whose currents carry liner, tramp and navy vessels towards China. Over the South China Seas in the late afternoon, the news flashed to the isolated island-port of Hong-Kong.

South-east of Hong-Kong is the Pacific Ocean. Out of the Pacific rise the reefs of Papua in the setting sun. The lights are beginning to shine along the wooded coast of Australia.

It is a cold night in the Southern capitals. The families are gathered round the fire after Sunday tea, listening for news from twelve thousand miles away. Before eight there is a significant message: "All officers and ratings to report to their ships at once!" We debate its meaning in terms of peace and war. The announcement is repeated. Suddenly we hear "Daventry Chamberlain Downing Street," and then the grave voice of Mr Chamberlain: ". . . and consequently this country is at war." We listen in tense silence to the end. "It is evil things we shall be fighting." Two Anzac sons turn to their father. "I suppose we shall be fighting too, Dad." "We'll soon know." The radio breaks in. "In approximately an hour we shall broadcast the Prime Minister of Australia, Mr Menzies."

Rt. Hon. R. G. Menzies: "It is my melancholy duty to inform you officially that in consequence of a persistence of Germany in her invasion of Poland, Great Britain has declared war upon her, and that, as a result, Australia is also at war. No harder task can fall to the lot of a democratic leader than to make such an announcement. Great Britain and France, with the co-operation of the British Dominions, have struggled to avoid this tragedy. They have, as I

The Australian War Cabinet in session, September 1939. R. G. Menzies third from right.

firmly believe, been patient. But in the result their efforts have failed, and we are therefore, as a great family of nations, involved in a struggle which we must at all costs win and which we believe in our hearts that we will win. Australia is ready to see it through."

Little more than a thousand miles away across the starlit Tasman Sea lie the twin islands of New Zealand. Immediately the Government cabled the Secretary of State for Dominion Affairs to say that New Zealand stood by Britain's side.

At night the islands rise up dark out of the quiet Pacific—the Gilbert and Ellice Islands, the Solomon Islands and Fiji—beloved of writers of romantic tales.

South-east down the Pacific and round the tempestuous Horn you go from night to day, from tropical heat to freezing cold. In the bleak Falkland Islands, scene of one of the greatest naval battles of the century, the news arrived at six-fifteen.

North-west from the Falklands, following the green coast of South America, we find British Guiana.

Only a little way north-eastward in the Atlantic lies the Island of Trinidad, and northward now runs our line. past the West Indies, Barbados, the Windward and Leeward Islands, Jamaica, the Bahamas, the islands of flowers and sugar cane. Wooded British Honduras is left far to the west. Over the cold grey Atlantic our path runs straight to Canada. Canada's answer to the challenge is told in the words of an ex-officer.

On Friday, September 1, Canadians are heading southward from their summer homes. The armies of tourists and holidaymakers are saying goodbye to summer, and preparing to buckle down to another year's work.

In this mood struck the announcement of war. It came in the form of a statement from the Prime Minister that a state of emergency existed. In the drawing of a breath, Canada had turned from peace to war. By Sunday night, a full week before Canada's parliamentary declaration, the young men of the militia and air force, and the old soldiers of the last war, the men of Ypres, Vimy, Passchendale and Amiens, were in touch with their units.

Six days later, true to his promise to submit the decision of war to Parliament, Mr Mackenzie King stood amidst his Government on Parliament Hill at Ottawa and heard his House of Commons echo with the thunder of a nation's assent.

Rt. Hon. W. L. Mackenzie King: "There comes a time in the affairs of men when they must prepare to defend not only their homes but their tenets of faith and humanity on which their Churches, their Governments, and their very civilisation are founded."

Through the Gulf of St. Lawrence and across the Cabot Strait lies the island of Newfoundland, famous for its fishing banks, the most ancient colony in the Empire.

From all parts of the world the peoples of the Empire have answered the challenge. Now from London comes the voice of the Secretary of State for Dominion Affairs, the Right Hon. Anthony Eden:

William Lyon Mackenzie-King.

"Now we have spanned the earth, and have listened to the voices of statesmen and citizens in many lands that make up the British Commonwealth. We have heard the response of a great Empire to a great cause, a cause which is as much that of the small nation and the humblest citizen as it is of the greatest association of free peoples the world has ever known. What is the answer which the peoples of the British Empire has given? What is the spirit which breathes life into each one of these messages, that have come to us tonight from across the Seven Seas? It can be simply stated.

"We all share a determination that the rule of violence must cease, that the perpetual menace to the freedom of nations, small and great, must be removed, so that the peoples of the world may once more be -able to live their own lives in security and peace.

"To achieve this, we of the British Empire are prepared to devote the whole of our strength. Sacrifices will be demanded of us. We are resolved in calmness and with fortitude to make them. We are not fighting to preserve an old world, but to build a new.

"All human progress is a record of man's endeavour to outlaw the rule of force. This is a war to redeem hope, to give the peoples of the world a chance to live and breathe, to free our children from the haunting dread that shadows our own time, to create for them a future where moral and spiritual values shall prevail. Twenty years ago we thought that we had won such a victory. This time—God willing—we shall not fail.

"We cannot live for ever armed to the teeth, or at the mercy of the next act of robber violence. No country should have to say to itself: 'Shall I be the next victim of attack, or shall I be lucky enough to gain six months' respite while someone else is gobbled up?'

"In each of the many lands to which you have travelled in thought tonight the inspiration is the same. It is freedom; the oldest, the most hallowed, the most vital of our traditions; our fairest earthly fame.

"It is the hall-mark of civilisation; it carries with it a tolerance, a restraint, a willingness to live and let live.

"To preserve that freedom for ourselves, to gain it for others, to create out of present wars an understanding and enduring peace, is the task to which we have set our hand.

"A family of peoples united in faith and in purpose, we will not, we cannot, fail."

· · · · ·

Meanwhile, the Polish army was fighting desperately against overwhelming German forces. The Polish Ambassador in London, Count Raczynski, spoke on 9 September about Poland's struggle.

THE WAR IN POLAND

Home Service, September 9 1939

Germany attacked Poland suddenly and without any declaration of war on Friday, September 1 in the early hours of the morning. This date will go down in history as a day of shame for the aggressors and as the opening of a new chapter in the life of Europe.

Since that day my country has been incessantly battered by practically the whole of the German army, and continuously bombed by its entire air force. Immense mechanised columns were launched against Poland simultaneously from the west in a powerful frontal attack, from the north through East Prussia, and from the south through Slovakia, which has been previously overpowered by the Germans. The Polish Army was outnumbered from the very beginning and exposed to relentless attacks from the air. In spite of that the soldiers of Poland are fighting steadfastly, displaying the bravery that was expected from them by everyone knowing the traditions of the Polish Army.

Why do men of many nations declare their support for the Polish cause? Because there never was a clearer case of unprovoked aggression than that of September 1. No complicated quarrels divided us from Germany. On the contrary, we had a solemn non-aggression pact with the Third Reich, valid until 1944. The one excuse invented by the fertile brain of the German Fuehrer was the alleged maltreatment of the German minority in Polish lands. The excuse is poor and the accusation slander. All who knew the position of the German minority in Poland stand amazed at the impudence of German mendacity. The day of aggression was fixed by the enemy beforehand with ruthless precision. It was known to be planned for the beginning of September, and some excuse or other had to be found by that time.

It seems the simplest thing that could be done to defend the homes of Poland against a cruel and unscrupulous aggressor. And yet, by doing it, Poland turned a new leaf in recent European history. For Poland was the first nation which dared to defy Hitler's challenge and meet his attack with fire. This act of courage, which has already cost Poland the lives of many of her best sons, and the devastation of some of her provinces and towns, was a great service rendered to all the free nations of the world. The time was bound to come when the Nazi methods of extortion would meet with strong resistance. But the fact is that Poland was the first nation to do it, and she accepted an unequal struggle rather than join in the ranks of those who allowed themselves to be victims of Nazi blackmail.

Poland today is determined to carry the struggle on to the end and until a complete and decisive victory.

By the middle of September nearly all Western Poland had been overrun. On 17 September Russian forces entered Poland from the east and the Polish armies collapsed. In less than a month, Poland had disappeared from the map of Europe.

A winter followed of deceptive calm and of strange illusions in Britain and France. Very few were able to see the Finnish campaign as only a small preparatory move for the inevitable life-and-death struggle between Germany and Soviet Russia.

With the French Army manning the Maginot Line and the small British Expeditionary Force on the Belgian frontier, England and France were still thinking in terms of the First World War. Meanwhile the German war factories were working night and day, and the mighty armies of the enemy were preparing for the two campaigns by which Hitler reckoned to decide the war in the West.

So passed the winter. The British Navy bore the brunt of the war through these months, and it kept command of the sea. There were losses such as the aircraft carrier *Courageous*, and the battleship *Royal Oak*, but also brilliantly fought engagements as the battle of the River Plate against the *Graf Spee*.

On 9 April Germany launched her long-prepared aggression against Denmark and Norway.

KMS *Admiral Graf Spee* retired to Montevideo after being damaged by an action with British cruisers *Exeter*, *Ajax* and *Achilles* on 13 December 1939. Rather than face a larger British force, the battleship was scuttled.

Denmark was overrun within a day and capitulated under protest. Only the Danish sailors on the seas of the free world were able to take up the challenge of Germany. They did.

Norway declared war on the German aggressors, but the Luftwaffe decided the issue of the battle by its command of the Skagerak and of Norway's coastal waters. The small British reinforcements had to be withdrawn.

King Haakon and his Ministers left Norway with powers from their parliament to continue the struggle from England.

The Norwegian campaign had two very important results: it brought Winston Churchill to supreme power, and it gave the Allies the support during the rest of the war, of the great Norwegian merchant navy.

After the stormy debate in Parliament on 8 May, Neville Chamberlain resigned. He was succeeded by Winston Churchill, who formed a three-party coalition government, and at once set up a Ministry of Aircraft Production with the purpose of making the aircraft industry the largest in Britain.

On the same day as Winston Churchill came into power Germany had started her big offensive in the West.

CHAPTER II

The Battle of Britain

May—October, 1940

On 10 May Germany invaded Holland and Belgium. The attack was carried out with overwhelming mechanised forces and with large numbers of parachutists and glider-troops, and ruthless bombing of all points of resistance. The Dutch Army held out gallantly for four and a half days. The Queen succeeded in reaching England together with the Dutch Government.

The main German offensive came through the Belgian Ardennes. Here the German armoured forces crossed the Meuse between Sedan and Mézières, turning the flank of the Maginot Line. The British Army had to fall back towards the sea.

In France and Belgium the Germans were continuing their advance.

The German flying column turned northwards from Abbeville along the Channel coast with the purpose of annihilating the British Army that was falling back on Dunkirk.

England had reached the most dangerous moment in her history, but she did not waver. Hitler had reckoned neither with the fighting strength and working power of the British people, nor with Winston Churchill as its leader. In his speech in the House of Commons on 13 May, Churchill said, "I would say to the House as I said to those who have joined this Government: I have nothing to offer but blood, toil, tears and sweat. You ask what is our policy? I will say: It is to wage war by sea, land and air with all our might and with all the strength that God can give us, to wage war against a monstrous tyranny never surpassed in the dark lamentable catalogue of human crime. That is our policy. You ask, What is our aim? I can answer in one word: Victory—victory at all costs, victory in spite of all terror, victory, however long and hard the road may be.; for without victory, there is no survival. But I take up my task with buoyancy and hope. I feel sure that our cause will not be suffered to fail among men. At this time I feel entitled to claim the aid of all and I say, Come, then, let us go forward together with our united strength."

Britain responded to the call. The following day the Secretary of State for War, Mr Anthony Eden, made his appeal for "Local Defence Volunteers"—the "Home Guard," as it later came to be called.

THE FORMATION OF THE HOME GUARD

Anthony Eden, Home Service, May 14 1940

I want to speak to you tonight about the form of warfare which the Germans have been employing so extensively against Holland and Belgium, namely, the dropping of troops by parachute behind the main defensive lines.

The success of such an attack depends on speed. Consequently, the measures to defeat such an attack must be prompt and rapid. It is upon this basis that our plans have been laid. You will not expect me to tell you, or the enemy, what our plans are, but we are confident that they will be effective. However, in order to leave nothing to chance, and to supplement, from sources as yet untapped, the means of defence already arranged, we are going to ask you to help us in a manner which I know will be welcome to thousands of you. Since the war began the Government have received countless inquiries from all over the Kingdom from men of all ages who are for one reason or another not at present engaged in military service and who wish to do something for the defence of the country.

Anthony Eden in conversation with US Secretary of State, Cordell Hull.

Now is your opportunity. We want large numbers of such men in Great Britain who are British subjects between the ages of 17 and 65 to come forward now and offer their service in order to make assurance double sure. . . .

. . . . .

At the end of two weeks the number of volunteers had reached one and a half millions.

"Thought must be the harder: the heart the keener,
Courage shall be greater as our strength grows less."

"The Battle of Maldon," AD 993

On 19 May Churchill broadcast to the British people.

CHURCHILL'S FIRST BROADCAST AS PREMIER

Home Service, May 19 1940

I speak to you for the first time as Prime Minister in a solemn hour for the life of our country, of our Empire, of our Allies, and, above all, of the cause of Freedom. A tremendous battle is raging in France and Flanders. The Germans, by a remarkable combination of air bombing and heavily-armoured tanks, have broken through the French defences north of the Maginot Line, and strong columns of their armoured vehicles are ravaging the open country, which for the first day or two was without defenders. They have penetrated deeply and spread alarm and confusion in their track. Behind them there are now appearing infantry in lorries, and behind them, again, the large masses are moving forward. The regrouping of the French armies to make head against, and also to strike at, this intruding wedge has been proceeding for several days, largely assisted by the magnificent efforts of the Royal Air Force.

It would be foolish, however to disguise the gravity of the hour. It would be still more foolish to lose heart and courage or to suppose that well-trained, well-equipped armies numbering three or four millions of men can be overcome in the space of a few weeks, or even months, by a scoop, or raid of mechanised vehicles, however formidable. For myself, I have invincible confidence in the French Army and its leaders. Only a very small part of that splendid army has yet been heavily engaged; and only a very small part of France has yet been invaded. There is good evidence to show that practically the whole of the specialised and mechanised forces of the enemy have been already thrown into the battle; and we know that very heavy losses have been inflicted upon them. No officer or man, no brigade or division, which grapples at close quarters with the enemy, wherever encountered, can fail to make a worthy contribution to the general result. The armies must cast away the idea of resisting behind concrete lines or natural obstacles, and must realise that mastery can only be gained by furious and unrelenting assault. And this spirit must not only animate the High Command, but must inspire every fighting man.

In the air— often at serious odds hitherto thought overwhelming—we have been clawing down three or four to one of our enemies; and the relative balance of the British and German Air Forces is now considerably more favourable to us than at the beginning of the battle. In cutting down the German bombers we are fighting our own battle as well as that of France. My confidence in our ability to fight it out to the finish with the German Air Force has been strengthened by the fierce encounters which have taken place and are taking place. At the same time, our heavy bombers are striking nightly at the tap-root of German mechanised power, and have already inflicted serious damage upon the oil refineries on which the Nazi effort to dominate the world directly depends.

We must expect that as soon as stability is reached on the Western Front the bulk of that hideous apparatus of aggression which gashed Holland into ruin and slavery in a few days will be turned upon us. I am sure I speak for all when I say we are ready to face it; to endure it; and to retaliate against it—to any extent that the unwritten laws of war permit. There will be many men, and many women, in this island who when the ordeal comes upon them, as come it will, will feel comfort, and even a pride-that they are sharing the perils of our lads at the Front—soldiers, sailors and airmen, God bless them—and are drawing away from them a part at least of the onslaught they have to hear. Is not this the appointed time for all to make the utmost exertions in their power? If the battle is to be won we must provide our men with ever-increasing quantities of the weapons and ammunition they need. We must have, and have quickly, more aeroplanes, more tanks, more shells, more guns. There is imperious need for these vital munitions. They increase our strength against the powerfully armed enemy. They replace the wastage of the obstinate struggle; and the knowledge that wastage will speedily be replaced enables us to draw more readily upon our reserves and throw them in now that everything counts so much.

Our task is not only to win the battle—but to win the war. After this battle in France abates its force there will come the battle for our island—for all that Britain is, and all that Britain means. That will be the struggle. In that supreme emergency we shall not hesitate to take every step, even the most drastic, to call from our people the last ounce and the last inch of effort of which they are capable. The interests of property, the hours of labour, are nothing compared with the struggle for life and honour, for right and freedom, to which we have vowed ourselves.

I have received from the Chiefs of the French Republic, and in particular from its indomitable Prime Minister, M. Reynaud, the most sacred pledges that whatever happens they will fight to the end, be it bitter or be it glorious. Nay, if we fight to the end, it can only be glorious.

Haring received His Majesty's commission, I have formed an administration of men and women of every party and of almost every point of view. We have differed and quarrelled in the past; but now one bond unites us all—to wage war until victory is won, and never to surrender ourselves to servitude and shame, whatever the cost and the agony may be. This is one of the most awe-striking periods in the long history of France and Britain. It is also beyond doubt the most sublime. Side by side, unaided except by their kith and kin in the great Dominions and by the wide Empires which rest beneath their shield—side by side, the British and French peoples have advanced to rescue not only Europe but mankind from the foulest and most soul-destroying tyranny which has ever darkened and stained the pages of history. Behind them —behind us—behind the armies and fleets of Britain and France —gather a group of shattered States and bludgeoned races: the Czechs, the Poles, the Norwegians, the Danes, the Dutch, the Belgians—upon all of whom the long night of barbarism will descend, unbroken even by a star of hope, unless we conquer, as conquer we must; as conquer we shall.

Today is Trinity Sunday. Centuries ago words were written to be a call and a spur to the faithful servants of Truth and Justice: "Arm yourselves, and be ye men of valour, and be in readiness for the conflict; for it is better to perish in battle than to look upon the outrage of our nation and our altar. As the Will of God is in Heaven, even so let it be."

. . . . .

On 22 May Churchill flew to France to discuss the desperate situation with M. Reynaud and General Weygand. On the same day, the House of Commons, in less than three hours, passed the most far-reaching law in the history of British democracy, the Emergency Powers (Defence) Act, 1940. The Deputy Prime Minister, Mr Attlee, spoke in a broadcast about this new law.

CLEMENT ATTLEE ON THE EMERGENCY POWERS BILL

Home Service, May 22 1940

I am sure that you all realise that the war has reached a critical stage. A great battle is proceeding in the north of France. We cannot tell yet what will be the issue. The effects of the next few weeks, or even the next few days, will be vitally important. We cannot forecast what will be the enemy's next step. Whatever may be the difficulties and dangers which confront us, I know that you will meet them with the same calm courage and confidence which the British people have shown in the past. Our men at sea, on land, and in the air, have shown the bravery, devotion and skill which we expected of them. We must be worthy of them.

Today, on your behalf, Parliament has given to the Government full power to control all persons and property. There is no distinction between rich and poor, between worker and employer; between man and woman; the services and property of all must be at the disposal of the Government for the common task. This does not mean that everyone should give up what he is doing, or that everybody's property will immediately be seized. On the contrary; everyone should continue doing his or her ordinary work till other orders are given. But the Government now has the right to call upon any citizen to do the work that is most immediately required in the national interest. It has power to control any business, factory, mine, shop or bank, and to order it to be carried on in the way desired. It can take property of every kind.

Business engaged in munitions, aircraft and other industries essential for carrying on the war will be specially controlled, and excess profits duty will be at the rate of 100 per cent. These very wide powers will be exercised by the competent authority, which will in every sphere of activity be the appropriate Minister of the Crown. The direction of persons to perform services will be under the Minister of Labour, Mr Ernest Bevin.

. . . . .

ADDRESS BY ERNEST BEVIN, MINISTER OF LABOUR AND NATIONAL SERVICE

Home Service, May, 1940

This is the first time that I have had the opportunity of addressing the citizens of this country as Minister of Labour and National Service.

I was convinced from the beginning that the only argument that Hitler and the Nazi régime would understand would be that of overwhelming force. While this country has every right to be proud (indeed such a term cannot adequately express our feelings), it is thankful for the amazing courage, ability, and resourcefulness of our Navy, Air and Military Forces, Mercantile Marine, Trawler-Men, and all those who have been defending us. Their very courage has made an increasing demand upon us to preserve such wonderful manhood by equipping them with the weapons and materials necessary to enable them adequately to defend themselves and the country.

Consequent upon the break-through in France, I am sure no one in this country is surprised, or taken aback, at the act of the Government in coming forward and asking Parliament for the drastic powers which were passed last week. We cannot afford to take any chance. We will not, by the exhibition of any weakness, risk the lives of the men in the Forces or the civilian population at home. Many of the powers which have been taken have devolved upon me, as Minister of Labour, a heavy and grave responsibility; for I have the most difficult material to handle—that is, the human being. The insured population who are working day by day to produce the sinews of war and the necessary commodities for the nation, number no less than fifteen million. But the Act goes beyond the insured population; it covers all persons; and it will become my duty, as the demands are made upon me by the Service and Supply Departments, to find the necessary personnel to man the factories, workshops and mines, to do agricultural work, and to serve in the armed Forces.

In this great task I believe that I shall have the confidence, co-operation and sympathy of all those who will be affected. My first task has been to create the most efficient machine I possibly could—the pivot of which is the Production Council. It is this Council which must balance the supply of material and the plant available, and have knowledge of the strategy of war, together with the available labour supply, so that the whole national effort may move in a cohesive and disciplined way. In my own particular Department I have established a Labour Supply Board, the members of which will not only have experience of Labour, but of production and lay-out. Machine tools and other instruments of production are more valuable than gold at the present time. We cannot afford that they shall be idle for one moment. Our effort will be to link and check up one against the other, to ensure that there shall be no idle material or idle moments.

I must try to secure for the people who are to work on the various shifts, adequate transport facilities and all the amenities that I can to make their lives as comfortable as possible. To that end I have established Regional Councils.

It is vital that every form of training shall be brought into being. I must pool many of the munition factories for the purpose of employment, so that the personnel is not merely employed by one factory, but by the State, and then the services of the worker can be switched from one factory to another as necessity requires. I am glad that the question of rates of pay and conditions has been settled. I want to preserve the joint negotiating machinery—additions to this machinery will probably be necessary in the interests of the State—but I want to ask the Trade Unions, and the employers, to operate this joint machinery in this crisis as trustees on behalf of the State.

The Minister of Mines has the task of increasing coal production. The men must be brought back to the mines and at the same time a feeling of security created. Many men have left the industry, and I am anxious that they shall volunteer to return to assist the country now. No employee should leave the mines; your place is to remain there; and if you are tempted to seek employment in other industries—don't. Stick to the production of coal, which is so vital at this moment.

In the countryside, in conjunction with the Minister of Agriculture, we are reviewing the whole situation. More food must be produced. The stigma of servitude and the old traditional conception of the farm worker must go, and go immediately. Interchangeability between the rural population must be secured. I know it can be done—without compulsion.

Time does not permit me to deal more fully with this comprehensive proposal. Therefore the question I want to put to you all is this: Do you want to secure victory? Do you want to smash Hitlerism? Do you want to do it in quick time? Do you want your husbands, sons and brothers home by your sides following their normal civilian life? They did not want to go to war; they are performing a disagreeable duty. You can give your answer in the field, factory and workshop. We have heard a great deal about the "Fifth Column." I want another column— a National Service Column—resolved to win, and win quickly, and which will deal drastically with anyone who seeks to hinder us in our great crusade. Always remember that when these boys do come back, it is not words they want or empty promises; it is for us, in the designing of our scheme, to keep an eye on the conditions which have been created to see that they can readily be adapted to reabsorb them into normal civil life and to secure the ushering in of a better age, based upon social justice and peace.

A call for arms was made by the Minister of Supply, Mr Herbert Morrison.

HERBERT MORRISON: A CALL FOR ARMS

Home Service, May, 1940

Today we are at grips with a more deadly menace than has threatened the people of these islands since Philip's great Armada set out to storm our coasts and bring us under his yoke. Indeed, the present threat looms nearer. Today there is not "time enough to finish the game and beat the enemy too"; there is time for nothing but an intense concentrated effort of muscle and mind and will. It must begin now.

We have our backs to the wall surely enough. You know that, all of you—men and women. Our heavy industry has been replanned. Stocks of raw materials have been built up. Thousands of men have worked long intense hours on the benches and machines at the Royal Ordnance and other factories. I am fully mindful of their devoted effort. But the enemy had a long start in the race to prepare for this war; and we have not yet caught him up. You read and hear, day by day, how our magnificent young men are striving to buy with their flesh and blood the time that we need to build up our strength. At this hour of all hours we at home cannot take things easy; for whether we have deserved it or not, the men of our fighting forces are struggling to give us time to make up leeway, to their undying honour. What are we going to do with it—with this crucial time that we yet possess? The question answers itself. We, men and women alike, are going to work our fingers to the bone for our sons and for their future. We are going to do whatever lies in our power to match, and to be worthy of, the sacrifices that are being made for us. We are going to cut down our leisure, cut down our comfort, blot out of our thought every private and sectional aim. We must! We are going to guard our health and strength; for these are assets in the fight. But we shall be careless of all else—thinking only of arms for the men, arms for victory, arms for liberty.

Whatever our past mistakes have been, there are, deep within us, stronger and richer than we ourselves may realise, resources of mind and spirit that cannot be matched by the feverish propaganda-fed, self-deluded spirit of our enemies. Let us count on that. Let us refresh ourselves with the realisation of our own strength; and let us express that strength now—tonight— tomorrow, every moment, until victory is won. "Work" is the call. "Work at war speed." Go to it.

. . . . .

On 27 May the Belgian Army surrendered. The hard-pressed, encircled British Expeditionary Force succeeded in holding a bridgehead round Dunkirk, and on 29 May the evacuation began.

Here are three descriptions from the days of Dunkirk, one by a Royal Air Force pilot (broadcast in 1942), one by "Bartimeus," about the British Army, and the last by the Minister of Shipping, Mr Ronald Cross, about the work of the British Merchant Navy during the evacuation.

In 1940 Herbert Morrison was appointed the first Minister of Supply by Winston Churchill.

DOG-FIGHTS OVER DUNKIRK

Royal Air Force Pilot, Home Service, 1942

The days of Dunkirk when France finally capitulated are far behind, but some of those battles, high up in the sky, have left vivid memories in the minds of many pilots.

I can remember the glorious spring evenings when the sun was going down, lighting the evening with a deep red glow, and our squadron pilots stood outside the dispersal huts, still in full flying kit, waiting for the release from readiness which came only with the darkness.

We stood there at nights watching the endless stream of heavy bombers droning south-eastwards over our heads; the ground crews who stayed by to check our machines after dark, ready for the next day, were counting the heavy chaps as they went out, and a throaty cheer went up as the hundredth ploughed majestically on its way, becoming ever smaller until it was lost to sight in the darkness of the east.

Donald and Ralph, my two friends, were beside me—we were a little apart from the rest, and Ralph spoke: "Things are pretty grim over there. I wonder when our turn will come?"

"Old boy, don't you worry," replied Donald. "We'll be in the thick of it in the next fortnight; the French won't be able to hold out, and then we will have to fight like hell to stop the darned Huns from walking into London."

For once I was quiet—amazed at the sudden turn of events on the Continent. War up to now had been just one terrific thrill, but now it was looming up into a threat against Britain, which appeared likely to end in complete and utter disaster.

It was dark and the telephone rang, but instead of the expected release from readiness we were ordered to eat our supper as soon as possible and to arrange for six pilots to be at readiness throughout the night. I was second off the ground that night, so I rolled up in my flying clothes and tried to get some sleep. It was after midnight when someone shook me. It was my Commanding Officer.

"What's the matter, sir? Are we going to France?" I asked. "No," came the quiet reply. "The Army is evacuating from France. It has started already, and we are going to cover the withdrawal."

I tried to snatch some more sleep but it was useless. All the time through my mind rushed those few words—"the army is evacuating." I was relieved when at last it was time to go out to our aircraft.

It was just growing light. Our Spitfires were standing looking slim and eager to get into the air. There was no wind; a white mist was drifting over the Fens and it was rather chilly and damp.

In this war, by far the most vivid memories are not those of fierce fighting, or firing guns or aeroplanes—they are of quiet moments at the beginning and end of each day when dawn is breaking or night falls. Some of the sunrises that I have seen have been among the most beautiful moments that I can remember.

At last we were airborne, packed in tight formation. Already in the east the sun was rising over the North Sea. It was all so strangely beautiful, and yet, ever present, was the thought of the grim and dangerous work soon to be done.

Our job was to patrol at 20,000 feet to stop the German Messerschmitt fighters from protecting their bombers below. Underneath us three squadrons of Hurricanes were to deal with the bombers. Above us another squadron of Spitfires patrolled.

We flew straight into the sun on the way over, and I could see very little as my eyes watered with the strain of looking for the enemy. We passed Dunkirk—a huge column of black smoke rising straight up to 15,000 feet, hardly moving in the still morning. For thirty-five minutes we flew round inside France when suddenly we saw black dots a little to the north-east of us. We rushed towards them, and in a moment the sky was full of whirling aircraft, diving, twisting and turning. Too late, both squadrons realised that we were friends, and although we had not opened fire at one another, it was going to be almost impossible to form up again in our own squadrons.

Round and round we went looking for our sections. I noticed queer little straight lines of smoke very close together as I flew past them. Suddenly I woke up. "Someone is shooting; it's smoke from incendiary bullets," I told myself. I gave up all thought of trying to find the rest of the squadron and started searching all round. The French Curtis flying across my front: I went closer to have a look at them. Wow! They weren't Frenchmen, they were Huns—Me.109s. They turned towards me, and went into a steep climbing turn. Up the two of them went. Gosh! How they could climb! They were level with me about 400 yards away; another one joined them. I could see no other aeroplanes by now—just the three 109s.

It was a question of who could get the most height first. I opened the throttle as far as it could go. I was gaining a little now, and with my more manoeuvrable Spitfire I could turn inside the 109s. Slowly in giant spirals, we gained height, and suddenly I found myself up sun of all three of them. I quickly turned the other way, and they lost me.

Round I came at 26,000 feet, and I was right behind the last 109—too far away to shoot yet. I gained—oh, so slowly!—but sure enough, I was gaining. How long could I wait before firing or before the leader saw me? He was weaving about pretty violently now looking for me. At last, I was in range. I pressed the button, and my whole aeroplane shuddered as the eight guns fired. Nothing happened. The 109 flew on. Then suddenly there was a flash, and the enemy aircraft flicked over: his port aileron had been hit and had come off. He jettisoned his hood to jump out, and I turned quickly when showers of tracer bullets flew past me. I had forgotten the other two 109s. I flicked over into a quick turn and lost them. It was getting late, and I had not much petrol left, so I dived for home.

Re-arming a Hurricane.

Oil tanks burn at Dunkirk.

I crossed the Channel at 500 feet. It was an amazing sight, with hundreds of vessels of all sorts of shapes and sizes ploughing backwards and forwards across the Straights. It was incredible to see little 15-ft. motor-boats sailing steadily across towards Dunkirk, unarmed, to face the fury and strength of the Huns.

At last my aerodrome came in sight. I landed just as another of the squadron was touching down. By ten o'clock three more pilots had returned, making five in all, and we sat down to a terrific breakfast of bacon and eggs and champagne (the chef had produced the champagne). One by one the pilots came back; practically everyone had shot something down, and many had been damaged slightly.

There were only two pilots missing, and our squadron score was 10 destroyed, three probables, and three damaged. By four o'clock it was known that the two missing pilots had not got back to this country. They were Donald and Ralph, my two friends. We never heard of them again.

HOW THE B.E.F. CAME BACK

"Bartimeus," June 1 1940

All day Thursday I spent at the South Coast base where the ships that brought off the British Expeditionary Force came and went. For days and nights there had been a continuous stream to and fro of transports and destroyers, sloops and trawlers, coming back crammed to their utmost capacity with men. They had been shelled by coastal batteries and bombed almost ceaselessly from the air. They embarked thousands from beaches, men wading out to their armpits to reach the boats. They embarked tens of thousands from piers and jetties, beating off the German bombers with their guns while the troops climbed on board. They told me of men of a Scottish Regiment who scrambled on to a destroyer's fo'c'sle in the last stages of exhaustion and joined in the fusillade with their rifles, trying to shoot down the low-diving bombers.

I was on board a destroyer in the afternoon that had just come back from the beaches. She had had fifty-two bombs dropped over her, and she had lost her captain, but she came back crammed to capacity. They had only one boat, a whaler, to bring them off—the other boats were splintered and out of action. What seemed to worry them most was the behaviour of a German bomb that burst in shallow water on the bottom of the sea and deluged the whole ship and everybody on board with grey mud. The gunner's mate was the happiest man on board; he'd found a Bren gun abandoned on the beach; it was full of sand, and he spent a blissful afternoon taking it to bits and oiling it and putting it together again. "We'll have some fun with this tomorrow," he said. "I've never owned a Bren gun before." I remember, while I watched his fingers fiddling with the complicated mechanism, a little sloop came past us, having just landed her troops, on her way to take in fuel. Her funnel and upper works were so riddled with bomb splinters that she looked like a colander. Her captain's face was covered with bandages, leaving a hole for one eye, and he was conning his ship with that. But they were all laughing at our baptism of grey mud—so my hosts laughed back at their splinter-holes, though that grey mud rankled rather—and wished them luck next trip.

I sailed in another destroyer about midnight. We riddled our way through the minefields till we were nearing Dunkirk. The oil tanks were still blazing furiously, and there was an occasional sound of distant gunfire. Once a shell landed in one of those blazing tanks and a huge red glare blazed up almost to the zenith. It died down again and the moon came out from behind a cloud, giving the sea and the sky a queer semblance of peace, in contrast to the blazing inferno ashore. It was light enough to see the outlines of the town buildings still standing, black against the glare of the fire, and the vast clouds of smoke billowing away eastward. And it was light enough to see, assembled on the whole length of the Mole, thousands of men of the British Expeditionary Force waiting patiently for embarkation. There was a French destroyer already alongside filled up with men. There was a trawler alongside also; but she had been sunk by bombs, and only her masts and funnels were above water. The White Ensign was still flying bravely at her mast-head. We went alongside between them, watched by those thousands of patient eyes under the shrapnel helmets. It was nearly low water, and the top of the Mole was level with our bridge. Scaling ladders were lowered, and down they came as fast as fully-equipped, fully-armed men could climb. This was no army in defeat: they looked in magnificent fettle, ruddy and burly, and wearing full equipment; dog-tired after fighting rear-guard action day and night for a week, as well they might be; but for the matter of that, the Navy that was bringing them off could have done with a bit of sleep themselves. Every man as he got on board grinned and said, "Thank God," and settled down quietly on a bit of deck space, like a well-behaved school-treat packing into a motor-coach for an outing.

Then a bomber appeared overhead and we opened fire. A French destroyer came in through the entrance, firing as she came, followed by a British destroyer. The embarkation continued as calmly as if nothing out of the ordinary was happening. German shells began bursting at the end of the Mole with methodical regularity, hitting nobody—about one a minute. The English Channel was an extraordinary sight as the sun rose. It looked something like Henley Regatta, as if every craft on the south coast that could float was heading for Dunkirk and the beaches to finish off the job. There were barges and wherries, yachts and launches, little boats in tow of bigger boats, and presently up through the middle of them came an overseas convoy from the other side of the world. There was something about them—their bright Red Ensigns, and their guns cocked up on the stern, that suggested an indescribable jauntiness. On board our ship, every inch of space on deck and below was crammed with men. Already many of them were asleep where they lay, and many of those who slept had smiles on their faces as if they were congratulating themselves, even in sleep, on a good job well done. They were just a haphazard collection of men from any number of regiments, but in physique and bearing they might have been the pick of the crack of an army. We all felt happier that morning than we had felt since the war started. "Give us a chance for a wash and brush-up and a bit of sleep, and let's get back: we've got Jerry beat." That is, in effect, what they all said.

THE MERCHANT NAVY AT DUNKIRK

The Minister of Shipping, Mr Ronald Cross, Home Service

I want to tell you something of the almost unbelievable work which the Merchant Navy did.

You will remember that the merchant seaman is not subject to Naval discipline; he's not a trained, fighting man—he's just a British volunteer who, the moment the call came, gave his skill, his energy, perhaps his life, to go and fetch the lads from the other side.

There was only one port left—and that was badly damaged by the bombardment—and so we had to use the beaches as well; and that meant collecting at a moment's notice all the small craft we could lay our hands on—ships of such shallow draught that they could get close inshore. The ports from the Humber to Southampton were scoured: something like a thousand small craft took part. We shall never have a complete list of all the vessels employed. Never was there a more fantastic armada: never did a weirder collection of vessels set sail.

There were pleasure steamers; coasting craft; tugs; trawlers; drifters; motor-boats and launches; and motor and sailing barges. Every tug from the River Thames was taken. At our request the Royal National Lifeboat Institution sent twenty lifeboats, collected from ports between Lowestoft and Poole. A father and his son would take their yacht across from some south coast port without a word to anybody, and bring it back full of troops. There was a Deal boatman who took his motor-boat across with several open rowing boats in tow, and brought them all back full of troops. And so I could go on, giving you story after story of these brave volunteers.

But, alas: great military operations cannot be carried through without loss. The First Lord of the Admiralty has announced the losses of Naval vessels: in addition to these losses about twenty merchant craft met a glorious and self-sacrificing end. But let us be thankful that when we compare these losses with the wonderful work that was done—335,000 Allied troops carried to British ports in that little time, and under constant fire—we can only conclude that these losses were remarkably light. Not a soldier, French or British, who could get to the coast was left behind.

But it is the work of the men themselves that grips our imagination, inspires our minds and tears at our heart-strings. On the map it looks a short distance from Dunkirk to our south-east ports, but only the tiny craft could go direct. In order to avoid minefields and enemy bombardment the round trip for the rather larger vessels from Dover to Dunkirk was at times as much as 160 miles. The men on these ships worked till they dropped. Without sleep, often without proper meals, for days on end they passed to and fro the Channel, under attack by enemy batteries on the coast, by enemy aircraft with bombs and machine-guns, by enemy submarines and motor torpedo boats. In order to provide relief for these exhausted men a pool of seamen was arranged by the Shipping Federation at Dover, and an appeal was made for volunteer deck and engine-room officers. These appeals were magnificently answered.

Engineers are now almost all engaged on work of national importance—if not at sea, they are making munitions or building aircraft or ships. We appealed to engineers with sea-going experience to come for a few days to help in evacuating the troops. We could promise them nothing but fatigue and danger. But the response was immediate. Within a few hours we received the names of about three hundred and fifty volunteers. There was one factory at Ramsgate on which we called for volunteers; and the appeal was "You are going into hell—you'll be bombed and machine-gunned; will you fetch back the lads?" There was no hesitation. Tools were thrown down and the engineers went straight down to ships they had never seen before, and within twenty minutes had sailed to the bomb-ridden waters of Dunkirk.

In spite of the constant strain and danger to which they were subjected, the officers and crews were always ready to take on an extra risk. One ship was badly holed above the water line, and would almost certainly have sunk had the sea got rougher; nevertheless, without hesitation, the crew turned her round and went back to Dunkirk once more. Two others were so badly damaged that they could not be sent out again—the crews immediately volunteered to take on another ship. On occasion, on the Dunkirk beaches, it was difficult to get the troops out from the shore to the ships, and merchant seamen swam ashore with lines in order to help the troops to embark.

The acts of courage and devotion were so numerous, and so many of them have not been reported, that it would be invidious for me to select any here. Just as a sample I might instance an elderly Chief Officer, well past the prime of life. Three of the four boats on his ship had been blown away by bombs: he spent the whole night in the remaining boat picking up survivors from another ship which had been sunk. He and his boat's crew rescued a hundred and fifty men. In consequence of his efforts he became partially paralysed in the legs, but was perfectly ready to make another trip if called upon.

And then there was a young Fifth Engineer who had only been four months
at sea. After a long series of bomb attacks he came up from the engine-room to
get a breath of fresh air. An officer suggested that he might man a Bren gun for
a short time. A German bomber swung round to repeat an attack—the young
engineer released a burst of fire and brought the bomber down into the sea—
and then returned to the engine-room to get on with his job.

. . . . .

On 3 June the evacuation had been completed; 250,000 British soldiers, no
less than four-fifths of the British Expeditionary Force, had been rescued
together with 112,000 Allied troops, but all their equipment had been lost.

This is how an eye-witness described the arrival of the British soldiers:

"All of them were tired, some were completely exhausted, but the most
amazing thing was that practically every man was reasonably cheerful. Even
when a man was obviously on the verge of collapse from sheer fatigue, you
could still tell by his eyes that his spirit was irrepressible. On the station I
watched the men climbing into the long waiting trains. It was astounding to
walk along carriage after carriage full of soldiers, and to find in each one—
silence. For most of the men were fast asleep where they sat. In the dining cars
they sat most of them with their heads on the tables or on pillows improvised
out of their equipment. Train after train puffed out of the station, all full of
sleeping men. All the way along the line, the people of England stood at the
level-crossings and in the back gardens, to wave to them. And so the men of the
B.E.F. came home."

A striking feature in the BBC broadcasts of the summer, 1940, were the Sunday
postscripts by J. B. Priestley. In the first of them, on 5 June, he looked back on
the evacuation of Dunkirk.

J. B. PRIESTLEY: DUNKIRK

Home Service, June 5 1940

I wonder how many of you feel as I do about this great battle and evacuation
of Dunkirk. The news of it came as a series of surprises and shocks, followed
by equally astonishing new waves of hope. It was all, from beginning to end,
unexpected. And yet now that it's over, and we can look back on it, doesn't it
seem to you to have an inevitable air about it—as if we had turned a page in the
history of Britain and seen a chapter headed "Dunkirk" and perhaps seen, too,
a picture of the troops on the beach, waiting to embark?

And now that this whole action is completed, we notice that it has a definite shape, and a certain definite character. What strikes me about it is how typically English it is. Nothing, I feel, could be more English than this Battle of Dunkirk, both in its beginning and its end, its folly and its grandeur. It was very English in what was sadly wrong with it; this much has been freely admitted, and we are assured will be freely discussed when the proper moment arrives. We have gone sadly wrong like this before; and here and now we must resolve never, never to do it again. Another such blunder may not be forgiven us.

But having admitted this much, let's do ourselves the justice of admitting, too, that this Dunkirk affair was also very English (and when I say English I really mean British) in the way in which, when apparently all was lost, so much was gloriously retrieved. Bright honour was almost "plucked from the moon." What began as a miserable blunder, a catalogue of misfortunes and miscalculations, ended as an epic of gallantry. We have a queer habit—and you can see it running through our history—of conjuring up such transformations. Out of a black gulf of humiliation and despair, rises a sun of blazing glory. This is not the German way. They don't make such mistakes (a grim fact that we should bear in mind) but also—they don't achieve such epics. There is never anything to inspire a man either in their victories or their defeats; boastful when they are winning, quick to whine when threatened with defeat—there is nothing about them that ever catches the world's imagination. That vast machine of theirs can't create a glimmer of that poetry of action which distinguishes war from mass murder. It's a machine—and therefore has no soul.

But here at Dunkirk is another English epic. And to my mind what was most characteristically English about it—so typical of us, so absurd and yet so grand and gallant that you hardly know whether to laugh or to cry when you read about them—was the part played in the difficult and dangerous embarkation— not by the warships, magnificent though they were—but by the little pleasure steamers. We've known them and laughed at them, these fussy little steamers, all

J. B. Priestley at the
BBC microphone.

our lives. We have called them "the shilling sicks." We have watched them load and unload their crowds of holiday passengers—the gents full of high spirits and bottled beer, the ladies eating pork pies, the children sticky with peppermint rock. Sometimes they only went as far as the next seaside resort. But the boldest of them might manage a Channel crossing, to let everybody have a glimpse of Boulogne. They were usually paddle steamers, making a great deal more fuss with all their churning than they made speed; and they weren't proud, for they let you see their works going round. They liked to call themselves "Queens" and "Belles"; and even if they were new, there was always something old-fashioned, a Dickens touch, a mid-Victorian air about them. They seemed to belong to the same ridiculous holiday world as pierrots and piers, sand castles, palmists, automatic machines, and crowded, sweated promenades. But they were called out of that world, and—let it be noted—they were called out in good time and good order. Yes, these "Brighton Belles" and "Brighton Queens" left that innocent, foolish world of theirs—to sail into the inferno, to defy bombs, shells, magnetic mines, torpedoes, machine-gun fire—to rescue our soldiers. Some of them alas—will never return. Among those paddle steamers that will never return was one that I knew well, for it was the pride of our ferry service to the Isle of Wight—none other than the good ship "Gracie Fields," for she was the glittering queen of our local line, and instead of taking an hour over her voyage, used to do it, churning like mad, in forty-five minutes. And now never again will we board her at Cowes and go down into her dining saloon for a fine breakfast of bacon and eggs. She has paddled and churned away for ever. But now—look—this little steamer, like all her brave and battered sisters, is immortal. She'll go sailing proudly down the years in the epic of Dunkirk. And our great grand-children, when they learn how we began this war by snatching glory out of defeat, and then swept on to victory, may also learn how little holiday steamers made an excursion to hell and came back glorious.

. . . . .

On 10 June, Italy declared war on France and Britain. On the 14th the Germans entered Paris. Two days later the French Premier, M. Reynaud, resigned, and Marshal Pétain formed a new Government.

On 17 June, Marshal Pétain sued for peace. The same evening Winston Churchill broadcast to the British people.

The news from France is very bad, and I grieve for the gallant French people who have fallen into this terrible misfortune. Nothing will alter our feelings towards them or our faith that the genius of France will rise again. What has happened in France makes no difference to our actions and purpose. We have become the sole champions now in arms to defend the world cause. We shall do our best to be worthy of this high honour. We shall defend our island home, and with the British Empire we shall fight on unconquerable until the curse of Hitler is lifted from the brows of mankind. We are sure that in the end all will come right.

On the following evening Churchill, in another broadcast, gave a fuller account of the situation.

CHURCHILL: THE FRENCH DISASTER AND BRITAIN

Home Service, June 18 1940

I spoke the other day of the colossal military disaster which occurred when the French High Command failed to withdraw the Northern Armies from Belgium at the moment when they knew that the French front was decisively broken at Sedan and on the Meuse. This delay entailed the loss of fifteen or sixteen French divisions and threw out of action for the critical period the whole of the British Expeditionary Force. Our Army and 120,000 French troops were indeed rescued by the British Navy from Dunkirk, but only with the loss of their cannon, vehicles and modern equipment.

A fortnight ago I made it perfectly clear that whatever happened in France would make no difference to the resolve of Britain and the British Empire to fight on, "if necessary for years, if necessary alone." During the last few days we have successfully brought off the great majority of the troops we had on the lines of communication in France; and seven-eighths of the troops we have sent to France since the beginning of the war—that is to say, about 350,000 out of 400,000 men are safely back in this country.

We have, therefore, in this island today a very large and powerful military force. This force comprises all our best trained and our finest troops. We have under arms at the present time in this island over a million and a quarter men. Behind these we have the Local Defence Volunteers numbering half a million, only a portion of whom, however, are yet armed with rifles or other firearms. We have incorporated into our Defence Forces every man for whom we have a weapon. We expect very large additions to our weapons in the near future, and in preparation for this we intend forthwith to call up, drill and train further large numbers. Those who are not called up, or else are employed upon the vast business of munitions production in all its branches—and their ramifications are innumerable—will serve their country best by remaining at their ordinary work until they receive their summons. We have also here Dominions armies. The Canadians had actually landed in France, but have now been safely withdrawn, much disappointed, but in perfect order, with all their artillery and equipment. And these very high-class forces from the Dominions will now take part in the defence of the Mother Country.

Lest the account which I have given of these large forces should raise the question: Why did they not take part in the great battle in France? I must make it clear that, apart from the divisions training and organising at home, only 12 divisions were equipped to fight upon a scale which justified their being sent abroad. And this was fully up to the number which the French had been led to expect would be available in France at the ninth month of the war. The rest of our forces at home have a fighting value for home defence which will, of course steadily increase every week that passes. Thus, the invasion of Great Britain would at this time require the transportation across the sea of hostile armies on a very large scale, and after they had been so transported they would have to be continually maintained with all the masses of munitions and supplies which are required for continuous battle as continuous battle it will surely be.

Here is where we come to the Navy—and after all, we have a Navy. Some people seem to forget that we have a Navy. We must remind them. At the beginning of the last war, the Germans had a magnificent battle fleet, whereas now they have only a couple of heavy ships worth speaking of.

Therefore, it seems to me, that as far as seaborne invasion on a great scale is concerned, we are far more capable of meeting it today than we were at many periods in the last war and during the early months of this war, before our other troops were trained, and while the B.E.F. had proceeded abroad. Now, the Navy have never pretended to be able to prevent raids by bodies of 5,000 or 10,000 men flung suddenly across or thrown ashore at several points on the coast some dark night or foggy morning. The efficacy of sea-power, especially under modern conditions, depends upon the invading force being of large size. It has to be of large size, in view of our military strength, to be of any use. If it is of large size, then the Navy have something they can find and meet and, as it were, bite on. Now we must remember that even five divisions, however lightly equipped, would require 200 to 250 ships, and with modern air reconnaissance and photography it would not be easy to collect such an armada, marshal it, and conduct it across the sea without any powerful naval forces to escort it; and there would be very great possibilities, to put it mildly, that this armada would be intercepted long before it reached the coast, and all the men drowned in the sea or, at the worst, blown to pieces with their equipment while they were trying to land. We also have a great system of minefields.

It seems quite clear that no invasion on a scale beyond the capacity of our land forces to crush speedily is likely to take place from the air until our Air Force has been definitely overpowered. In the meantime, there may be raids by parachute troops and attempted descents of airborne soldiers. We should be able to give those gentry a warm reception, both in the air and on the ground, if they reach it in any condition to continue the dispute. But the great question is: Can we break Hitler's air weapon? We have a very powerful Air Force which has proved itself far superior in quality, both in men and in many types of machines to what we have met so far in the numerous and fierce air battles which have

The German Wehrmacht invades France, May 1940.

been fought with the Germans. Anyone who looks at the photographs which were published a week or so ago of the re-embarkation, showing the masses of troops assembled on the beach and forming an ideal target for hours at a time, must realise that the re-embarkation would not have been possible unless the enemy had resigned all hope of recovering air superiority at that time and at that place.

During the great battle in France, we gave very powerful and continuous aid to the French Army, both by fighters and bombers; but in spite of every kind of pressure we never would allow the entire metropolitan fighter strength of the Air Force to be consumed. This decision was painful, but it was also right, because the fortunes of the battle in France could not have been decisively affected even if we had thrown in our entire fighter force. That battle was lost by the unfortunate strategical opening, by the extraordinary and unforeseen power of the armoured columns and by the great preponderance of the German Army in numbers. Our fighter Air Force might easily have been exhausted as a mere accident in that great struggle, and then we should have found ourselves in a very serious plight. But as it is our fighter strength is stronger at the present time relatively to the Germans, who have suffered terrible losses, than it has ever been; and consequently we believe ourselves possessed of the capacity to continue the war in the air under better conditions than we have ever experienced before. I look forward confidently to the exploits of our fighter pilots—these splendid men, this brilliant youth—who will have the glory of saving their native land, their island home, and all they love, from the most deadly of all attacks.

There remains, of course, the danger of bombing attacks, which will certainly be made very soon upon us by the bomber forces of the enemy. It is true that the German bomber force is superior in numbers to ours; but we have a very large bomber force also, which we shall use to strike at military targets in Germany without intermission. I do not at all underrate the severity of the ordeal which lies before us; but I believe our countrymen will show themselves capable of standing up to it, like the brave men of Barcelona.

I have thought it right upon this occasion to give the country some indication of the solid practical grounds upon which we base our inflexible resolve to continue the war. There are a good many people who say, "Never mind. Win or lose, sink or swim, better die than submit to tyranny—and such a tyranny." And I do not dissociate myself from them. But I can assure them that our professional advisers of the three Services unitedly advise that we should carry on the war, and that there are good and reasonable hopes of final victory. We have fully informed and consulted all the self-governing Dominions, these great communities far beyond the oceans who have been built up on our laws and on our civilisation, and who are absolutely free to choose their course, but are absolutely devoted to the ancient Motherland, and who feel themselves inspired by the same emotions which lead me to stake our all upon duty and honour. We have fully consulted them, and I have received from their Prime Ministers, Mr Mackenzie King of Canada, Mr Menzies of Australia, Mr Fraser of New Zealand, and General Smuts of South Africa—that wonderful man, with his immense, profound mind, and his eye watching from a distance the whole panorama of European affairs—I have received from all these eminent men, who all have Governments behind them elected on wide franchises, who are all there because they represent the will of their people, messages couched in the most moving terms in which they endorse our decision to fight on, and declare themselves ready to share our fortunes and to persevere to the end. That is what we are going to do.

During the first four years of the last war the Allies experienced nothing but disaster and disappointment. That was our constant fear: one blow after another, terrible, losses, frightful dangers. Everything miscarried. And yet at the end of those four years the morale of the Allies was higher than that of the Germans, who had moved from one aggressive triumph to another, and who stood everywhere triumphant invaders of the lands into which they had broken. During that war we repeatedly asked ourselves the question: How are we going to win? and no one was able ever to answer it with much precision, until at the end, quite suddenly, quite unexpectedly, our terrible foe collapsed before us, and we were so glutted with victory that in our folly we threw it away.

We do not yet know what will happen in France or whether the French resistance will be prolonged, both in France and in the French Empire overseas.

The French Government will be throwing away great opportunities and casting adrift their future if they do not continue the war in accordance with their treaty obligations, from which we have not felt able to release them. You will have read the historic declaration in which, at the desire of many Frenchmen—and of our own hearts—we have proclaimed our willingness at the darkest hour in French history to conclude a union of common citizenship in this struggle. However matters may go in France or with the French Government, or other French Governments, we in this island and in the British Empire will never lose our sense of comradeship with the French people. If we are called upon to endure what they have been suffering, we shall emulate their courage, and if final victory rewards our toils they shall share the gains, aye, and freedom shall be restored to all. We abate nothing of our just demands; not one jot or tittle do we recede. Czechs, Poles, Norwegians, Dutch, Belgians have joined their causes to our own. All these shall be restored.

What General Weygand called the Battle of France is over. I expect that the Battle of Britain is about to begin. Upon this battle depends the survival of Christian civilisation. Upon it depends our British life and the long continuity of our institutions and our Empire. The whole fury and might of the enemy must very soon be turned on us. Hitler knows that he will have to break us in this island or lose the war. If we can stand up to him, all Europe may be free and the life of the world may move forward into broad, sunlit uplands. But if we fail, then the whole world, including the United States, including all that we have known and cared for, will sink into the abyss of a new Dark Age made more sinister, and perhaps more protracted, by the lights of perverted science. Let us therefore brace ourselves to our duties, and so bear ourselves that, if the British Empire and its Commonwealth last for a thousand years, men will still say, "This was their finest hour."

. . . . .

On 18 June Hitler and Mussolini met at Munich to agree on terms for France. But on that same day, while German troops were marching down the Champs Elysées, General de Gaulle made his famous appeal from London to all Frenchmen, not to give up hope, and to unite in resistance to the enemy.

GENERAL DE GAULLE'S APPEAL FOR RESISTANCE

European Service, June 18 1940

The leaders who, for many years past, have been at the head of the French armed forces, have set up a government.

Alleging the defeat of our armies, this government has entered into negotiations with the enemy with a view to bringing about a cessation of hostilities. It is quite true that we were, and still are, overwhelmed by enemy mechanised force, both on the ground and in the air. It was the tanks, the planes, and the tactics of the Germans, far more than the fact that we were outnumbered, that forced our armies to retreat. It was the German tanks, planes, and tactics that provided the element of surprise which brought our leaders to their present plight.

But has the last word been said? Must we abandon all hope? Is our defeat final and irremediable? To those questions I answer—No!

Speaking in full knowledge of the facts, I ask you to believe me when I say that the cause of France is not lost. The very factors that brought about our defeat may one day lead us to victory.

For, remember this, France does not stand alone. She is not alone. Behind her is a vast Empire, and she can make common cause with the British Empire, which commands the seas and is continuing the struggle. Like England, she can draw unreservedly on the immense industrial resources of the United States.

This war is not limited to our unfortunate country. The outcome of the struggle has not been decided by the Battle of France. This is a world war. Mistakes have been made, there have been delays and untold suffering, but the fact remains that there still exists in the world everything we need to crush our enemies some day. Today we are crushed by the sheer weight of mechanised force hurled against us, but we can still look to a future in which even greater mechanised force will bring us victory. The destiny of the world is at stake.

I, General de Gaulle, now in London, call on all French officers and men who are at present on British soil, or may be in the future, with or without their arms; I call on all engineers and skilled workmen from the armaments factories

General Charles de Gaulle.

who are at present on British soil, or may be in the future, to get in touch with me.

Whatever happens, the flame of French resistance must not and shall not die.

. . . . .

On 21 June Hitler received the French plenipotentiaries in Marshal Foch's railway carriage in the Forest of Compiègne and dictated his armistice terms.

In order to prevent the French fleet from falling into the hands of the enemy the British Navy immobilised a number of French capital ships (3 July, *Oran*: 8 July, *Dakar*). Churchill's foresight and faith were expressed in his broadcast on 14 July, the date of the national festival of France.

CHURCHILL ON BRITAIN AND FRANCE

Home Service, July 14 1940

During the last fortnight the British Navy, in addition to blockading what is left of the German Fleet and chasing the Italian Fleet, has had imposed upon it the sad duty of putting effectually out of action for the duration of the war the capital ships of the French Navy. These, under the Armistice terms, signed in the railway coach at Compiègne, would have been placed within the power of Nazi Germany. The transference of these ships to Hitler would have endangered the security of both Great Britain and the United States. We therefore had no choice but to act as we did, and to act forthwith. Our painful task is now complete. Although the unfinished battleship the *Jean Bart* still rests in a Moroccan harbour and there are a number of French warships at Toulon and in various French ports all over the world, these are not in a condition or of a character to derange our preponderance of naval power. As long, therefore, as they make no attempt to return to ports controlled by Germany or Italy, we shall not molest them in any way. That melancholy phase in our relations with France has, so far as we are concerned, come to an end.

Let us think rather of the future. Today is the fourteenth of July, the national festival of France. A year ago in Paris I watched the stately parade down the Champs Elysées of the French Army and the French Empire. Who can foresee what the course of other years will bring? Faith is given to us, to help and comfort us when we stand in awe before the unfurling scroll of human destiny. And I proclaim my faith that some of us will live to see a fourteenth of July when a liberated France will once again rejoice in her greatness and in her glory, and once again stand forward as the champion of the freedom and the rights of man. When the day dawns, as dawn it will, the soul of France will turn with comprehension and with kindness to those Frenchmen and Frenchwomen, wherever they may be, who in the darkest hour did not despair of the Republic.

In the meantime, we shall not waste our breath nor cumber our thought with reproaches. When you have a friend and comrade at whose side you have faced tremendous struggles, and your friend is smitten down by a stunning blow, it may be necessary to make sure that the weapon that has fallen from his hands shall not be added to the resources of your common enemy. But you need not bear malice because of your friend's cries of delirium and gestures of agony. You must not add to his pain, you must work for his recovery. The association of interest between Britain and France remains. The cause remains. Duty inescapable remains. So long as our pathway to victory is not impeded, we are ready to discharge such offices of goodwill towards the French Government as may be possible, and to foster the trade and help the administration of those parts of the great French Empire which are now cut off from captive France, but which maintain their freedom. Subject to the iron demands of the war which we are waging against Hitler and all his works, we shall try so to conduct ourselves that every true French heart will beat and glow at the way we carry on the struggle; and that not only France, but all the oppressed countries in Europe may feel that each British victory is a step towards the liberation of the Continent from the foulest thraldom into which it has ever been cast.

And now it has come to us to stand alone in the breach, and face the worst that the tyrant's might and enmity can do. Bearing ourselves humbly before God, but conscious that we serve an unfolding purpose, we are ready to defend our native land against the invasion by which it is threatened. We are fighting BY ourselves alone; but we are not fighting FOR ourselves alone. Here in this strong City of Refuge which enshrines the title-deeds of human progress and is of deep consequence to Christian civilisation; here, girt about the seas and oceans where the Navy reigns; shielded from above by the prowess and devotion of our airmen we await undismayed the impending assault. Perhaps it will come tonight. Perhaps it will come next week. Perhaps it will never come. We must show ourselves equally capable of meeting a sudden violent shock, or what is perhaps a harder test, a prolonged vigil. But be the ordeal sharp or long, or both, we shall seek no terms, we shall tolerate no parley; we may show mercy—we shall ask for none.

All depends now upon the whole life-strength of the British race in every part of the world and of all our associated peoples and of all our well-wishers in every land, doing their utmost night and day, giving all, daring all, enduring all—to the utmost—to the end. This is no war of chieftains or of princes, of dynasties or of national ambition; it is a War of peoples and of causes. There are vast numbers not only in this island but in every land, who will render faithful service in this War, but whose names will never be known, whose deeds will never be recorded. This is a War of the Unknown Warriors; but let all strive without failing in faith or in duty, and the dark curse of Hitler will be lifted from our age.

· · · · ·

By 2 July, orders were issued by the German High Command for the invasion of Britain, with ten German divisions to be put into action on British soil in ten days. Landing barges were concentrated along the north coast of France, Belgium and Holland. Complete air superiority was demanded from Goering, whose task it was first to paralyse the RAF and then to attack and neutralise the British Navy.

At the same time the huge Italian armies in Libya and Abyssinia were closing in on Egypt, and the Italian Navy controlled the Mediterranean. It was at this moment of supreme danger to Britain that Churchill took the decision to send off the only armoured land-forces in the country on the long voyage round the Cape. They reached Egypt just in time to hold the Italian drive on Suez.

All through July and the first week of August the Germans continued their preparations. On 8 August began the Battle of Britain. It has been divided into four phases, the first from 8-18 August, where the German attacks were mainly directed against ports and coastal aerodromes; the second from 24 August to 5 September, with attacks on inland aerodromes; the third stage from 6 September to 5 October, with the great air offensive against London; and finally the fourth stage from 6 October to 31 October, with the Luftwaffe in retreat and the daylight raids gradually giving way to increasing night bombing. In the whole period the number of German aircraft certainly brought down in daylight was 2,375, besides a large number of "probables." The RAF lost in all 375 pilots killed and 358 wounded.

It was in the House of Commons on 20 August that Churchill spoke the famous words about the Royal Air Force: "The gratitude of every home in our Island, in our Empire, and indeed throughout the world, except in the abodes of the guilty, goes out to the British airmen who, undaunted by odds, unwearied in their constant challenge and mortal danger, are turning the tide of the world war by their prowess and their devotion. Never in the field of human conflict was so much owed by so many to so few."

Little was spoken at the time by the pilots of the RAF. The following two descriptions by a Wing-Commander and a Squadron-Leader were broadcast about two years after the Battle of Britain had been fought and won.

THE BATTLE OF BRITAIN

A WING-COMMANDER SPEAKS

Home Service, 1942

In those days the only time we saw the pilots of other squadrons was at night after long hours at readiness, when we met in the bar for a quick one. So often just as one was becoming friendly with a pilot he would get shot down, and we would see him no more. Our Air Force term was, and still is, that So-and-so had "bought it." Meaning that he was dead, or at best lying wounded in some hospital.

When we met the Hun we mixed it good and proper; we generally waited for a moment or two until we were in the most favourable position before making the first attack. After the first attack it was every man for himself. There were nearly always many more Huns than ourselves. We whirled around, taking squirts at as many machines as possible; sometimes when they burst into flames the crew baled out or we were lucky enough to see where they hit the ground; then we were able to claim victories.

After the battle we would rush back to the drome, tell our stories to the Intelligence Officer, tell him to buck up and get through to the hospitals to find out if So-and-so had got any confirmed before he was shot down, and ask him to try and salvage something from the Hun wrecks.

Often at the height of the blitz, when we returned we could not remember what on earth had happened, not even what we had fired our guns at; one of the pilots in my Flight, fighting nine Messerschmitt 109s, swore that he had only fired his guns for a one-second burst, yet he had actually finished his ammunition, sixteen seconds' worth.

I do remember clearly seeing the Hun bombers, flying in tight mass formation, crossing the English coast, and thinking to myself that they were about to drop their bombs on my country, my friends, perhaps even my mother, and that I was in a Hurricane and that with God's will I could stop them. I dived to attack and

A ground crew to arm a Spitfire.

laughed as they broke formation; the crew of a Heinkel baled out; the others turned and ran, spraying me with tracer. Five bullet holes in my plane that time. Within the hour the ground crews had fixed it, and my plane was ready for action.

We always had a devil-may-care sort of happiness. Lying in the sun waiting at readiness, there were moments of great beauty; the colours in the fields seemed brightest and the sky the deepest blue just before taking off for a big blitz. At dusk everything became peaceful. We were all happy at the thought of another day accomplished, our Hurricanes standing silhouetted against the sky, looking strong and confident, the darkness hiding their patched-up paintwork. In the morning whilst it was still dark, the roar of the engines being tested woke us for another day's work.

A SQUADRON LEADER SPEAKS

A long time has passed since the Battle of Britain, and yet it seems only yesterday that we all crowded round the radiogram in the mess on the night of September 15th, and listened to the scores of the day's fighting—185 German aircraft destroyed, only 27 of ours missing.

When the Battle of Britain began I was stationed in the Midlands: our squadron was fresh and ready to go and have a crack at the Huns as they raided Dover and our Channel convoys, but days went by and we began to despair, feeling that we were to be left out of the show.

At last our chance came. On a hot September morning, Operations rang— "Squadron to go to F. at once."

Then at our new station the first time over the loud-speaker, "Squadrons scramble London 20,000 feet."

It all came so quickly. One instant I was asleep on the grass by my aeroplane; a short moment while fumbling fingers strapped me in my Spitfire—my inside felt cold and seemed to be turning over—then bumping across the aerodrome in formation. I do not know what happened after that until a queer artificial voice came over the radio, "Two hundred bandits crossing Dover flying north at 20,000 feet; some more very high up." The sky was empty, and everything below us seemed still, as if the world was asleep.

Then suddenly we saw them, a huge great rectangle of black bombers, ack-ack bursting all around them, and we were diving towards them. I remember a 110 flying across my nose so close that I saw the pilot looking at me. There were aircraft all around—bombers falling out of formation, black dots of fighters climbing and diving. Away on the left a long black trail of smoke and a blazing dot going straight down. Then it was all over, and I was back at the aerodrome. Excited pilots were recounting their experiences. I only realised then that I had fired my guns. I felt it had been a good day—little did I know that twice

Scramble!

more that day I would climb up over London, fight, and come home again. They were wonderful, weird, exciting days. Days when aircraft left beautiful curving vapour trails high in the sky, days when some of our friends took off and never came back, when others came back maimed and burnt, never to fight again. Days when the Germans at their bases back in France must have sat and wondered, when their High Command must have been appalled at their growing losses, until at long last into the bullying German mind there came the realisation that they had lost their first battle—the Battle of Britain.

> Be great in act, as you have been in thought;
> Be stirring as the time; be fire with fire;
> Threaten the threatener, and outface the brow
> Of bragging horror—
>
> Shakespeare: King John.

London was the main target of the Luftwaffe's powerful attacks by night and day, when Churchill broadcast on the Battle of Britain on 11 September.

CHURCHILL ON THE BATTLE OF BRITAIN

Home Service, September 11 1940

A great air battle is being fought out between our fighters and the German Air Force. Whenever the weather is favourable, waves of German bombers, protected by fighters, often three or four hundred at a time, surge over this island, especially the promontory of Kent, in the hope of attacking military and other objectives by daylight. However, they are met by our fighter squadrons and nearly always broken up; and their losses average three to one in machines and six to one in pilots.

This effort of the Germans to secure daylight mastery of the air over England is, of course, the crux of the whole war. So far it has failed conspicuously. It has cost them very dear.

On the other hand, for him to try to invade this country without having secured mastery in the air would be a very hazardous undertaking. Nevertheless, all his preparations for invasion on a great scale are steadily going forward. Several hundreds of self-propelled barges are moving down the coasts of Europe, from the German and Dutch harbours to the ports of Northern France; from Dunkirk to Brest; and beyond Brest to the French harbours in the Bay of Biscay.

Besides this, convoys of merchant ships in tens of dozens are being moved through the Straits of Dover into the Channel, dodging along from port to port under the protection of the new batteries which the Germans have built on the French shore. There are now considerable gatherings of shipping in the German, Dutch, Belgian and French harbours—all the way from Hamburg to Brest. Finally, there are some preparations made of ships to carry an invading force from the Norwegian harbours.

Behind these clusters of ships or barges, there stand very large numbers of German troops, awaiting the order to go on board and set out on their very dangerous and uncertain voyage across the seas. We cannot tell when they will try to come; we cannot be sure that in fact they will try at all; but no one should blind himself to the fact that a heavy, full-scale invasion of this island is being prepared with all the usual German thoroughness and method, and that it may be launched now—upon England, upon Scotland, or upon Ireland, or upon all three.

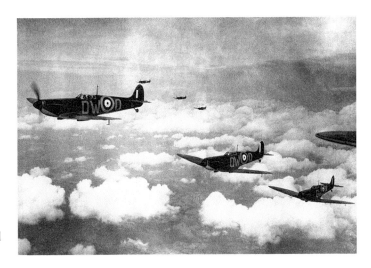

Spitfires of 610
Squadron based
at Biggin Hill.

If this invasion is going to be tried at all, it does not seem that it can be long delayed. The weather may break at any time. Besides this, it is difficult for the enemy to keep these gatherings of ships waiting about indefinitely, while they are bombed every night by our bombers, and very often shelled by our warships which are waiting for them outside.

Therefore, we must regard the next week or so as a very important period in our history. It ranks with the days when the Spanish Armada was approaching the Channel, and Drake was finishing his game of bowls; or when Nelson stood between us and Napoleon's Grand Army at Boulogne. We have all read about this in the history books; but what is happening now is on a far greater scale and of far more consequence to the life and future of the world and its civilisation than these brave old days of the past.

Every man and woman will therefore prepare himself to do his duty, whatever it may be, with special pride and care. Our fleets and flotillas are very powerful and numerous; our Air Force is at the highest strength it has ever reached; and it is conscious of its proved superiority, not indeed in numbers, but in men and machines. Our shores are well fortified and strongly manned, and behind them, ready to attack the invaders, we have a far larger and better equipped mobile Army than we have ever had before.

Besides this, we have more than a million and a half men of the Home Guard, who are just as much soldiers of the Regular Army as the Grenadier Guards, and who are determined to fight for every inch of ground in every village and in every street.

It is with devout but sure confidence that I say: Let God defend the Right.

Vapour trails from
a dogfight over
London.

These cruel, wanton, indiscriminate bombings of London are, of course, a part of Hitler's invasion plans. He hopes, by killing large numbers of civilians, and women and children, that he will terrorise and cow the people of this mighty imperial city, and make them a burden and an anxiety to the Government and thus distract our attention unduly from the ferocious onslaught he is preparing. Little does he know the spirit of the British nation, or the tough fibre of the Londoners, whose forbears played a leading part in the establishment of Parliamentary institutions and who have been bred to value freedom far above their lives. This wicked man, the repository and embodiment of many forms of soul-destroying hatred, this monstrous product of former wrongs and shame, has now resolved to try to break our famous island race by a process of indiscriminate slaughter and destruction. What he has done is to kindle a fire in British hearts, here and all over the world, which will glow long after all traces of the conflagration he has caused in London have been removed. He has lighted a fire which will burn with a steady and consuming flame until the last vestiges of Nazi tyranny have been burnt out of Europe, and until the Old World—and the New—can join hands to rebuild the temples of man's freedom and man's honour upon foundations which will not soon or easily be overthrown.

Our fighting forces know that they have behind them a people who will not flinch or weary of the struggle—hard and protracted though it will be; but that we shall rather draw from the heart of suffering itself the means of inspiration and survival, and of a victory won not only for ourselves but for all; a victory won not only for our own time but for the long and better days that are to come.

. . . . .

J. B. Priestley was a regular broadcaster at the BBC and became a household name from his contributions to the Home Service.

"The Battle of London" was the subject of J. B. Priestley in his postscript on Sunday night, 15 September.

PRIESTLEY ON THE BATTLE OF LONDON

Home Service, September 15 1940.

There is no evidence to suggest that Herr Hitler and Marshal Goring are well-read in English literature, and I should doubt if they ever spent much time with *Pickwick Papers*. But their attention ought to be drawn to chapter ten of that immortal work, in which chapter Samuel Weller makes his first appearance.

He was, if you remember, cleaning boots in the yard of the White Hart Inn, when a smart chambermaid called over the balustrade of the gallery, "Sam;" "Hello," replied Sam. "No. 22 wants his boots." Sam replied: "Ask 22 whether he'll have them now or wait till he gets 'em." "Come, don't be a fool, Sam," said the girl coaxingly, "the gentleman wants his boots directly." "Well, you are a nice young 'ooman for a musical party, you are," said Sam. "Look at these 'ere boots; eleven pair of boots, and one shoe as belongs to No. 6 with a wooden leg. The eleven boots is to be called at half-past eight and the shoe at nine. Who's No. 22 that's to put all the others out? No, no, 'regular rotation,' as Jack Ketch said when he tied the man up. 'Sorry to keep you a-waiting, Sir, but I'll attend to you directly.'"

That's Sam Weller, and there seems to me nearly all the true cockney spirit, independence, ironic humour, cheek and charm shown in that tiny bit of dialogue.

A lot of us, especially if we are from the North, and thought we knew everything, imagined that that old cockney spirit was dead and gone. We thought the Londoner of today, catching his tubes and electric trains, was a different kind of fellow altogether, with too many of his corners rubbed off, too gullible, easily pleased, too soft; and we were wrong. This last grim week has shown us how wrong we were. The Londoners, as the Americans say, can take it, and London itself—this grey sea of a city—can take it. The fact that the savage, indiscriminate bombing of the city has seized the world's imagination, is itself a tribute to the might and majesty of London. There was a time when, like many north-countrymen who came South, I thought I disliked London; it had vast colourless suburbs that seemed to us even drearier than the ones we had left behind. We hated the extremes of wealth and poverty that we found, cheek by jowl in the West End, where at night the great purring motor-cars filled with glittering women passed the shadowy rows of the homeless, the destitute, the down-and-out.

The life here in London seemed to us to have less colour, less gaiety than life in capitals abroad, and at the same time to have less character and flavour than the life we remembered in our provincial cities. And so on and so forth. But on these recent nights, when I have gone up to high roofs and have seen the fires like open wounds on the vast body of the city, I've realised, like many another settler here, how deeply I've come to love London, with its misty, twilit charm, its hidden cosiness and companionship, its smoky magic. The other night, when a few fires were burning so fiercely that half the sky was aglow, and the tall terraces around Portland Place were like pink palaces in the Arabian Nights, I saw the Dome and Cross of St. Paul's, silhouetted in sharpest black against the red flames and orange fumes, and it looked like an enduring symbol of reason and Christian ethics seen against the crimson glare of unreason and savagery. "Though giant rains put out the sun, here stand I for a sign."

In a supreme battle for the world's freedom, and there can be no doubt that you and I are now in the midst of such a battle, there are only two capital cities in the world that are worthy of figuring in its portrait—one of them is Paris, city of quick barricades and revolutions, now temporarily out of the fight, not because its brave people lost heart but rather because they lost interest and so allowed banal men, intriguers greedy for wealth and power and all the enemies of a people on the march, to deceive and betray them.

The other great city is London, which during the last thousand years—and what are the wobblings and timidities of the last ten years compared with the nine hundred and ninety that went before—has many a time given itself a shake and risen to strike a blow for freedom, and not only its own freedom but that of men everywhere. In this capacity, as any European history book will show

Burning warehouses in London Docklands.

you, it is in sharp contrast to Berlin, which has never yet been regarded as a beacon light by the free spirit of mankind. But London has often been seen as such a beacon light. Even the chief revolutionaries of our time lived here in their day and were nourished on books paid for by London citizens. And now, in the darkest hour, it blazes again; yes, because the incendiary bombs have been rained upon it, but also because of its proud defiance and unconquerable spirit have brought to men and women all over the world renewed hope and courage.

This, then, is a wonderful moment for us who are here in London, now in the roaring centre of the battlefield, the strangest army the world has ever seen, an army in drab civilian clothes, doing quite ordinary things, an army of all shapes and sizes and ages of folk, but nevertheless a real army, upon whose continuing high and defiant spirit the world's future depends.

We have not suddenly entered upon a new and quite lunatic way of living with the prospect of months and months and months of sirens and shelters and bombs before us, but we have been flung into a battle. As a kind of civilian life, this is hellish, but as battles go, it is not at all bad-with some shelter, meals arriving fairly regularly and a quick rescue of the wounded. But I am not giving advice to the cockneys. They can say to Herr Hitler and Marshal Goring what Sam Welter said: "Sorry to keep you waiting, Sir, but I'll attend to you directly."

. . . . .

A Wing-Commander in the Royal Air Force gave, after the end of the war, a survey of life in the RAF before and during the Battle of Britain.

MEMORIES OF THE BATTLE OF BRTTAIN

Wing-Commander Ronald Adams, Home Service, June, 1945

When I was ordered to report to Hornchurch in 1939 and first entered the Operations Room I wondered how long it would take me to assimilate and understand all the details of this queer room.

After a few weeks I found myself transferred to the Controller's Chair with all the business of radio-telephony patter to learn, and how to guide our own pilots to make contact with the enemy; for instance, "bandits" meant German aircraft; so many "angels" meant so many thousand feet in height, and the electric phrase "tally-ho" from the pilot meant that your directions to him had been successful, and he had sighted the enemy and was going to engage him.

The days of that "phoney" war were interesting because we were learning a new job. We practised with our aircraft incessantly, and every now and then the enemy obligingly put in an appearance over the North Sea and more often than not was successfully engaged. The radio stations round our coast—those tall masts that puzzled people before the war—were able to pick up and identify the enemy. The information was passed to us and our plotters plotted it with arrows on a great table map below us. We could find out the position of our own fighters from their radio transmissions, and so a thrilling game of hide-and-seek developed, while we waited for the "tally-ho." Radar was in its infancy in those days, and the enemy certainly did not appreciate its possibilities; nor, thank goodness, did we in Ops fully appreciate its limitations, or we might have been more worried. The technicians knew, of course, but they did not split. For it was not all that accurate, and there were times when it could fail to give any information at all. If the enemy had known just how to outwit it, which he could have done quite simply, the Battle of Britain would have had to be fought in a very different way, with perhaps a different ending.

The Battle of Holland, and of Belgium, and of France, developed and things were pretty tough, but it was Dunkirk that made my spirits rise again: I cannot believe that the much-vaunted Luftwaffe did not put out its best efforts to prevent the evacuation from those Dunkirk beaches, and it was then that the fighter boys showed just what they could do to the Luftwaffe. For the handful of them that were available "clawed the enemy out of the sky." I know that the army wondered where the aircraft were. They could not be expected to realise that a few dozen fighters were engaging hundreds of the enemy out of sight over the sea. I thought then: "If that's what the fighters can do there's a hope for us, if only we can get some more."

Then came the astonishing lull during July that puzzled us. We all knew how limited our resources were, how few aircraft and trained pilots we had got ready for action, and we did not—and we could not—understand why the enemy did not come for us at once. There was about a six weeks' pause. We held our breath during it, and then early in August, 1940, the radar plots began to show the enemy assembling in the air behind Cape Gris-nez in France. There he was milling around as one formation after another joined up, and we went to our loud-speakers when our Group Headquarters gave the order telling the squadron to take off. "Scramble" was the word we used: "Scramble" we would say, and Spitfires would tear into the sky and go off on their course over Maidstone, climbing up to twenty thousand feet, to meet the oncoming enemy. As he came, we would sit there on the ground and watch the plots and gather such information as we could from the Royal Observer Corps and from our liaison officers. We would pass information to the pilots, telling them all changes in the enemy's direction, how he was splitting up into different formations, what height he was flying at, and guiding our fighters to the most advantageous position up in the eye of the sun, ready to attack. The Battle of Britain is summarised for me in one snatch on the radio-telephone from a famous New Zealand fighter who is still alive. I heard his voice in my ear as he sighted the enemy: "Christ Almighty, tally-ho, whole bloody hordes of them." That will for ever be to me the Battle of Britain—"whole hordes of them."

During the next six weeks, as so many of us watched the battle in our skies in the south-east corner of England, from just before dawn until after last light of those days of outstanding summer weather, the Spitfires flew and flew, and the air crackled, not only with the explosions, but with the voices of the controllers on the radio and the answers of the pilots, and the breathless messages they passed to one another.

When we came out of that strange bungalow-building so near the main hangars of the aerodrome, we would stroll around in the sunlight to the pilots' dispersal huts on the other side and see them stretched out on beds, or in wicker chairs fast asleep, with the Mae Wests slung loosely upon them, and their clumsy flying boots on their feet. Every time the telephone bell rang in the dispersal hut, or every time a voice was heard booming on the loud-speaker, all the sleeping figures would wake up and listen, and if it was not an urgent call for them, they would fall back and be asleep in an instant. Generally, the radio was on at full blast. That did not disturb them. The roar of aircraft taking off and the clatter of vehicles passing by—those did not disturb them either. But a telephone bell had them alert and grabbing for their flying helmets before it had stopped ringing. Often, they were pretty nearly out on their feet. For instance, after a long day's flying, one of our boys landed and the Spitfire trundled along the ground and came to rest—and nobody got out of it. The ground-crew rushed out and tried to help their pilot, but he was slumped in his cockpit. He was not wounded; he was just fast asleep. The ground-crews themselves, stripped to the waist, worked day and night re-arming and re-fuelling and repairing, because the stock of replacements kept going down and the margin was getting narrower and narrower as the days went by. Occasionally, some lone ferry-pilot would arrive with a replacement—a new or patched-up Spitfire—but that was only on rare occasions. In those days and at the beginning of September, 1940, although I did not know it at the time, we were actually down to a few days' replacements; and that was all that stood between us and many grim possibilities.

I do not think the boys had any conscious idea of being heroic. We none of us had any real knowledge of how desperate things were, in fact, but we realised without needing facts that this would be the end if it could not be withstood. The boys' abounding high spirits were rather stilled by September: they were strained and silent, but never for one instant did they fail to leap for their aircraft like scalded cats the moment the "Scramble" was given. But when a Wing went up, instead of the normal thirty-six aircraft taking the air, we would be lucky if we could scrape up ten. Solidly and speedily the enemy poured across the Straits of Dover, and still that magic eye of the radar spotted him and still the tired pilots went up to shoot him down, while he bombed their landing-grounds

A Luftwaffe bomber, looking like a Dornier Do 215 in flames, August 1940.

beneath them. I remember getting the depleted squadrons off the ground to meet an oncoming raid—and they were all off except the last section of three, when the bombs fell. All three aircraft had opened their throttles to take off; the first was blown upside down and slid about two hundred yards on its cockpit; the second was blown in the air and both its wings fell off; the third was blown clean out of the aerodrome and into a nearby brook. In the middle of the smoke and confusion, a pitched battle raged in the middle of the aerodrome. The undamaged pilot of the second aircraft had run to the first one: he had managed to pull the pilot of it out and was trying to carry him. Eric was a little fellow; he had a great admiration for the big, husky pilot he was trying to save, but the husky pilot had no wish to be saved by Eric, and the protests he made ended in a furious battle. This raid drove operations room from its aerodrome to an emergency pitch some four miles away, in a small unoccupied grocer's shop, where we almost sat on one another's laps to control! We were bombed there within a few days of setting up. So the heat was turned on, and grew throughout August and the opening days of September, until the historic day of September 15. I was controller on duty that night when my group rang through to give the score—a hundred and eighty-five enemy aircraft destroyed, fourteen pilots lost on our side. It was not the end of the Battle of Britain, but it was the beginning of the end. Less and less enemy bombers came, with more and more enemy fighters trying to protect them. And now, more ferry pilots arrived with more aircraft and more pilots to fly them. Still we knew there was much ahead to endure, but we also knew that what we had suspected at Dunkirk had come true. We had taken the measure of the Luftwaffe and thrashed his hordes with a handful of fighter pilots, perhaps as many people as you would see collected round the field at a village cricket match.

CHAPTER III

Hitler, Master of the Continent

October, 1940—May, 1941

The German invasion plans for Great Britain had failed. The Luftwaffe turned to night-bombing, and for nine months the cities of Britain were subjected to incessant air attacks. At the same time the Germans intensified the U-boat blockade to starve England into submission. They failed again. Most important of all, Hitler failed in uniting Europe behind Germany, for the Germans made themselves hated wherever they came, and the resistance was nourished by England's unbending will to continue the struggle.

Through the following years London was not only the capital of the United Kingdom and the mother city of the British Commonwealth. It became the seat of more than half a dozen European Governments: the Dutch, the Belgian, the Luxemburg, the Norwegian, the Free French, the Polish, the Czechoslovak, the Greek and the Yugoslav, and their peoples looked to them as their leaders and true representatives during the years of occupation.

Queen Wilhelmina first spoke from England to her people in the opening programme of the Dutch Government's broadcasting service at the BBC, Radio Oranje.

QUEEN WILHELMINA TO HOLLAND

European Service, July 28 1940

First of all, I wish to join you in a solemn commemoration of the fatherland that has been so heavily afflicted by the calamity of war. Deeply moved, we think at this moment of the endless sorrows that have come upon our people and that continue to weigh on their hearts. We render homage to the heroes who fell in the execution of their duty to the fatherland, to the courage of our armed forces on land, at sea and in the air who with the exertion of their utmost strength resisted the overwhelmingly powerful assailant much longer than we had expected.

After all that has already been said and written about the war in which we have become involved, you will not expect me in these few moments to deal with the war itself and its many related problems. But what we must do is to realise that the war reveals itself more and more clearly as being essentially a war between good and evil, a battle between God and our conscience on the one side, and the forces of darkness now in the ascendant on the other side. It is a battle, I need hardly tell you, which belongs to the realm of the spirit fought in the deepest recesses of the human heart, but now in the most distressing and loathsome manner come to the surface in the form of this immense world struggle of which we have become the innocent victims and all peoples suffer.

What is at stake in this war is the liberty of those all the world over who wish to work for the good of mankind to do so without being frustrated by the evildoers. Those who think that the spiritual value acquired through the ages can be destroyed with the sword must learn to realise the idleness of such beliefs. They must be made to understand that crude violence cannot deprive a people of its conviction.

Just as in earlier days neither force of arms nor the flames of the stake nor impoverishment and suffering have ever succeeded in exterminating our love of liberty, our freedom of conscience and religion, so I remain convinced that once again we and all those of whatever nation who think like us shall emerge from this ordeal strengthened and chastened through our sacred sufferings.

May the knowledge that already thousands of our brave compatriots gave their all for this high purpose and that this sacrifice has not been in vain, be a source of solace to their kith and kin and to all of us.

Queen Wilhelmina of the Netherlands visiting New York, 14 July 1942.

Even though the enemy has occupied our native soil, the Netherlands will carry on the war till the morrow of a free and happy future dawns for us. Our beloved flag flies proudly on the seas, in great Netherland in the East and the West. Side by side with our allies our gallant men continue the struggle.

The Empire overseas which has given such striking proof of its sympathy in the calamity which struck the motherland is more closely attached to us in its thinking and feeling than ever before. With unshakable unity we intend to vindicate our freedom, our independence and all our territories.

I call on my compatriots at home and wherever they may be, however dark and difficult the times may be, to keep faith in the final victory of our cause, a cause which is strong not only because it is served by strength in battle but also because of the profound belief that our most sacred values are at stake.

. . . . .

On 25 September, when the Reich Commissar Terboven had taken over all power in Norway and had replaced the legal Government by installing members of the Norwegian Nazi Party, King Haakon broadcast the following speech from London to the Norwegian people:—

KING HAAKON TO NORWAY

European Service, September 26 1940

The liberty and independence of the Norwegian people are for me the first injunction of the Constitution, and it is my intention to follow this injunction and to take care of the interests of the Norwegian people in the best possible way by adhering to the position and the task which a free people gave me in 1905. I repeat today that I would not be true to my duty to our common Fatherland if I gave up that fight for the liberty of Norway which has been forced upon us.

I and my Government have been obliged to carry on this fight outside the country, but it is our greatest and dearest hope soon to be able to return home to rebuild the life of the people and the State which the war, in the undeserved attack on our country, has torn to pieces. I can foresee heavy and difficult days for the Norwegian people under the foreign régime of force, but I feel convinced that the people, with firmness and prudence, will bear the oppression, and that all Norwegian men and women will maintain a good spirit and hope and thereby prepare for the restoration which shall and must come.

We are fortunately neither without arms nor without friends, and, as we who are away will do everything possible to ease the condition for you who are at home, we ask you all to feel sure that we will never give up the work to create a new, free, and independent Norway.

I say today as I said in 1905, and as I will say all my life: "Everything for Norway, God bless Norway."

. . . . .

On 21 October Winston Churchill addressed the French people.

CHURCHILL TO THE FRENCH PEOPLE

Home Service, October 21 1940

Frenchmen! For more than thirty years in peace and war I have marched with you, and I am marching still along the same road. Tonight I speak to you at your firesides wherever you may be, or whatever your fortunes are. I repeat the prayer around the louis d'or, "Dieu protège la France." Here at home in England, under the fire of the Boche, we do not forget the ties and links that unite us to France, and we are persevering steadfastly and in good heart in the cause of European freedom and fair dealing for the common people of all countries, for which, with you, we drew the sword. When good people get into trouble because they are attacked and heavily smitten by the vile and wicked, they must be very careful not to get at loggerheads with one another. The common enemy is always trying to bring this about, and, of course, in bad luck a lot of things happen which play into the enemy's hands. We must just make the best of things as they come along.

Here in London, which Herr Hitler says he will reduce to ashes, and which his aeroplanes are now bombarding, our people are bearing up unflinchingly. Our Air Force has more than held its own. We are waiting for the long-promised invasion. So are the fishes. But, of course, this for us is only the beginning. Now, in 1940, in spite of occasional losses, we have, as ever, command of the seas. In 1941 we shall have the command of the air. Remember what that means. Herr Hitler with his tanks and other mechanical weapons, and also by Fifth Column intrigue with traitors, has managed to subjugate for the time being most of the finest races in Europe, and his little Italian accomplice is trotting along hopefully and hungrily, but rather wearily and very timidly, at his side. They both wish to carve up France and her Empire as if it were a fowl; to one a leg, to another a wing or perhaps part of the breast. Not only the French Empire will be devoured by these two ugly customers, but Alsace-Lorraine will go once again under the German yoke, and Nice, Savoy and Corsica—Napoleon's Corsica—will be torn from the fair realm of France. But Herr Hitler is not thinking only of stealing other people's territories, or flinging gobbets of them to his little confederate. I tell you truly what you must believe when I say this evil man, this monstrous abortion of hatred and defeat, is resolved on nothing less than the complete wiping out of the French nation, and the disintegration of its whole life and future. By all kinds of sly and savage means, he is plotting and working to quench for ever the fountain of characteristic French culture and of French inspiration to the world. All Europe, if he has his way, will be reduced to one uniform Boche-land, to be exploited, pillaged, and bullied by his Nazi gangsters. You will excuse me speaking frankly, because this is not a time to mince words. It is not defeat that France will now be made to suffer at German hands, but the doom of complete obliteration. Army, Navy, Air Force, religion, law, language, culture, institutions, literature, history, tradition, all are to be effaced by the brute strength of a triumphant army, and the scientific low-cunning of a ruthless police force.

Frenchmen—re-arm your spirits before it is too late. Remember how Napoleon said before one of his battles: "These same Prussians who are so boastful today were three to one at Jena, and six to one at Montmirail." Never will I believe that the soul of France is dead. Never will I believe that her place amongst the greatest nations of the world has been lost for ever! All these schemes and crimes of Herr Hitler's are bringing upon him and upon all who belong to his system a retribution which many of us will live to see. The story is not yet finished, but it will not be so long. We are on his track, and so are our friends across the Atlantic Ocean. If he cannot destroy us, we will surely destroy him and all his gang, and all their works. Therefore, we have hope and faith, for all will come right.

Now what is it we British ask of you in this present hard and bitter time? What we ask at this moment in our struggle to win the victory which we shall share with you, is that if you cannot help us, at least you will not hinder us. Presently you will be able to weight the arm that strikes for you, and you ought to do so. But even now we believe that Frenchmen wherever they may be, feel their hearts warm and a proud blood tingle in their veins when we have some success in the air or on the sea, or presently—for that will come—upon the land.

Remember we shall never stop, never weary, and never give in, and that our whole people and Empire have vowed themselves to the task of cleansing Europe from the Nazi pestilence and saving the world from the new Dark Ages. Do not imagine, as the German-controlled wireless tells you, that we English seek to take your ships and colonies. We seek to beat the life and soul out of Hitler and Hitlerism. That alone, that all the time, that to the end. We do not covet anything from any nation except their respect. Those Frenchmen who are in the French Empire, and those who are in so-called unoccupied France, may see their way from time to time to useful action. I will not go into details. Hostile ears are listening. As for those, to whom English hearts go out in full, because they see them under the sharp discipline, oppression, and spying of the Hun—as to those Frenchmen in the occupied regions, to them I say, when they think of the future let them remember the words which Gambetta, that great

Go to it! A cartoon of the Bulldog spirit.

Frenchman, uttered after 1870, about the future of France and what was to come: "Think of it always; speak of it never."

Good night then: sleep to gather strength for the morning. For the morning will come. Brightly it will shine on the brave and true, kindly upon all who suffer for the cause, glorious upon the tombs of heroes. Thus will shine the dawn. Vive la France! Long live also the forward march of the common people in all the lands towards their just and true inheritance, and towards the broader and fuller age.

. . . . .

The Vichy Government followed a policy of concession and collaboration, but the attitude of the French people was never in doubt.

GENERAL DE GAULLE TO FRANCE

European Service, December 28 1940

The hideous ambiguity imposed on France by the terms of the armistice is nearing its end. The semblance of sovereignty on which the men responsible for the capitulation pride themselves vanishes in its turn, giving place to shame and panic. Behind the crumbling façade, the nation now sees the reality. That reality is the enemy: an enemy exploiting his slaves in order to reduce them to still more abject servitude; an enemy bringing pressure to bear on his collaborators in order to gain still more active collaboration; an enemy trading on dishonour to impose still baser infamy.

Faced by this fresh lapse on the part of Vichy, we, the Free French, consider it our right and duty to speak our minds in no uncertain terms. We have the right to do so, because we have never for a moment submitted to the law imposed by the enemy. We have the right to do so, because enemy soldiers have been killed or captured, enemy ships sunk, and enemy planes shot down by our arms. We have the right to do so, because a thousand men from our Army, Navy and Air Force have given their lives for France since the Armistice. We have the right to do so, because France has been placed at the enemy's mercy, so that now, gagged and crushed, she has no voice but ours to speak for her.

We maintain that the enemy is still our foe. So long as the Germans are in Paris and Bordeaux, in Lille, Rheims, at Strasburg, so long as Germans and Italians seek to impose their will on the French nation, there is but one thing to do-fight. To treat with such enemies, accepting their control and collaborating with them, is treason in the true sense of the word.

We maintain that although the French Army may have lost a great battle through lack of proper organisation in accordance with the methods of modern warfare, France has not lost the war. For this is a world war. The enemy may have won initial successes, but he has not won the war, and he knows it. Already he is suffering severe reverses. All over the world vast forces are assembling to crush him. France's Allies have realised this—Poles, Czechs, Dutch, Belgians, Norwegians, Luxemburgers, and Greeks alike. Not a single Government of the belligerent countries has treated with the enemy, with the sole exception of the so-called Government of France!

We maintain that France must play a decisive part in this world war. Our Empire is intact. If, at this very moment, French North Africa, Syria, and the French Fleet were fighting for France, the great Battle of the Mediterranean would be decided forthwith by an overwhelming French victory.

We maintain that if only all Frenchmen, wherever they may be and whatever their situation, rank, or opinions, will take up arms again for France, we shall be with them unconditionally and without a moment's hesitation. We promise that all French leaders—whatever faults they may have committed in the past—

who decide to draw again the sword they sheathed, will find us at their side. To this we make no exceptions, and for ourselves we have no ambition. If French Africa rises at last to fight in the war, she will have the backing of the Free French territories.

By observing the Hour of Hope on January 1st, by not appearing in the streets between 2 and 3 p.m. in unoccupied France, and between 3 and 4 p.m. in occupied France; by deserting the streets of our towns and villages for sixty minutes, the French people will show the enemy that they still regard him as their foe. By this vast plebiscite of silence, France will show the world that for her there can be no future save in liberty, no greatness save in independence, no salvation save in victory.

· · · · ·

Meanwhile the German air offensive against Britain was continued night after night through autumn, winter and spring, first against London, then also against the other cities and towns of Britain. To begin with, London was raided on 82 out of 85 consecutive nights and had 10,000 casualties in September alone.

The well-known author and playwright Emlyn Williams, in one of the Sunday postscripts, gave a vivid description from London under the blitz.

PORTRAIT OF A LONDONER

Home Service, Autumn, 1940

I am going to talk about a woman I know. She's forty-seven, below normal in height and in breadth, and lives in London; her calling is both the humblest and the most independent of all. She doesn't answer to the name of 'A Lady Help.' Oh, no. When she answers the 'phone, all you hear is: 'This is the charwoman speaking; yes?'

Her face, in repose, is melancholy and a little vague; her grey hair curls quite prettily over the temples, but her looks are spoilt by one protruding tooth which her married daughter keeps begging her to have out, but she won't hear of it.

Any fine morning she is to be seen kneeling on the steps, 'doing' them; the heels of the little boots tapping against each other as she leans to and fro. She doesn't talk much, and when she does, it's mostly superfluous. For instance, I have never yet known the air-raid warning die away without her face coming slowly round the corner and her saying, with a look as if she really meant to mispronounce the word that way, 'That was the Serene.' She has been told her pronunciation is not correct, and that nothing could be less serene than what she is describing; but, no, it's like her tooth, she is sticking to it.

She has two vices: one is singing, while she is washing up, in a very high completely tuneless voice, the most unsuitable songs. Some time ago it was 'The Night is Young and You're so Beautiful'; just lately, when one has become pretty well bomb-conscious, her choice is even more unsuitable: 'Give a Little Whistle.' 'Roll out the Barrel,' she won't hear of, as it somehow spells drink to her, and she's got a prejudice. The other vice is bomb stories told in the most spiritless manner. It's the same ritual every time; I have to play up to her, but it's quite easy, as it just means saying 'yes' over and over again. 'You know the big stores, sir, next the pillar box?' 'Yes.' 'You know the picture 'ouse next the stores?' 'Yes.' 'You know the little garridge which stands on the other corner?' 'Yes.' 'Well, it's gawn.'

I said her face was melancholy in repose—but when something really interests her, those eyes suddenly brighten and dart about like a bird's. And she even talks. That something which interests her isn't the war, which she ignores, and has only mentioned once. When somebody asked her if she didn't think somebody's Austrian maid was a fifth-columnist, she looked more severe than I've ever seen her look, and the old tooth stuck out further than ever as she said: 'There's only one man that knows all those things, and that's Mr Churchill, God bless 'im; you better drop 'im a line.'

No, there's only one interest in her life, and that's Reg. Reg is her only son, aged fifteen, an office boy in the city. It isn't that she praises him: on the contrary, she's always running him down. 'That lad'll be the death o' me; people say it's 'igh spirits, but 'e's a bad boy.' I gather that Reg's great accomplishment is combing his hair forward, raising one arm, and giving an impersonation of Hitler, which is apparently, war or no war, the talk of the Stock Exchange; he sounds to me rather a trying young chap. But he is her whole life; the only time

Business as usual — 'Our oranges came through Musso's lake'.

she is in any hurry to finish her work is on Reg's half-day, when she has to get home for his dinner—'only 'e'll bolt it all,' and 'off on that bike again, sixty miles an hour; naughty boy. The Serene's gawn, sir.'

But I'm telling you all this in the present, when some of it ought to be in the past. Because on Thursday morning she was late. She was so late that when I left the house she still hadn't come in. I missed that steady, careful climb down the steps, the discreet little cough, the bomb story, and Reg's latest escapade: it seemed odd not to see those delicate veined hands scampering like mice after the dust under my desk, with the little boots somewhere in the rear.

When I got back about twelve, though, I was relieved to hear the clatter of dishes in the sink; but no singing. I called out, 'Everything all right?' She called out, 'Yes'; and I thought no more about it. And then I realised, suddenly, that the noise of dish-washing had stopped; there wasn't a sound. I was mystified and walked into the kitchen.

She was standing perfectly still, in front of the sink; her hands wrist-deep in the soapy water; looking out of the window. I spoke her name, and with a great and simple dignity, she turned her head. She looked at me, and I knew my presentiment had been right. She smiled; I noticed with a slight shock that her poor old tooth had gone, but that didn't spoil the smile, somehow.

'You know, sir,' she said, 'You know the way you teased me about me bomb stories? Well, I got me own bomb story now.' She was obviously shaken, but no worse. 'What about Reg?' I said. 'Well,' she said, looking out of the window almost absentmindedly, ''e's all right. As soon as 'e saw I was O.K., 'e went off on 'is bike, the naughty thing, to 'elp with another fire in the next street, an' a wall fell on 'im an' 'e fell in a crater, an' 'e's in the 'ospital with 'is leg broken; but 'e's all right. When I left 'e got the nurses in stitches with the imitation of 'Itler, 'e's all right.'

She was still looking out of the window, quite without movement, a single tear rolling into the wrinkles under one eye, when slowly and unconsciously almost, she said two things which I don't think should be forgotten. She said, 'You know, sir, 'e's a very small boy for 'is age, but 'e's got spirit.' Then came the only comment on the war I've ever heard her make. 'That 'Itler," she said, thoughtfully, still looking out of the window, 'that 'Itler, dropping bombs on Reg and me an' such . . . you know, 'e's a bad loser.'

After a lot of difficulty I persuaded her to go back to Reg and her own affairs for the rest of the day. She finished washing up, dried her hands methodically on the roller-towel, folded up her apron, put it carefully in its drawer, made up the laundry, perched the little toque on top of her head, and set off.

I watched that tiny unobtrusive figure going its way along the street. She got to the fallen masonry strewn on the corner, stopped, gave one firm twitch to her fur tippet, the black boots proceeded to pick their way steadily through the rubble, and she was gone: the toughest, bravest little fighter of us all.

. . . . .

Apart from the war by air and by sea the main events of the war from October to May took place round the Mediterranean. In hope of an easy victory Mussolini attacked Greece from Albania on 28 October, but the Italians were not only stopped but thrown back. In November the British Navy and its carrier-borne planes ended Italian naval supremacy at Taranto. And in December a small British force of only 30,000 men, under General Wavell, drove the Italians out of Egypt and conquered Cyrenaica, capturing 133,000 prisoners together with 1,300 guns. Suez had been saved for the time being.

The heroic fight of the Greeks, and the Greek tradition were the subject of a broadcast by the Greek scholar, Professor Gilbert Murray.

"Now, sons of Hellas, now!
Set Hellas free, set free your wives, your homes,
Your gods' high altars and your fathers' tombs.
Now all is in the stake!

Aeschylus: The Persians.

GILBERT MURRAY ; GREECE AND HER TRADITION

Home Service, December, 1940

Just now we are all thinking about Greece. While the small nations of the West have been conquered one by one, and the nations of the East bullied into submission without daring to raise their heads, one alone—the smallest among them—has dared to stand up against the giants, and is not only standing up but has actually been winning victory after victory. One cannot tell how long the victories will last. But Greece has at least great allies, not only powerful help from Britain and the sympathy of the world; she has her mountains and her sea, and the inspiration of her own great traditions. It is a tradition to which, as the Greek Prime Minister said the other day, honour matters more than success. Reading those words I thought of Demosthenes, the undaunted champion of Greek freedom, who in the very hour of his failure was presented by his fellow citizens with a golden crown in gratitude for the lead he had given them.

That ancient Greek tradition, the thing called Hellenism—I apologise for the rather highbrow word—almost covers the cause we are now fighting for. Historically it is the spirit which existed in a little country for a brief time, about one hundred years, some two thousand five hundred years ago; but it has remained a memory and an inspiration for after-ages and nations utterly remote in time and customs. People of all nations throughout Europe have looked back on fifth-century Athens as a sort of Golden Age—a Golden Age of freedom and simple living—a Golden Age of art, poetry, philosophy, of all kinds of intellectual life. Of course, there has been some exaggerated sentiment in all this. The ideal Hellenism, like all ideals, is very different from the reality on which it is based. I want to speak to you for a few minutes about what, in my opinion, the Ancient Greeks were really like, and why some people still feel excited and enthusiastic about them.

A great deal I will take for granted. Everybody knows that the little country in that short time produced some of the finest buildings and statues in the world. For my own part, no building I have seen moves me as the Parthenon in Athens. Again, I am interested in poetry. There is nothing that goes out of fashion so quickly as poetry; yet those people over two thousand years ago produced poems which people still love and learn by heart, comedies at which people still laugh aloud, tragedies by which people are thrilled and to use the old Greek word, "purified." They produced books on philosophy which all the universities of Europe are still reading and arguing about. And even in science which depends so much on continuous discovery, their books lasted on for well over fifteen hundred years. And as for war, now as we hear day by day about the fighting in Mount Pindus and around Dodona, we think of those old battles whose names are famous throughout the civilised world—the glorious victories of Marathon and Salamis and the even more glorious defeat of Thermopylae, a defeat which made final victory possible.

There is an inscribed stone at Athens, inscribed in the year 458 B.C., giving the names of the members of one Athenian tribe who had fallen fighting on five different battle fronts: Cyprus, Egypt, Halieis, Ægina, Megara; five battle fronts in one year: what terrific energy for that one city! And to think that at the same time Pericles was building the Parthenon, and Sophocles producing his great tragedies!

But I will take all that for granted. I want to speak of something else. We are many of us considering what sort of society, what attempt at a better world, we can dare to aim at after the war. I wonder if we can get any hints—they will not be more than hints—from thinking about that old Hellenic Society which seems to have done such wonders with so little material.

Our own civilisation, say, in modern England and America, is in some ways very Hellenic and in others extraordinarily un-Hellenic. Historically we are more than we know, the children of the Greeks, in literature, art, thought, ethics, politics, and hardly less so in religion. On the other hand, we are an age of quite extraordinary and unparalleled material civilisation; an age of great possessions and inventions, an age of machinery, of mass production, of economic complexity and immense governmental strength. Greece was the very opposite in material things. They were almost primitive. Their clothes consisted of two garments, roughly speaking, a shirt and a blanket, which they managed somehow to wear gracefully. As for boots and shoes, they mostly could not afford them; they called the Persians and Lydians "tenderfooted," because they could not walk barefoot. They had no proper roads. The Assyrians and Hittites had made good roads before; the Romans made magnificent roads afterwards.

But the Greek cities seem never to have had the necessary capital and labour for these large undertakings. When the King of Persia wanted to make a bridge from Asia to Europe, or cut a canal through Mount Athos he could provide the capital and the labour; but he needed Greek engineers to show how the work should be done. Materially, we have nothing whatever to learn from them; except perhaps the important lesson that material possessions and inventions do not matter as much as we think they do, certainly not nearly as much as the quality of the human beings who use them. It is entirely by their qualities as human beings that the Greeks count, by character, brains and imagination.

Think first of their freedom. It is freedom for which we are now fighting, freedom against the claims of despots who are above the law, like the Roman Emperors who were worshipped as gods. There was never in Greece a superhuman semi-divine Great King, as there was in Babylon and Egypt and in Rome afterwards. The Greeks had kings and leaders—some good, some bad— but they are always sharply warned that they are not superhuman and will only get into trouble if they think they are. They must not put up megalomaniac inscriptions about their glory. They must not expect to have concubines and attendants sacrificed on their graves. They must not expect people to kiss the earth on entering their presence or to walk backwards on leaving it. They must not seize other men's wives and daughters. They are never above the law; the law is always above them. The meanest of their citizen-fellows has the right of free speech and cannot be condemned unheard. Take another significant fact. The Romans, as we all know, rejoiced in gladiatorial games, where sometimes professional gladiators fought to the death to amuse the mob; sometimes it was criminals or slaves who were butchered or thrown to wild beasts. The taste for these games spread everywhere; the degraded mobs in most countries liked them, and it was a regular form of flattery to Rome to adopt the great Roman institution; it spread everywhere except to Greece. In Greece only one city gave in—the rather disreputable city of Corinth. When it was proposed to build an amphitheatre for gladiators in Athens a philosopher who was present moved an amendment: before building the amphitheatre, he said, they should destroy the Altar of Pity in the market-place. They did not have gladiators; they did not destroy the Altar of Pity.

Even in war, when most moral rules tend to disappear, the Greeks recognised certain rules. There must be no killing of prisoners, no torture, no boasting over the dead. All such doings would be what they called "hybris"—pride, insolence—the sin of sins, the sin of tyrants and conquerors who forget that they are men like other men. For example—in a Roman triumph the victorious general dragged his conquered enemies behind him in chains. The crowd mocked at them. Afterwards they were taken to a dungeon and strangled. The Assyrian conqueror put up gigantic limestone reliefs, still extant after three thousand years, showing himself in superhuman size receiving tribute from his enemies, making pyramids of skulls, impaling prisoners and leading kings through the streets by fish-hooks through their noses. That was "hybris" in perfection. Just what the Greeks most hated. The Greek conqueror must have no "triumph." He must put up no permanent war memorial, only what they call a "trophy" a wooden pole and cross-bar with armour upon it to mark the site of the victory. The conquered were bound in honour never to pull down the trophy, and the conqueror never to repair it. Both sides allowed it gradually to break up and sink into the earth as the memory of the old battles faded. Deeds of enmity, they said, had better be forgotten; deeds of goodwill remembered. Again, roughly speaking, in the great monarchies of antiquity there was only one duty—obedience. "Among the barbarians," said the Greek proverb, "all are slaves but one." That is the system against which the Greeks fought, and against which we are fighting today. How is this insistence on freedom, free speech, equality before the law, connected with the great achievements of the Greeks in art, thought and literature? We can see at least this connection, that if freedom does not of itself necessarily produce great art or thought, the absence of freedom makes great art and thought impossible. It is not for nothing that the tyrants of Germany and Italy today have driven out their great writers and men of science and are taking the trouble to murder university students. In fighting for freedom the Greeks fought not merely for the right to be unpersecuted in their daily lives; they fought for the right to think and to speak, to write poems and plays and books on philosophy and to build temples like the Parthenon. And so do we.

Is there another lesson we can learn from that short-lived splendid civilisation of ancient Hellas? Alas, there is. They did not solve the problem of war; and consequently war destroyed them. The free Greek cities so valued their sovereign independence that they did not learn to co-operate. The little nations tried again and again to form a great league or union—concord was what they called it—but they were not in time. The big military monarchies conquered them before their concord was complete.

. . . . .

Britain under the German air attacks, the events in the Balkans and the Middle East, the Battle of the Atlantic and the growing help from the United States (Lend-Lease Law enacted in U.S., 11 March), were the main subjects in Winston Churchill's great survey on 27 April.

CHURCHILL: SURVEY OF THE WAR, APRIL 27 1941

Home Service, April 27 1941

I was asked last week whether I was aware of some uneasiness which it was said existed in the country on account of the gravity, as it was described, of the war situation. So I thought it would be a good thing to go and see for myself what this "uneasiness" amounted to, and I went to some of our great cities and seaports which had been most heavily bombed, and to some of the places where the poorest people had got it worst. I have come back not only reassured, but refreshed. To leave the offices in Whitehall with their ceaseless hum of activity and stress, and to go out to the front, by which I mean the streets and wharves of London or Liverpool, Manchester, Cardiff, Swansea or Bristol, is like going out of a hothouse on to the bridge of a fighting ship. It is a tonic which I should recommend any who are suffering from fretfulness to take in strong doses when they have need of it.

It is quite true that I have seen many painful scenes of havoc, and of fine buildings and acres of cottage homes blasted into rubble-heaps of ruin. But it is just in those very places where the malice of the savage enemy has done its worst, and where the ordeal of the men, women and children has been most severe, that I found their morale most high and splendid. Indeed, I felt encompassed by an exaltation of spirit in the people which seemed to lift mankind and its troubles above the level of material facts into that joyous serenity we think belongs to a better world than this.

Of their kindness to me I cannot speak, because I have never sought it or dreamed of it, and can never deserve it. I can only assure you that I and my colleagues, or comrades rather—for that is what they are—will toil with every scrap of life and strength, according to the lights that are granted to us, not to fail these people or to be wholly unworthy of their faithful and generous regard. The British nation is stirred and moved as it has never been at any time in its long, eventful, famous history, and it is no hackneyed trope of speech to say that they mean to conquer or to die.

Night time during the Blitz.

What a triumph the life of these battered cities is, over the worst that fire and bomb can do. What a vindication of the civilised and decent way of living we have been trying to work for and towards in our Island. What a proof of the virtues of free institutions. What a test of the quality of our local authorities, and of institutions and customs and societies so steadily built. This ordeal by fire has even in a certain sense exhilarated the manhood and womanhood of Britain. The sublime but also terrible and sombre experiences and emotions of the battlefield which for centuries had been reserved for the soldiers and sailors, are now shared for good or ill, by the entire population. All are proud to be under the fire of the enemy. Old men, little children, the crippled veterans of former wars, aged women, the ordinary hard-pressed citizen or subject of the King, as he likes to call himself, the sturdy workmen who swing the hammers or load the ships; skilful craftsmen; the members of every kind of A.R.P. service, are proud to feel that they stand in the line together with our fighting men, when one of the greatest of causes is being fought out, as fought out it will be, to the end. This is indeed the grand heroic period of our history, and the light of glory shines on all.

You may imagine how deeply I feel my own responsibility to all these people; my responsibility to bear my part in bringing them safely out of this long, stern, scowling valley through which we are marching, and not to demand from them their sacrifices and exertions in vain.

I have thought in this difficult period, when so much fighting and so many critical and complicated manoeuvres are going on, that it is above all things important that our policy and conduct should be upon the highest level, and that honour should be our guide. Very few people realise how small were the forces with which General Wavell, that fine Commander whom we cheered in good days and will back through bad—how small were the forces which took the bulk of the Italian masses in Libya prisoners. In none of his successive victories could General Wavell maintain in the desert more than two divisions, or about 30,000 men. When we reached Benghazi, and what was left of Mussolini's legions scurried hack along the dusty road to Tripoli, a call was made upon us which we could not resist. Let me tell you about that call.

You will remember how in November the Italian Dictator fell upon the unoffending Greeks, and without reason and without warning invaded their country, and how the Greek nation, reviving their classic fame, hurled his armies back at the double quick. Meanwhile Hitler, who had been creeping and worming his way steadily forward, doping and poisoning and pinioning, one after the other, Hungary, Rumania and Bulgaria, suddenly made it clear that he would come to the rescue of his fellow-criminal. The lack of unity among the Balkan States had enabled him to build up a mighty army in their midst. While nearly all the Greek troops were busy beating the Italians, the tremendous German military machine suddenly towered up on their other frontier. In their mortal peril the Greeks turned to us for succour. Strained as were our resources, we could not say them nay. By solemn guarantee given before the war, Great Britain had promised them her help. They declared they would fight for their native soil even if neither of their neighbours made common cause with them, and even if we left them to their fate. But we could not do that. There are rules against that kind of thing; and to break those rules would be fatal to the honour of the British Empire, without which we could neither hope nor deserve to win this hard war. Military defeat or miscalculation can be redeemed. The fortunes of war are fickle and changing. But an act of shame would deprive us of the respect which we now enjoy throughout the world, and this would sap the vitals of our strength.

Let us see what has happened. We knew, of course, that the forces we could send to Greece would not by themselves alone be sufficient to stem the German tide of invasion. But there was a very real hope that the neighbours of Greece would by our intervention be drawn to stand in the line together with her while time remained. How nearly that came off will be known some day. The tragedy of Yugoslavia has been that these brave people had a government who hoped to purchase an ignoble immunity by submission to the Nazi will. Thus when at last the people of Yugoslavia found out where they were being taken, and rose in one spontaneous surge of revolt, they saved the soul and future of their country: but it was already too late to save its territory. They had no time to mobilise their armies. They were struck down by the ruthless and highly-mechanised Hun before they could even bring their armies into the field. Great disasters have occurred in the Balkans. Yugoslavia has been beaten down. Only in the mountains can she continue her resistance. The Greeks have been overwhelmed. Their victorious Albanian Army has been cut off and forced to surrender, and it has been left to the Anzacs and their British comrades to fight their way back to the sea, leaving their mark on all who hindered them.

While these grievous events were taking place in the Balkan Peninsula and in Greece, our forces in Libya have sustained a vexatious and damaging defeat. The Germans advanced sooner and in greater strength than we or our Generals expected. The bulk of our armoured troops, which had played such a decisive part in beating the Italians, had to be refitted, and the single armoured brigade which had been judged sufficient to hold the frontier till about the middle of May was worsted and its vehicles largely destroyed by a somewhat stronger German armoured force. Our infantry, which had not exceeded one division, had to fall back upon the very large Imperial armies that have been assembled and can be nourished and maintained in the fertile delta of the Nile. Tobruk—the fortress of Tobruk—which flanks any German advance on Egypt, we hold strongly.

We must now expect the war in the Mediterranean, on the sea, in the desert, and above all in the air, to become very fierce, varied and widespread. The war may spread to Spain and Morocco. It may spread eastwards to Turkey and Russia. The Huns may lay their hands for the time upon the granaries of the

Ukraine and the oil-wells of the Caucasus. They may dominate the Black Sea. They may dominate the Caspian. Who can tell? We shall do our best to meet them and fight them wherever they go. In order to win this war, Hitler must either conquer this Island by invasion, or he must cut the ocean life-line which joins us to the United States.

Let us look into these alternatives. When I spoke last, in February, many people believed the Nazi boastings that the invasion of Britain was about to begin. It has not begun yet, and with every week that passes we grow stronger on the sea, in the air, and in the numbers, quality, training and equipment of the great Armies that now guard our Island. When I compare the position at home as it is today with what it was in the summer of last year, I feel that we have very much to be thankful for, and I believe that provided our exertions and our vigilance are not relaxed even for a moment, we may be confident that we shall give a very good account of ourselves. More than that it would be boastful to say. Less than that it would be foolish to believe.

But how about our life-line across the Atlantic? What is to happen if so many of our merchant ships are sunk that we cannot bring in the food we need to nourish our brave people? That is what is called the Battle of the Atlantic, which in order to survive we have got to win on salt water just as decisively as we had to win the Battle of Britain last August and September in the air.

Wonderful exertions have been made by our Navy and Air Force; by the hundreds of mine-sweeping vessels which with their marvellous appliances keep our ports clear in spite of all the enemy can do; by the men who build and repair our immense fleets of merchant ships; by the men who load and unload them; and need I say by the officers and men of the Merchant Navy who go out in all weathers and in the teeth of all dangers to fight for the life of their native land and for a cause they comprehend and serve. Still, when you think how easy it is to sink ships at sea and how hard it is to build them and protect them, and when you remember that we have never less than two thousand ships afloat and three or four hundred in the danger zone; when you think of the great armies we are maintaining and reinforcing in the East, and of the world-wide traffic we have to carry on—when you remember all this, can you wonder that it is the Battle of the Atlantic which holds the first place in the thoughts of those upon whom rests the responsibility for procuring the victory?

It was therefore with indescribable relief that I learned of the decisions lately taken by the President and people of the United States. The American Fleet and flying boats have been ordered to patrol the wide waters of the Western Hemisphere, and to warn the peaceful shipping of all nations outside the combat zone of the presence of lurking U-boats or raiding cruisers belonging to the two aggressor nations. We British shall therefore be able to concentrate our protecting forces far more upon the routes nearer home, and to take a far heavier toll of the U-boats there. The President and Congress of the United

States, having newly fortified themselves by contact with their electors, have solemnly pledged their aid to Britain in this war because they deem our cause just, and because they know their own interests and safety would be endangered if we were destroyed. They are taxing themselves heavily. They have passed great legislation. They have turned a large part of their gigantic industry to making the munitions which we need. They have given us or lent us valuable weapons of their own. I could not believe that they would allow the high purposes to which they have set themselves to be frustrated and the products of their skill and labour sunk to the bottom of the sea. U-boat warfare as conducted by Germany is entirely contrary to international agreements freely subscribed to by Germany only a few years ago. There is no effective blockade, but only a merciless murder and marauding over wide, indiscriminate areas utterly beyond the control of the German seapower. When I said ten weeks ago: "Give us the tools and we will finish the job," I meant give them to us: put them within our reach—and that is what it now seems the Americans are going to do. And that is why I feel a strong conviction that though the Battle of the Atlantic will be long and hard, and its issue is by no means yet determined, it has entered upon a more grim but at the same time a far more favourable phase.

It is worthwhile therefore to take a look on both sides of the ocean at the forces which are facing each other in this awful struggle, from which there can be no drawing back. No prudent and far-seeing man can doubt that the eventual and total defeat of Hitler and Mussolini is certain, in view of the respective resolves of the British and American democracies. There are less than seventy millions malignant Huns—some of them are curable and others killable—many of whom are already engaged in holding down Austrians, Czechs, Poles, French, and the many other ancient races they now bully and pillage. The peoples of the British Empire and of the United States number nearly two hundred millions in their homelands and in the British Dominions alone. They possess the unchallengeable command of the oceans, and will soon obtain decisive superiority in the air. They have more wealth, more technical resources, and they make more steel, than the whole of the rest of the world put together.

When we face with a steady eye the difficulties which lie before us, we may derive new confidence from remembering those we have already overcome. Nothing that is happening now is comparable in gravity with the dangers through which we passed last year. Nothing that can happen in the East is comparable with what is happening in the West.

Last time I spoke to you I quoted the lines of Longfellow which President Roosevelt had written out for me in his own hand. I have some other lines which are less well known but which seem apt and appropriate to our fortunes tonight, and I believe they will be so judged wherever the English language is spoken or the flag of freedom flies:

> For while the tired waves, vainly breaking,
>> Seem here no painful inch to gain,
> Far back, through creeks and inlets making,
>> Comes silent, flooding in, the main.
>
> And not by eastern windows only,
>> When daylight comes, comes in the light;
> In front the sun climbs slow, how slowly!
>> But westward look, the land is bright.

. . . . .

The first month of 1941 saw the beginning of the famous V-campaign. Through the BBC European Service the V-sign became the symbol for all the peoples under the German yoke, of their common will to resist the Germans. The campaign was started by M. de Laveleye, the BBC's Belgian programme organiser, in the following broadcast.

THE "V" SIGN

European Service, January 14 1941

Our young children in Belgium have found, we are told, a new way—one more way—of infuriating the Boche.

They cut out in paper the three letters R A F, the initials of the Royal Air Force, the British Air Arm, and stick them up in our streets. Well done, children!

But don't you grown-ups run away with the idea that it's all a bit of childishness. We all know, of course, that little bits of paper won't drive the Germans out. But a gesture like this, repeated again and again as a manifestation of your confidence in victory and a simple tribute of admiration to the British airmen, wears down the courage of your oppressors by showing them that your faith lives and grows daily.

I have something else to suggest to you tonight. It is up to you to do what you wish with it. Here it is.

It is in your interests to know how many of you want deliverance. Belgian patriots must have a sign to rally round, a sign which they should multiply about them so that seeing the sign written up everywhere they may come to know their strength. And the continual sight of this same sign, repeated indefinitely, must make the enemy realise that he is surrounded and hemmed in by a mighty army of Belgian citizens who wait patiently for the first slip and watch for the first sign of weakness. Don't think it's futile. It will be a permanent encouragement to you, a means of recognition, a way of knowing your number, a tangible witness of the moral resistance which animates and sustains you.

As your rallying-sign I suggest the letter V.

Why V? Because V is the first letter of 'Victoire' in French and of 'Vrijheid' (Freedom) in Flemish. Victory and Freedom—two things which go together, just as Walloons and Flemings march forward today hand in hand, two things which are complementary; victory which will restore your freedom, the victory of our great English friends. And the English for 'Victoire' is 'Victory' which begins with the same letter. You see how well it works out in every way. The letter V is thus the perfect symbol of the Anglo-Belgian entente.

I suggest the letter V for yet another reason; it can be scribbled easily and quickly. A mark with a pencil or a piece of chalk on a wall, a fence or a hoarding, one stroke down and one stroke up; the front of a building touched lightly in passing, the quick pencil stroke, the work of a second, done too quickly to be observed. In this way you can plaster the V sign over the walls of our towns, on German posters on any of a thousand places you might choose. Your impudence might even be pushed to carving V's—with a pen-knife, a pen, a nail, the sharp end of a stone, an old trouser button—on the bodies of German cars. But take care. The point of the game is to infuriate the enemy without being caught.

What a fine show Belgium would make covered with V's, and what a striking affirmation it would be of your confidence and your patriotism.

You could go even further too and make the V a sign of mutual recognition, the patriot's salute to patriot.

Raise the right hand—or the left hand if you're left-handed—to the level of your chest, the palm turned towards you, the fingers stretching upwards. Separate the forefinger and middle finger, lowering the thumb and the two other fingers. The two fingers pointing to the sky form a V.

One more symbol to add to the list.

Victory announced on the walls of Belgium, victory proclaimed by the very hands of our good people at home, victory which is already in every heart, and will soon be there in deed.

· · · · ·

Before many weeks the V's were chalked on the walls in all the occupied countries of Europe. The second stage of the campaign began with the broadcasts of "Colonel Britton" in the Friday night talks for English-speaking listeners in Europe. He issued directions for the 17-campaign. The third stage was begun on the night of June 27 when the V-symbol was transcribed into sound by the Morse signal for V (. . . -), the rhythmic theme of the opening of Beethoven's Fifth Symphony. Broadcasting on 18 July Colonel Britton announced for 20 July the mobilisation of the "V Army," the innumerable battalions of underground resistance. On that date Winston Churchill sent this message to the people of Europe:

"The V sign is the symbol of the unconquerable will of the people of the occupied territories and a portent of the fate awaiting Nazi tyranny. So long as the peoples of Europe continue to refuse all collaboration with the invader, it is sure that his cause will perish and that Europe will be liberated."

It is a remarkable fact that even through these early years of the war, where the people of Britain were fighting for their very existence, their thoughts were continually occupied with the future Europe they wanted to see, with reconstruction at home and abroad and with reforms. It is probably also true that never was there in any country, during a long and perilous war, such freedom of speech and writing and such freedom from fanaticism as in Britain through these years. The virtue of tolerance—to foreigners such a striking quality in English life—was the subject of a broadcast by the author and humanist E. M. Forster in the summer of 1941.

E. M. FORSTER: THE UNSUNG VIRTUE OF TOLERANCE

Overseas Service, July, 1941

Everybody today is talking about reconstruction. Our enemies have their schemes for a new order in Europe, maintained by their secret police, and we on our side talk of rebuilding London or England, or western civilisation, and we make plans how this is to be done—five-year plans or seven-year, or twenty-year. Which is all very well, but when I hear such talk, and see the architects sharpening their pencils and the contractors getting out their estimates, and the statesmen marking out their spheres of influence, and everyone getting down to the job, as it is called, a very famous text occurs to me: "Except the Lord build the house they labour in vain who build it." Beneath the poetic imagery of these words lies a hard scientific truth, namely, unless you have a sound attitude of mind, a right psychology, you cannot construct or reconstruct anything that will endure. The text is true, not only for religious people, but for workers whatever their outlook, and it is significant that one of our historians, Dr Arnold Toynbee, should have chosen it to preface his great study of the growth and decay of civilisations.

We shall probably agree on this point; surely the only sound foundation for a civilisation is a sound state of mind. Architects, contractors, international commissioners, marketing boards, broadcasting corporations will never, by themselves, build a new world. They must be inspired by the proper spirit, and there must be the proper spirit in the people for whom they are working. For instance, we shall never have a beautiful new London until people refuse to live in ugly houses. At present, they don't mind; they demand comfort, but are indifferent to civic beauty; indeed they have no taste. I live myself in a hideous block of flats, but I can't say it worries me, and until we are worried, all schemes for reconstructing London beautifully must automatically fail.

But about the general future of civilisation we are all worried. We want to do something about it, and we agree that the basic problem is psychological, that the Lord must build if the work is to stand, that there must be a sound state of mind before diplomacy or economics or trade-conferences can function. What state of mind is sound? Here we may differ. Most people, when asked what spiritual quality is needed to rebuild civilisation, will reply "Love." Men must love one another, they say; nations must do likewise, and then the series of cataclysms which is threatening to destroy us will be checked.

Respectfully, but firmly, I disagree. Love is a great force in private life; it is indeed the greatest of all things: but love in public affairs simply does not work. It has been tried again and again: by the Christian civilisations of the Middle Ages, and also by the French Revolution, a secular movement which reasserted the Brotherhood of Man. And it has always failed. The idea that nations should love one another, or that business concerns or marketing boards should love one another, or that a man in Portugal, say, should love a man in Peru of whom he has never heard—is absurd, it is unreal, worse, it is dangerous. It leads us into perilous and vague sentimentalism. "Love is what is needed," we chant, and then sit back and the world goes on as before. The fact is we can only love what we know personally. And we cannot know much. In public affairs, in the rebuilding of civilisation, something much less dramatic and emotional is needed, namely, tolerance. Tolerance is a very dull virtue. It is boring. Unlike love, it has always had a bad press. It is negative. It merely means putting up with people, being able to stand things. No one has ever written an ode to tolerance, or raised a statue to her. Yet this is the quality which will be most needed after the war. This is the sound state of mind which we are looking for. This is the only force which will enable different races and classes and interests to settle down together to the work of reconstruction.

The world is very full of people—appallingly full; it has never been so full before—and they are all tumbling over each other. Most of these people one doesn't know and some of them one doesn't like; doesn't like the colour of their skins, say, or the shapes of their noses, or the way they blow them or don't blow them, or the way they talk, or the smell of their clothes, or their fondness for jazz, and so on. Well, what is one to do? There are two solutions. One of them is the Nazi solution. If you don't like people, kill them, banish them, segregate them, and then strut up and down proclaiming that you are the salt of the earth. The other way is much less thrilling, but it is on the whole the way of the democracies, and I prefer it. If you don't like people, put up with them as well as you can. Don't try to love them: you can't, you will only strain yourself. But try to tolerate them. On the basis of that tolerance a civilised future may be built. Certainly I can see no other foundation for the post-war world.

For what it will most need is the negative virtues: not being huffy, touchy, irritable, revengeful. I have no more faith in positive militant ideals; they can so seldom be carried out without thousands of human beings getting maimed or imprisoned. Phrases like "I will purge this nation," "I will clean up this city," terrify and disgust me. They might not have mattered so much when the world was emptier: they are horrifying now, when one nation is mixed up with another, when one city cannot be organically separated from its neighbours. And, another point: reconstruction is unlikely to be rapid. I do not believe that we are psychologically fit for it, plan the architects never so wisely. In the long run, yes, perhaps: the history of our race justifies that hope. But civilisation has its mysterious regressions, and it seems to me that we are fated now to be in one of them, and must recognise this and behave accordingly. Tolerance, I believe, will be imperative after the establishment of peace. It's always useful to take a concrete instance: and I have been asking myself how I should behave if, after peace was signed, I met Germans who had been fighting against us. I shouldn't try to love them: I shouldn't feel inclined. They have broken a window in my ugly little flat for one thing, and they have done other things which I need not specify. But I shall try to tolerate them, because it is common-sense, because in the post-war world we shall have to live with Germans. We can't exterminate them, any more than they have succeeded in exterminating the Jews. We shall have to put up with them, not for any lofty reason, but because it is the next thing that will have to be done.

I don't regard Tolerance as a great eternally established divine principle, though I might perhaps quote "In My Father's House are many Mansions" in support of such a view. It is just a makeshift of an over-crowded and over-heated planet. It carries on when love gives out, and love generally gives out as soon as we move away from our home and our friends—and stand in a queue for potatoes. Tolerance is wanted in the queue; otherwise: we think, "Why will people be so slow?"; it is wanted in the tube, "Why will people be so fat?"; it is wanted at the telephone, or we say "Why are they so deaf?" or conversely, "Why do they mumble?" It is wanted in the street, in the office, at the factory, and it is wanted above all between classes, races and nations. It's dull. And yet it entails imagination. For you have all the time to be putting yourself in someone else's place. Which is a desirable spiritual exercise.

I was saying that Tolerance has a bad press. This ceaseless effort to put up with other people seems tame, almost ignoble, so that it sometimes repels generous natures, and I don't recall many great men who have recommended it. St. Paul certainly didn't. Nor did Dante. However, a few names occur to me, and I will give them, to lend some authority to what I say. Going back over two thousand years, and to India, there is the great Buddhist Emperor Asoka, who set up inscriptions all over India, recording not his own exploits but the need for mercy and mutual understanding and peace. Going back four hundred years, to Holland, there is the Dutch scholar Erasmus, who stood apart from

E. M. Forster
at the BBC
microphone.

the religious fanaticism of the Reformation and was abused by both parties, Catholic and Lutheran, in consequence. In the same century there was the Frenchman Montaigne, subtle, intelligent, witty, who lived in his quiet country house and wrote essays which still delight the civilised. And England, too: there was John Locke, the philosopher; there was Sydney Smith, the Liberal and liberalising divine; there was a man who recently died, Lowes Dickinson, writer of a little book called A Modern Symposium, which might be called the Bible of Tolerance. And Germany, too—yes, Germany: there was Goethe. All these men testify to the creed which I have been trying to express: a negative creed, but very necessary for the salvation of this crowded jostling modern world.

Two more remarks, and I have done. The first is that it's very easy to see fanaticism in other people, but difficult to spot in oneself. Take the evil of racial prejudice. We can easily detect it in the Nazis; their conduct has been infamous ever since they rose to power. But we ourselves—are we quite guiltless? We are far less guilty than they are. Yet is there no racial prejudice in the British Empire? Is there no colour question? I ask you to consider that, those of you to whom Tolerance is more than a pious word. My other remark is to forestall criticism. Tolerance is not the same as weakness. Putting up with people does not mean giving in to them. This complicates the problem. But the rebuilding of civilisation is bound to be complicated. I only feel certain that unless the Lord builds the House, they will labour in vain who build it. Perhaps, when the house is completed, love will enter it, and the greatest force in our private lives will also rule in public life.

. . . . .

The well-known American writer and journalist, Dorothy Thompson, came on a visit to England during the summer of 1941 to see for herself what life in Britain was like, and to be able to tell the American people of the urgent need of more help from the United States.

This as the tribute she paid to the women of Britain.

DOROTHY THOMPSON: THE WOMEN OF BRITAIN

Home Service, August, 1941

I did not come to England to speak but to listen, to see, to visit, to learn. And I have learned a great deal and hope to learn more before I go back to my country. I have a great story to tell the women of America, and my only apprehension is that I shall not tell it accurately or eloquently enough. I shall tell them about you. I shall tell them about the women I have seen at the air stations, in the uniforms of the Air Force, doing all the work accurately and brilliantly that can be taken off the shoulders of men; of the women I have met in the Army and the Admiralty, soldiers and sailors of a sort, of the wonderful women I have met in the relief stations and hospitals, in the fire stations and the A.R.P., proving in every case that when it comes to fortitude and presence of mind, cheerfulness and sheer endurance, the women of Britain justify their greatest poet, Shakespeare, who imagined and created the most winsome and proud women who ever walked the stages of the world. Thinking of these proud fighting and 'defending women reminds me of the words of the great Queen Elizabeth of your Renaissance, who, you remember, said:—

> Let tyrants fear; I have always behaved myself that under God I have placed my chiefest strength and safeguard in the ' loyal hearts and goodwill of my subjects; and therefore I am come amongst you as you see, not for my recreation and disport, but being resolved in the midst and heat of the battle to live or die amongst you all, to lay down for my God and for my Kingdom and my people my honour and my blood even in the dust. I know I have the body but of a weak and feeble woman; but I have the heart and stomach of a king, and of a King of England, too.

Yes, that is the way I shall think of the girls of the services, military and civilian—ladies with the heart and stomach of kings, and of Kings of England, too.

But I shall also tell the women of America and Canada about the other women of England who serve England's cause and the world's cause in the most inconspicuous way. I shall tell them of the miners' wives, who push their own bit of meat across the table to the man of the family to sustain him in his hard work; who back up and support the men who, having got free of the mines, are going back into the pits to dig the black diamonds that turn the wheels and heat the homes and factories of this overworked island. I shall tell them of the wives of the airmen who watch their husbands' planes speed out across the Channel and never show for an instant the anxiety in their hearts. I shall tell them of the mothers separated from their children and grieving for them. I shall tell them of all the women who by their cheerfulness and patience hold together the morale of the families of this nation that seems to me to be, indeed, one big family.

I have always been glad that I was born a woman, but never so proud to have been born one as in these weeks among you. I know—and I hope British men will not mind my saying this—that it is always the women who in the end determine whether a country stands fast or cracks. The women of England have never been servile creatures, who think that sacrifice is the lot to which they were born. You have had too many great queens for that attitude, and you are a spunky breed. That is one difference between you and the German women, who think that father is always right. Perhaps that's one trouble with Germany: no woman has ever had the audacity to tell her husband to stop that nonsense, or, much better, to laugh at him when he becomes overblown. The woman who sticks by her man as a comrade and equal is the woman who will see Britain through.

But I am not going home merely to praise you, but to use the only weapons I have, a pen and a voice, to get more help for you. My job is not here; it is over there. It is to support the President, to press for more speed, and to help in my small way to put increased heart into our effort. Everything in this world runs on heart and emotion. Intellect can show the way, but it is feeling that impels the action. And I know that if I can make the women of America imagine the women of Britain, they will get a move on.

. . . . .

The German air offensive against Britain continued up to 16 May with bombing of increasing violence. Then the Luftwaffe turned east.

But all through the raids the British population had stood up to the attacks with discipline, courage and an indomitable sense of humour.

TAXI IN THE BLITZ

A. H. Rasmussen, European Service, 1941

I was travelling by taxi the other night from Hampstead, rather late. The driver was tired, he told me, and would only take me because I was going in his direction. He was making for his home in Brixton, and bed.

I have often wondered how taxi-drivers were able to carry on for hours on end in the blackout, and asked him, through the sliding window, if he did not feel all in after a long night's work. This started us talking, and to make conversation possible, I perched on the little seat behind him.

"Well, guv'nor," he said, "it gets me dahn sometimes when it's too quiet. Then I gets sleepy an' me eyes ache. It's so 'umdrum too, sort of quiet an' sleepy, like meself.

"In the blitzes you 'ad to look alive, an' dodge abaht an' the roads allus chinged. There was new 'oles every die, new bypasses, an' the fares was different. There was one bloke I 'ad. Lumme, I shan't forget 'im. I fahnd meself in Oxford Street one night. Bombs was dropping all over the bloody place, 'eavy stuff an' incendiaries.

"'Ouses was coming dahn in front an' be'ind, an' I was wondering 'ow the 'ell to get aht of it when a bloke walks over an' calls 'Taxi.' Quite a toff, bowler 'at an' all that. I stops, thinking 'e was like me, wanting to get to 'ell aht of it. "Op in,' I yells to 'im, an' 'e 'ops in. 'Where to.' I calls aht, an' 'e 'ollers back as cool as a bloody chunk of ice: 'Oh, just drive me arahnd, I want to see this, it's quite interesting.'

"Interestin' me foot," I yells back, "this is not a bloody tank, it's a taxi. An' I stops." 'e calls back: "Do you mean to say that you won't drive me?' Crikey, 'e was a cool customer 'e was. I opens the door an' 'e steps aht just as a bloody 'ouse cime dahn a'ead of us. 'E turned to me sarcastic-like an' calls aht: 'I thought Cockneys 'ad guts.' That was too much for me guv'nor. I yells aht: "Op in, blast you, an' I'll show you.' I leans over to open the door for 'im when a bloody big chunk of shrapnel or bomb-splinter comes through the side screen where me 'ead 'ad been a second before.

"Then I took 'im for a drive I was too scared to remember much abaht. I was through the last war but in all the time I spent in France I was never so bloody scared as I was that night.

"But when I think back on it, I am glad that bloke turned up, an' I am glad I took 'im, an' 'e can't run arahnd an' say Cockneys ain't got guts.

"The only trouble is that life is very 'umdrum afterwards, an' you get fed up when nothing 'appens. "Well 'ere we are sir, Bush 'Ouse."

CHAPTER IV

Germany's Attack on the Soviet Union

June—December, 1941

At dawn, on 22 June 1941, Germany, supported by Finland, Hungary and Rumania (and later by Italy), attacked the Soviet Union on a front of 1,500 miles from Finland to the Black Sea. In the morning a proclamation from Hitler was broadcast to the German people: "In this very hour a movement of troops is taking place which in its extent and magnitude is the greatest that the world has ever seen." Hitler stated quite clearly the strategic reason why he had attacked Russia: "Thus came about the result intended by the British and Soviet Russian co-operation—namely the tying-up of such powerful German forces in the east that the radical conclusion of the war in the West, particularly as regards aircraft, could no longer be vouched for by the German High Command."

At 11.15 a.m. the Soviet Vice-Premier and Foreign Commissar, M. Molotov, said in a broadcast from Moscow: "This is not the first time that our country has had to deal with an arrogant invading foe. When Napoleon invaded Russia our country answered with the nationalist war, and Napoleon was beaten and met his doom. The same thing will happen to the arrogant Hitler, who has started a new attack on our country."

All the day Europe wondered what Britain's attitude would be. At 9 p.m. Churchill made his famous broadcast announcing that England would make common cause with the Soviet Union.

CHURCHILL ON THE INVASION OF RUSSIA

Home Service, June 22 1941

I have taken occasion to speak to you tonight because we have reached one of the climacterics of the war. The first of these intense turning-points was a year ago when France fell prostrate under the German hammer, and when we had to face the storm alone. The second was when the Royal Air Force beat the Hun raiders out of the daylight air, and thus warded off the Nazi invasion of our island while we were still ill-armed and ill-prepared. The third turning-point was when the President and Congress of the United States passed the Lease-and-Lend enactment, devoting nearly 2,000 millions sterling of the wealth of the New World to help us to defend our liberties and their own. Those were the three climacterics. The fourth is now upon us.

At four o'clock this morning Hitler attacked and invaded Russia. All his usual formalities of perfidy were observed with scrupulous technique. A non-aggression treaty had been solemnly signed and was in force between the two countries. No complaint had been made by Germany of its non-fulfilment. Under its cloak of false confidence, the German armies drew up in immense strength along a line which stretches from the White Sea to the Black Sea; and their air fleets and armoured divisions slowly and methodically took their stations. Then, suddenly, without declaration of war, without even an ultimatum, German bombs rained down from the air upon the Russian cities, the German troops violated the frontiers; and an hour later, the German Ambassador, who till the night before was lavishing his assurances of friendship, almost of alliance, upon the Russians, called upon the Russian Foreign Minister to tell him that a state of war existed between Germany and Russia.

Thus was repeated on a far larger scale the same kind of outrage against every form of signed compact and international faith which we have witnessed in Norway, Denmark, Holland and Belgium, and which Hitler's accomplice and jackal, Mussolini, so faithfully imitated in the case of Greece.

The initial attack in Operation Barbarossa, 21 July 1941.

All this was no surprise to me. In fact I gave clear and precise warnings to Stalin of what was coming. I gave him warning as I have given warning to others before. I can only hope that this warning did not fall unheeded. All we know at present is that the Russian people are defending their native soil and that their leaders have called upon them to resist to the utmost.

Hitler is a monster of wickedness, insatiable in his lust for blood and plunder. Not content with having all Europe under his heel, or else terrorised into various forms of abject submission, he must now carry his work of butchery and desolation among the vast multitudes of Russia and of Asia. The terrible military machine, which we and the rest of civilised world so foolishly, so supinely, so insensately allowed the Nazi gangsters to build up year by year from almost nothing, cannot stand idle lest it rust or fall to pieces. It must be in continual motion, grinding up human lives and trampling down the homes and the rights of hundreds of millions of men. Moreover it must be fed, not only with flesh but with oil.

So now this bloodthirsty guttersnipe must launch his mechanised armies upon new fields of slaughter, pillage and devastation. Poor as are the Russian peasants, workmen and soldiers, he must steal from them their daily bread; he must devour their harvests; he must rob them of the oil which drives their ploughs; and thus produce a famine without example in human history. And even the carnage and ruin which his victory, should he gain it—he has not gained it yet—will bring upon the Russian people, will itself only be a stepping-stone to the attempt to plunge the four or five hundred millions who live in China, and the three hundred and fifty millions who live in India, into that bottomless pit of human degradation over which the diabolic emblem of the Swastika flaunts itself. It is not too much to say here this summer evening that the lives and happiness of a thousand million additional people are now menaced with brutal Nazi violence. That is enough to make us hold our breath. But presently I shall show you something else that lies behind, and something that touches very nearly the life of Britain and of the United States.

The Nazi régime is indistinguishable from the worst features of Communism. It is devoid of all theme and principle except appetite and racial domination. It excels all forms of human wickedness in the efficiency of its cruelty and ferocious aggression. No one has been a more consistent opponent of Communism than I have for the last twenty-five years. I will unsay no word that I have spoken about it. But all this fades away before the spectacle which is now unfolding. The past with its crimes, its follies and its tragedies, flashes away. I see the Russian soldiers standing on the threshold of their native land, guarding the fields which their fathers have tilled from time immemorial. I see them guarding their homes where mothers and wives pray yes, for there are times when all pray—for the safety of their loved ones, the return of the breadwinner, of their champion, of their protector. I see the ten thousand villages of Russia, where the means of existence was wrung so hardly from the soil, but where there are still primordial human joys, where maidens laugh and children play. I see advancing upon all this in hideous onslaught the Nazi war machine, with its clanking, heel-clicking, dandified Prussian officers, its crafty expert agents fresh from the cowing and tying-down of a dozen countries. I see also the dull, drilled, docile, brutish masses of the Hun soldiery plodding on like a swarm of crawling locusts. I see the German bombers and fighters in the sky, still smarting from many a British whipping, delighted to find what they believe is an easier and safer prey.

Behind all this glare, behind all this storm, I see that small group of villainous men who plan, organise and launch this cataract of horrors upon mankind. And then my mind goes back across the years to the days when the Russian armies were our allies against the same deadly foe; when they fought with so much valour and constancy, and helped to gain a victory from all share in which, alas, they were—through no fault of ours—utterly cut off. I have lived through all this, and you will pardon me if I express my feelings and the stir of old memories.

But now I have to declare the decision of His Majesty's Government—and I feel sure it is a decision in which the great Dominions will, in due course, concur—for we must speak out now at once, without a day's delay. I have to make the declaration, but can you doubt what our policy will be? We have but one aim and one single, irrevocable purpose. We are resolved to destroy Hitler and every vestige of the Nazi régime. From this nothing will turn us—nothing. We will never parley, we will never negotiate with Hitler or any of his gang. We shall fight him by land, we shall fight him by sea, we shall fight him in the air, until with God's help we have rid the earth of his shadow and liberated its peoples from his yoke. Any man or State who fights on against Nazidom will have our aid. Any man or State who marches with Hitler is our foe. This applies not only to organised States but to all representatives of that vile race of quislings who make themselves the tools and agents of the Nazi régime against their fellow-countrymen, and the lands of their birth. They—these quislings— like the Nazi leaders themselves, if not disposed of by their fellow-countrymen, which would save trouble, will be delivered by us on the morrow of victory to the justice of the Allied tribunals. That is our policy and that is our declaration. It follows, therefore, that we shall give whatever help we can to Russia and the Russian people. We shall appeal to all our friends and allies in every part of the world to take the same course and pursue it, as we shall, faithfully and stead-fastly to the end.

We have offered the Government of Soviet Russia any technical or economic assistance which is in our power, and which is likely to be of service to them. We shall bomb Germany by day as well as by night in ever-increasing measure, casting upon them month by month a heavier discharge of bombs, and making the German people taste and gulp each month a sharper dose of the miseries they have showered upon mankind. It is noteworthy that only yesterday the

Royal Air Force, fighting inland over French territory, cut down with very small loss to themselves 28 of the Hun fighting machines in the air above the French soil they have invaded, defiled and profess to hold. But this is only a beginning. From now forward the main expansion of our Air Force proceeds with gathered speed.

In another six months the weight of the help we are receiving from the United States in war materials of all kinds, and especially in heavy bombers, will begin to tell.

This is no class war, but a war in which the whole British Empire and Commonwealth of Nations is engaged without distinction of race, creed or party. It is not for me to speak of the action of the United States, but this I will say: if Hitler imagines that his attack on Soviet Russia will cause the slightest division of aims or slackening of effort in the great Democracies who are resolved upon his doom, he is woefully mistaken. On the contrary, we shall be fortified and encouraged in our efforts to rescue mankind from this tyranny. We shall be strengthened and not weakened in determination and in resources.

This is no time to moralise on the follies of countries and governments which have allowed themselves to be struck down one by one, when by united action they could have saved themselves and saved the world from this catastrophe. But when I spoke a few minutes ago of Hitler's blood-lust and the hateful appetites which have impelled or lured him on his Russian adventure, I said there was one deeper motive behind his outrage. He wishes to destroy the Russian power because he hopes that if he succeeds in this, he will be able to bring back the main strength of his army and air force from the East and hurl it upon this Island, which he knows he must conquer or suffer the penalty of his crimes. His invasion of Russia is no more than a prelude to an attempted invasion of the British Isles. He hopes, no doubt, that all this may be accomplished before the winter comes, and that he can overwhelm Great Britain before the fleet and air power of the United States may intervene. He hopes that he may once again repeat, upon a greater scale than ever before, that process of destroying his enemies one by one, by which he has so long thrived and prospered, and that then the scene will be clear for the final act, without which all his conquests would be in vain—namely, the subjugation of the Western Hemisphere to his will and to his system.

The Russian danger is therefore our danger, and the danger of the United States, just as the cause of any Russian fighting for his hearth and home is the cause of free men and free peoples in every quarter of the globe. Let us learn the lessons already taught by such cruel experience. Let us redouble our exertions, and strike with united strength while life and power remain.

. . . . .

On 3 July, Stalin, in a broadcast to the Russian people, expressed the determination of the Soviet Union to fight to the last drop of blood. The main contents of this broadcast from Moscow was given by the BBC.

STALIN TO THE SOVIET UNION

The entire Soviet people is rising in defence of the Fatherland at the side of the Red Army. It is a question of life and death for the Soviet State, for the people of the USSR—a question whether the peoples of the Soviet Union shall be free or reduced to slavery.

Great Lenin, who founded our State, used to say that the basic qualities of the Soviet men should be valour and daring: they should be fearless in battle and resolved to fight against the enemies of our country. The Red Army and Navy and all the citizens of the Soviet Union must defend every inch of the Soviet soil, fight to the last drop of their blood, defend their towns and villages, and show their daring and ingenuity—qualities that are characteristic of our people.

In the event of the retreat of the Red Army all railway rolling stock must be brought away. We must not leave a single engine to the enemy, nor a single railway coach. We must not leave a single pound of grain or a single gallon of petrol to the enemy. The collective farmers must take away all their cattle and place their corn in the care of State organisations to be transported to the rear zone. All valuable materials which cannot be taken away must be resolutely destroyed.

In the areas occupied by the enemy, foot and horse guerrilla detachments must be created, as well as groups of saboteurs entrusted with fighting against the units of the enemy army, with the launching of guerrilla warfare everywhere, with blowing up bridges and roads, with wrecking telephone and telegraph communications, and with setting forests, depots and trains on fire. It is necessary to create in invaded areas conditions unbearable for the enemy and all his accomplices.

The war against Fascist Germany cannot be regarded as an ordinary war. It is not only a war between two armies; it is at the same time a great war of the whole Soviet people against German
Fascist troops. The object of this national war against the Fascist invaders is not only to avert the danger overhanging our country but also to help all the peoples of Europe groaning under the yoke of German Fascism.

In this war of liberation we shall not be alone. In this great war we shall have faithful allies in the person of the peoples of Europe and America. Our war for the freedom of our Fatherland is merged into the struggle of the peoples of Europe and America for their independent freedom. It is the united front of the peoples who stand for freedom against the threat of enslavement by Hitler's Fascist armies.

'Digging in' shortly after the advance into Russia.

In this connection the historic utterance of the British Prime Minister, Mr Churchill, about aid to the Soviet Union, and the declaration of the Government of the United States signifying readiness to give assistance to our country are fully comprehensible and symptomatic.

Comrades! Our forces are numberless. The overweening enemy will soon learn this to his cost. Side by side with the Red Army many thousand workers, collective farmers, and intellectuals are rising to fight the enemy aggressor. The masses of our people will rise up in their millions. The working people of Moscow and Leningrad have already commenced quickly to form popular levies in support of the Red Army. Such popular levies must be raised in every city which is in danger of enemy invasion; all working people must be roused to defend our freedom, our honour, our country, in our patriotic war against German Fascism.

. . . . .

Far from making England and America more friendly to Germany, Hitler's attack on Russia brought the United States even closer to the anti-Hitler Powers. On 14 August it was announced that Winston Churchill and President Roosevelt had met at sea and issued a statement of war aims known as the "Atlantic Charter."

In a broadcast on 24 August, Churchill gave an account of his meeting with the President of the United States.

THE ATLANTIC CHARTER

Read in the Home Service by the Deputy Prime Minister,
Mr C. R. Attlee, on August 14 1941

The President of the United States and the Prime Minister, Mr Churchill, representing His Majesty's Government in the United Kingdom, being met together, deem it right to make known certain common principles in the national policies of their respective countries on which they base their hopes for a better future for the world.

FIRST, their countries seek no aggrandisement, territorial or other.

SECOND, they desire to see no territorial changes that do not accord with the freely expressed wishes of the peoples concerned.

THIRD, they respect the right of all peoples to choose the form of Government under which they will live; and they wish to see sovereign rights and self-government restored to those who have been forcibly deprived of them.

FOURTH, they will endeavour with due respect for their existing obligations, to further enjoyment by all States, great or small, victor or vanquished, or access, on equal terms, to the trade and to the raw materials of the world which are needed for their economic prosperity.

FIFTH, they desire to bring about the fullest collaboration between all nations in the economic field, with the object of securing for all improved labour standards, economic advancement, and social security.

SIXTH, after the final destruction of Nazi tyranny, they hope to see established a peace which will afford to all nations the means of dwelling in safety within their own boundaries, and which will afford assurance that all the men in all the lands may live out their lives in freedom from fear and want.

SEVENTH, such a peace should enable all men to traverse the high seas and oceans without hindrances.

EIGHTH, they believe all of the nations of the world, for realistic as well as spiritual reasons, must come to the abandonment of the use of force. Since no future peace can be maintained if land, sea, or air armaments continue to be employed by nations which threaten, or may threaten, aggression outside of their frontiers, they believe, pending the establishment of a wider and permanent system of general security, that the disarmament of such nations is essential.

They will likewise aid and encourage all other practicable measures which will lighten for peace-loving peoples the crushing burden of armament.

CHURCHILL ON THE ATLANTIC MEETING

Home Service, August 24, 1941

I thought you would like me to tell you something about the voyage which I made across the ocean to meet our great friend, the President of the United States. Exactly where we met is a secret, but I don't think I shall be indiscreet if I go so far as to say that it was "somewhere in the Atlantic."

In a spacious landlocked bay which reminded me of the West Coast of Scotland, powerful American warships protected by strong flotillas and far-ranging aircraft awaited our arrival, and, as it were, stretched out a hand to help us in. Our party arrived in the newest or almost the newest British battleship, the *Prince of Wales*, with a modern escort of British and Canadian destroyers; and there for three days I spent my time in company, and I think I may say in comradeship, with Mr Roosevelt; while all the time the chiefs of the staff and the naval and military commanders both of the British Empire and of the United States sat together in continual council.

President Roosevelt is the thrice-chosen head of the most powerful State and community in the world. I am the servant of King and Parliament at present charged with the principal direction of our affairs in these fateful times, and it is my duty also to make sure, as I have made sure, that anything I say or do in the exercise of my office is approved and sustained by the whole British Com-

Franklin D. Roosevelt and Winston Churchill, August 1941.

monwealth of Nations. Therefore this meeting was bound to be important, because of the enormous forces at present only partially mobilised but steadily mobilising which are at the disposal of these two major groupings of the human family: the British Empire and the United States, who, fortunately for the progress of mankind, happen to speak the same language, and very largely think the same thoughts, or anyhow think a lot of the same thoughts.

The meeting was therefore symbolic. That is its prime importance. It symbolises, in a form and manner which everyone can understand in every land and in every clime, the deep underlying unities which stir and at decisive moments rule the English-speaking peoples throughout the world. Would it be presumptuous for me to say that it symbolises something even more majestic— namely, the marshalling of the good forces of the world against the evil forces which are now so formidable and triumphant and which have cast their cruel spell over the whole of Europe and a large part of Asia?

This was a meeting which marks for ever in the pages of history the taking up by the English-speaking nations, amid all this peril, tumult and confusion, of the guidance of the fortunes of the broad toiling masses in all the continents; and our loyal effort without any clog of selfish interest to lead them forward out of the miseries into which they have been plunged, back to the broad highroad of freedom and justice. This is the highest honour and the most glorious opportunity which could ever have come to any branch of the human race.

Awful and horrible things are happening in these days. The whole of Europe has been wrecked and trampled down by the mechanical weapons and barbaric fury of the Nazis; the most deadly instruments of war—science have been joined to the extreme refinements of treachery and the most brutal exhibitions of ruthlessness, and thus have formed a combine of aggression the like of which has never been known, before which the rights, the traditions, the characteristics and the structure of many ancient honoured States and peoples have been laid prostrate, and are now ground down under the heel and terror of a monster. The Austrians, the Czechs, the Poles, the Norwegians, the Danes, the Belgians, the Dutch, the Greeks, the Croats and the Serbs, above all the great French nation, have been stunned and pinioned. Italy, Hungary, Rumania, Bulgaria have bought a shameful respite by becoming the jackals of the tiger, but their situation is very little different and will presently be indistinguishable from that of his victims. Sweden, Spain, and Turkey stand appalled, wondering which will be struck down next.

Here, then, is the vast pit into which all the most famous States and races of Europe have been flung and from which unaided they can never climb. But all this did not satiate Adolf Hitler; he made a treaty of non-aggression with Soviet Russia, just as he made one with Turkey, in order to keep them quiet till he was ready to attack them, and then, nine weeks ago today, without a vestige of provocation, he hurled millions of soldiers, with all their apparatus, upon the neighbour he had called his friend, with the avowed object of destroying

Russia and tearing her in pieces. This frightful business is now unfolding day by day before our eyes. Here is a devil who, in a mere spasm of pride and lust for domination, can condemn two or three millions, perhaps it may be many more, of human beings, to speedy and violent death. "Let Russia be blotted out—Let Russia be destroyed. Order the armies to advance." Such were his decrees. Accordingly from the Arctic Ocean to the Black Sea, six or seven millions of soldiers are locked in mortal struggle. Ah, but this time it was not so easy.

This time it was not all one way. The Russian armies and all the peoples of the Russian Republic have rallied to the defence of their hearths and homes. For the first time Nazi blood has flowed in a fearful torrent. Certainly a million-and-a-half, perhaps two millions of Nazi cannon-fodder have bit the dust of the endless plains of Russia. The tremendous battle rages along nearly two thousand miles of front. The Russians fight with magnificent devotion; not only that, our generals who have visited the Russian front line report with admiration the efficiency of their military organisation and the excellence of their equipment. The aggressor is surprised, startled, staggered. For the first time in his experience mass murder has become unprofitable. He retaliates by the most frightful cruelties. As his armies advance, whole districts are being exterminated. Scores of thousands—literally scores of thousands—of executions in cold blood are being perpetrated by the German police-troops upon the Russian patriots who defend their native soil. Since the Mongol invasions of Europe in the sixteenth century, there has never been methodical, merciless butchery on such a scale, or approaching such a scale. And this is but the beginning. Famine and pestilence have yet to follow in the bloody ruts of Hitler's tanks. We are in the presence of a crime without a name.

But Europe is not the only Continent to be tormented and devastated by aggressions. For five long years the Japanese military factions, seeking to emulate the style of Hitler and Mussolini, taking all their posturing as if it were a new European revelation, have been invading and harrying the five hundred million inhabitants of China. Japanese armies have been wandering about that vast land in futile excursions, carrying with them carnage, ruin and corruption and calling it the "Chinese Incident." Now they stretch a grasping hand into the southern seas of China; they snatch Indo-China from the wretched Vichy French; they menace by their movements Siam; menace Singapore, the British link with Australasia; and menace the Philippine Islands under the protection of the United States. It is certain that this has got to stop. Every effort will be made to secure a peaceful settlement. The United States are labouring with infinite patience to arrive at a fair and amicable settlement which will give Japan the utmost reassurance for her legitimate interests. We earnestly hope these negotiations will succeed. But this I must say: that if these hopes should fail we shall, of course, range ourselves unhesitatingly at the side of the United States.

And thus we come back to the quiet bay somewhere in the Atlantic where misty sunshine plays on great ships which carry the White Ensign, or the Stars and Stripes. We had the idea, when we met there—the President and I—that without attempting to draw up final and formal peace aims, or war aims, it was necessary to give all peoples, and especially the oppressed and conquered peoples, a simple, rough and ready war-time statement of the goal towards which the British Commonwealth and the United States mean to make their way, and thus make a way for others to march with them upon a road which will certainly be painful, and may be long.

The United States and Great Britain do not now assume that there will never be any more war again. On the contrary, we intend to take ample precautions to prevent its renewal in any period we can foresee by effectively disarming the guilty nations while remaining suitably protected ourselves.

Above all, it was necessary to give hope and the assurance of final victory to those many scores of millions of men and women who are battling for life and freedom, or who are already bent down under the Nazi yoke. Hitler and his confederates have for some time past been adjuring, bullying and beseeching the populations whom they have wronged and injured, to bow to their fate, to resign themselves to their servitude, and for the sake of some mitigations and indulgences, to "collaborate"—that is the word—in what is called the New Order in Europe.

What is this New Order which they seek to fasten first upon Europe and if possible—for their ambitions are boundless—upon all the continents of the globe? It is the rule of the Herrenvolk—the master race—who are to put an end to democracy, to parliaments, to the fundamental freedoms and decencies of ordinary men and women, to the historic rights of nations; and give them in exchange the iron rule of Prussia, the universal goose-step, and a strict, efficient discipline enforced upon the working-classes by the political police, with the German concentration camps and firing parties, now so busy in a dozen lands, always handy in the background. There is the New Order.

Napoleon in his glory and his genius spread his Empire far and wide. There was a time when only the snows of Russia and the white cliffs of Dover with their guardian fleets stood between him and the dominion of the world. Napoleon's armies had a theme: they carried with them the surges of the French Revolution. Liberty, Equality and Fraternity—that was the cry. There was a sweeping away of outworn medieval systems and aristocratic privilege. There was the land for the people, a new code of law. Nevertheless, Napoleon's Empire vanished like a dream. But Hitler, Hitler has no theme, nought but mania, appetite and exploitation. He has, however, weapons and machinery for grinding down and for holding down conquered countries which are the product, the sadly perverted product, of modern science.

Now Hitler is striking at Russia with all his might, well knowing the difficulties of geography which stand between Russia and the aid which the Western Democracies are trying to bring. We shall strive our utmost to overcome all obstacles and to bring this aid. We have arranged for a conference in Moscow between the United States, British and Russian authorities to settle the whole plan. No barrier must stand in the way. But why is Hitler striking at Russia, and inflicting and suffering himself or, rather, making his soldiers suffer, this frightful slaughter? It is with the declared object of turning his whole force upon the British Islands, and if he could succeed in beating the life and strength out of us, which is not so easy, then is the moment when he will settle his account, and it is already a long one, with the people of the United States and generally with the Western Hemisphere. One by one, there is the process.

We had a Church parade on the Sunday in our Atlantic bay. The President came on to the quarter-deck of the *Prince of Wales*, where there were mingled together many hundreds of American and British sailors and marines. The sun shone bright and warm while we all sang the old hymns which are our common inheritance and which we learned as children in our homes. We sang the hymn founded on the psalm which John Hampden's soldiers sang when they bore his body to the grave, and in which the brief, precarious span of human life is contrasted with the immutability of Him to Whom a thousand ages are but as yesterday, and as a watch in
the night. We sang the sailor's hymn "For those in peril—and there are very many—"on the sea." We sang "Onward, Christian Soldiers." And indeed I felt that this was no vain presumption, but that we had the right to feel that we were serving a cause for the sake of which a trumpet has sounded from on high.

When I looked upon that densely packed congregation of fighting men of the same language, of the same faith, of the same fundamental laws and the same ideals, and now to a large extent of the same interests, it swept across me that here was the only hope, but also the sure hope, of saving the world from measureless degradation.

And so we came back across the ocean waves, uplifted in spirit, fortified in resolve. Some American destroyers which were carrying mails to the United States Marines in Iceland happened to be going the same way, too, so we made a goodly company at sea together.

And when we were right out in mid-passage one afternoon a noble sight broke on the view. We overtook one of the convoys which carry the munitions and supplies of the New World to sustain the champions of freedom in the Old. The whole broad horizon seemed filled with ships; seventy or eighty ships of all kinds and sizes, arrayed in fourteen lines, each of which could have been drawn with a ruler, hardly a wisp of smoke, not a straggler, but all bristling with cannons and other precautions on which I will not dwell, and all surrounded by their British escorting vessels, while overhead the far-ranging Catalina air-boats soared—vigilant, protecting eagles in the sky. Then I felt that, hard and terrible and long drawn-out as this struggle may be, we shall not be denied the strength to do our duty to the end.

. . . . .

In Russia the German advance during the first weeks had been rapid, but the Russians inflicted terrible losses on the enemy. The Soviet Russian peoples were fighting with burning zeal and inspiration for the world they had built up, and the industrialisation of Russia through the five-year plans which had characterised the rule of Stalin, saved Russia and Europe from Nazism.

Time after time the Germans claimed to have encircled and annihilated the Russian armies, but again and again the Russian forces extricated themselves.

Early in October the Germans launched drives on a colossal scale against Moscow, the Donetz Basin and the Crimea, and on the 9th the Nazis told the world that Russia, as a military power was finished for good and all. Joseph Grigg, who was then a foreign correspondent in Berlin for the United Press of America, gave two years later in the Home Service of the BBC, the following description of the press conference in Berlin when this great news was given.

A GERMAN PRESS CONFERENCE

Home Service, October 9 1943

On 9 October I was summoned by a phone call to a special press conference at the Propaganda Ministry in Berlin. The girl secretary in the Foreign Press Department said there was to be a statement by Dr Otto Dietrich, the Reich's Press Chief, better known to the foreign correspondents as "Hitler's little Sir Echo." She said Dietrich had just returned from Hitler's headquarters and that the conference would be historic. It was set for 12 noon, and I was warned not to be late.

At noon some 200 foreign correspondents were assembled in the great ornate Propaganda Ministry "Theater," crowded with expensive red plush chairs, and with an eight-feet high map of Russia filling the stage. Behind the speaker's chair were grouped all Dr Dietrich's Yes-men and stooges, resplendent in Nazi uniforms, pompous and self-important and smirking with anticipation at the news their boss was about to reveal to the world.

just one half-hour late, Dr Dietrich bounced in, cocky and self-confident, flapping his right arm in an imitation of the salute Hitler uses at Nazi mass-meetings. The Nazi officials and Italians saluted and heiled. The rest of us just waited. Dr Dietrich is not the blonde Nordic giant type of Nazi. Actually, he is only a little man—about five foot three—with an ingratiating smile and cold, cynical eyes. Under Dr Goebbels his job is to run the whole tame Nazi press. He was wearing a grey uniform and high jack boots. He opened with a long, tiresome tirade against the allied leaders, whom he denounced as "liars" and "military illiterates." The American and other neutral correspondents—Swedes and Swiss—began to wonder whether this wasn't going to be just another

Hitler and Goebbels watch a propaganda film.

propaganda circus. I myself was beginning to think maybe I was wasting my time being there at all.

And then Dr Dietrich pulled out the rabbit he had been keeping in his hat to the very end. The great offensive, he announced, had resulted in the complete encirclement of Marshal Timoshenko's armies of some 60-70 Divisions in two mighty rings before Moscow. I'll quote his exact words as I noted them down at the time:

"The entire Soviet front is smashed. With the destruction of Timoshenko's armies now proceeding, the last Soviet army group will be disposed of and wiped out."

"The campaign in the East," he shouted dramatically, "is decided. Further developments will follow as we wish. With this last great blow we are dealing it, the Soviet Union is liquidated militarily. Gentlemen, I stake my professional reputation on this." The Nazi Yes-men and the Italians leapt up, cheering and heiling and scrambled to shake Dr Dietrich's hand. At the same time, the German radio began broadcasting with drums and trumpet fanfares a special communique telling the world the news Dr Dietrich had just told us. That afternoon and next morning the German papers came out with huge headlines splashed across their front pages proclaiming the military destruction of Russia.

. . . . .

A Fighter Wing of the Royal Air Force was stationed near Murmansk in the autumn of 1941, fighting side by side with their Russian brothers-in-arms. A RAF Flight-Lieutenant who took part, two years later gave the following description:

WITH THE ROYAL AIR FORCE AT MURMANSK

Hubert Griffith, November 7 1943

I had the luck to be in Russia as administrative officer—Wing Adjutant—with the chaps of the Fighter Wing of English Hurricanes that went out to Murmansk in the late summer of 1941. We were the first English contingent there in the first few weeks and months of Russia becoming our ally. We saw—in full measure—Russia at war. We lived and worked on an Arctic aerodrome with our Soviet opposite numbers-pilots, ground-crews, senior officers, administrative personnel—each to each. We got to know them through and through, and believed in them, and trusted them, and liked them; and they got to know us, in those months, and they got to believe in us, and trust us—and I sincerely think, to like us, too.

I remember first the impression on landing, of welcome and co-operation. Curious memories mix together—the memory of one of our airmen having a tunic button sewed on by a Russian
hospital nurse from a hospital train (with a couple of hundred Russians enthusiastically applauding). And the memory of the intensive and efficient arrangements made by high Soviet staff officers to get us to our destination, from Archangel up to Murmansk, in destroyers, and cargo ships, and Russian trains. I remember a serious and solemn occasion at the end of our stay—when our pilots had shot down fifteen German aircraft for the loss of only one of our own, and had done forty escorts to Soviet bombers and we had never let them lose a single bomber. At the farewell luncheon-party, our own Wing-Commander got up and proposed and drank the health of Marshal Stalin—and the Russian General-of-Aviation who had commanded us all the time we were out there got up and proposed and drank the health of the King. I am not overstating this when I say that that was a serious and impressive moment. And I also remember the day when the same Russian General arrived for one of our operational conferences bringing with him a little baby reindeer, about two feet high, as a friendly and living testimonial of his regard for our Wing.

The Russians have a passionate enthusiasm for aviation. They would fly in any weather. And they worked up an extreme enthusiasm for the British game of darts once we had taught it them. They would throw the dart as though it were a harpoon, and the dart-board the body of a German.

I wish I could give you an idea of the tremendous sense of "urgency" in war-time Russia. It impressed us, and shook us, and left something never to be forgotten in the memory. The Russian pilots gave our own pilots a series of parties, and nerve-shaking parties they were. Our own pilots gave the Russian pilots also some parties—and these were not bad parties either. And our senses of humour—British and Russian—turned out curiously the same. We had interpreters of course. But the pilots used to go and make diagrams in the snow. There were many lighter and off-the-record sides to the expedition. We'd laugh a lot but somehow we understood. But I still come back to that question of urgency. One day a little Soviet pilot—whom we knew well, and who had been to many of our parties—got into a fight with a couple of German machines. He shot down the first, and he rammed the second—and then, having baled out, he fought his two opponents on the ground; and killed them both—and then walked back, four days and four nights in the snow, with frostbitten feet and his face slashed to pieces and then retired to hospital, where we went down to see him. This seemed to us not abnormal, but typical. It stood for so much that we had seen, with our own eyes, of the intensity with which Russia is taking the war. Kindness and courtesy to us as guests—certainly! Cordiality, and co-operation, and fun, and the endless excitement that air-crews always seem to find in one another's society. But, at the heart, steel—and black hatred of the Hun. They are in the war to the death—and it will be the death of their enemies. Our Wing is scattered now. Some of them are dead, for the RAF is always in continuous action. But the rest are left, believing a lot of good things about Russia, and, from our own personal knowledge and experience.

. . . . .

By the middle of November the Germans were in Rostov, they had reached the outskirts of Moscow and Sevastopol, and had practically encircled Leningrad. The turn of the tide came with the battle of Moscow.

THE BATTLE OF MOSCOW

European Service, February, 1942

After the descriptions of correspondents in Moscow and after the return of the British Ambassador to Russia, Sir Stafford Cripps, it has now become possible to form a clearer picture of the battle of Moscow. It began with the terrible German offensive in the beginning of October. On the 15th the Russian Foreign Commissar, Molotov, sent for the British Ambassador and told him that the Germans were so dangerously near Moscow that all diplomatic corps would have to leave within six hours and go to Kuibyshev on the Volga. Although the Russians had thrown in large reinforcements, the Germans broke through to Mojaisk, only 65 miles from Moscow. As Stafford Cripps wrote: "It looked as if nothing could stop them, and nothing did stop them except the almost superhuman courage of the soldiers of the Red Army. Every policeman in Moscow was mobilised that night and sent to the front, and the front held."

But in the beginning of November, Hitler threw in 53 divisions in an attempt to take Moscow by envelopment and direct assault. These 53 German divisions, supported by 13 tank divisions (totalling 3,000 tanks) were hurled against the Russian capital. But only four or five days after this new and terrible onslaught had started, General Zhukov became convinced that the German attack would fail, and he conceived the outline of his December counter offensive. Unknown to the Germans, General Zhukov was receiving important reinforcements, so that the force with which he began his counter-offensive wore the symbolic aspect of an All-Union force, with Georgians, Siberians, Ukrainians, Cossacks, and White Russians fighting beside their Russian comrades-in-arms. Zhukov's tactics were directed towards wearing out the enemy by a steadily-planned withdrawal, inflicting terrible losses at a moment when the Germans were fully extended, and his own forces were sufficiently strengthened. Especially, Stalin had built up a large cavalry reserve of about 70,000 men; and then he bided his time. According to Sir Stafford Cripps, the critical moment came on the night of 6 December. Then the German troops were at one point within artillery range of the city, though they never had the chance to fire their guns. At that time Moscow was almost surrounded and the last great railway junction to the east was being attacked. This was the supreme moment and the Soviet cavalry under General Belov were thrown in to attack the Germans. Stalin had judged right. The Germans broke and started the retreat which later spread all along the front, while the temperature sank to a cold that was exceptional even for winter in Russia.

At the end of his article in the *Tribune*, Sir Stafford Cripps discusses the reasons for the German defeat: "How came it that the Russians succeeded and the Germans, with their wonderfully organised Blitz, failed? Not by means of a superb and highly accurate mechanism of organisation on the Russian side but by the brilliance of their young generals, by the initiative of their officers and soldiers, by the sure hand of their high command and of Stalin himself, the supreme director of their efforts, and because every man, woman and child throughout the areas where the fighting took place and along the lines of communication behind the front gave their most devoted service to the saving of their country."

CHAPTER V

The Climax of the Axis Efforts

December, 1941—January, 1943

At the same time as the Battle of Moscow reached its turning-point, the war spread to the Pacific. On 7 December, without warning, Japan attacked all American and British bases within her reach. Japanese planes bombed the US naval base at Pearl Harbor, Hawaii, with devastating effect.

On 8 December, Great Britain and the United States declared war on Japan, and three days later Germany and Italy declared war on the USA. On 8 December, Churchill spoke to the House of Commons, and he afterwards repeated his speech in a broadcast to the world.

CHURCHILL ON THE WAR WITH JAPAN

Home Service, December 8 1941

As soon as I heard last night, that Japan had attacked the United States, I felt it necessary that Parliament should be immediately summoned. It is indispensable to our system of government that Parliament should play its full part in all the important acts of State, and at all the crucial moments of the war. With the full approval of the nation, and of the Empire, I pledged the word of Great Britain, about a month ago, that should the United States be involved in war with Japan, a British declaration of war would follow within the hour. I therefore spoke to President Roosevelt on the Atlantic telephone last night, with a view to arranging the timing of our respective declarations. The President told me that he would this morning send a Message to Congress, which, of course, as is well known, can alone make a declaration of war on behalf of the United States, and I then assured him that we would follow immediately.

However, it soon appeared that British territory in Malaya had also been the object of Japanese attack, and later on it was announced from Tokyo that the Japanese High Command—a curious form; not the Imperial Japanese Government—had declared that a state of war existed with Great Britain and the United States. That being so, there was no need to wait for the declaration by Congress. American time is very nearly six hours behind ours. The Cabinet, therefore, which met at 12.30 today, authorised an immediate declaration of war upon Japan.

It is worth while looking for a moment at the manner in which the Japanese have begun their assault upon the English-speaking world. Every circumstance of calculated and characteristic Japanese treachery was employed against the United States. The Japanese envoys, Nomura and Kurusu, were ordered to prolong their mission in the United States, in order to keep the conversations going while a surprise attack was being prepared, to be made before a declaration of war could be delivered. The President's appeal to the Emperor, reminding him of the importance of preserving the peace of the Pacific, has received only this base and brutal reply.

Now that the issue is joined in the most direct manner, it only remains for the two great democracies to face their task with whatever strength God may give them.

It is of the highest importance that there should be no underrating of the gravity of the new dangers we have to meet, either here or in the United States. The enemy has attacked with an audacity which may spring from recklessness, but which may also spring from a conviction of strength. The ordeal to which the English-speaking world and our heroic Russian Allies are being exposed will certainly be hard, especially at the outset, and will probably be long, yet when we look around us over the sombre panorama of the world, we have no reason to doubt the justice of our cause or that our strength and will-power will be sufficient to sustain it. We have at least four-fifths of the population of the globe upon our side.

We are responsible for their safety and for their future. In the past we have had a light which flickered, in the present we have a light which flames, and in the future there will be a light which shines over all the land and sea.

. . . . .

Japan's first blow was directed against American naval power in the Pacific, the second against Malaya and Singapore. On 10 December, Japanese planes sank the British battleship *Prince of Wales* and the battle-cruiser *Repulse*. Japan had gained naval supremacy in the Pacific and the Japanese armies moved south and west. For a time their advance was sweeping, while the immense resources of the United States, now at war with all the Axis powers, were gradually being mobilised.

In a few months the Philippines, the Dutch East Indies and Malaya fell into the hands of the Japanese. The situation was grave indeed when Churchill, on

15 February made a survey over the events of the last months and announced the new blow which that very day had fallen upon the British Empire.

CHURCHILL ON FALL OF SINGAPORE

Home Service, February 15 1942

Nearly six months have passed since at the end of August I made a broadcast directly to my fellow-countrymen.

How do matters stand now? Taking it all in all, are our chances of survival better or are they worse than in August, 1941? The first and greatest of events is that the United States is now unitedly and whole-heartedly in the war with us. But there is another fact, in some ways more immediately effective. The Russian armies have not been defeated, they have not been torn to pieces. The Russian people have not been conquered or destroyed. Leningrad and Moscow have not been taken.

Here, then, are two tremendous fundamental facts which will in the end dominate the world situation and make victory possible in a form never possible before. But there is another heavy and terrible side to the account, and this must be set in the balance against these inestimable gains. Japan has plunged into the war, and is ravaging the beautiful, fertile, prosperous, and densely populated lands of the Far East. It would never have been in the power of Great Britain while fighting Germany and Italy—the nations long hardened and prepared for war—while fighting in the North Sea, in the Mediterranean and in the Atlantic—it would never have been in our power to defend the Pacific and the Far East single-handed against the onslaught of Japan. We have only just been able to keep our heads above water at home; only by a narrow margin have we brought in the food and the supplies; only by so little have we held our own in the Nile Valley and the Middle East. The Mediterranean is closed, and all our transports have to go round the Cape of Good Hope, each ship making only three voyages in the year. Not a ship, not an aeroplane, not a tank, not an anti-tank gun or an anti-aircraft gun has stood idle. Everything we have has been deployed either against the enemy or awaiting his attack. We are struggling hard in the Libyan Desert, where perhaps another serious battle will soon be fought. We have to provide for the safety and order of liberated Abyssinia, of conquered Eritrea, of Palestine, of liberated Syria, and redeemed Iraq, and of our new ally, Persia. A ceaseless stream of ships, men, and materials has flowed from this country for a year and a half, in order to build up and sustain our armies in the Middle East, which guard those vast regions on either side of the Nile Valley. We had to do our best to give substantial aid to Russia. We gave it her in her darkest hour, and we must not fail in our undertaking now. How then in this posture, gripped and held and battered as we were, could we have

Winston Churchill in his 'siren suit'.

provided for the safety of the Far East against such an avalanche of fire and steel as has been hurled upon us by Japan?

Tonight I speak to you at home; I speak to you in Australia and New Zealand, for whose safety we will strain every nerve; to our loyal friends in India and Burma; to our gallant Allies, the Dutch and Chinese; and to our kith and kin in the United States. I speak to you all under the shadow of a heavy and far-reaching military defeat. It is a British and Imperial defeat. Singapore has fallen. All the Malay Peninsula has been overrun. Other dangers gather about us out there, and none of the dangers which we have hitherto successfully withstood at home and in the East are in any way diminished. This, therefore, is one of those moments when the British race and nation can show their quality and their genius. This is one of those moments when it can draw from the heart of misfortune the vital impulses of victory. Here is the moment to display that calm and poise combined with grim determination which not so long ago brought us out of the very jaws of death. Here is another occasion to show—as so often in our long history—that we can meet reverses with dignity and with renewed accessions of strength. We must remember that we are no longer alone. We are in the midst of a great company. Three-quarters of the human race are now moving with us. The whole future of mankind may depend upon our action and upon our conduct. So far we have not failed. We shall not fail now. Let us move forward steadfastly together into the storm and through the storm.

. . . . .

Also in Europe, 1942 saw the climax of the expansion of the Axis powers. But the subdued peoples of Europe never reconciled themselves to the German invaders. The following description from France reached Britain in the spring of 1942.

. . . . .

HOSTAGES IN FRANCE

European Service, May 20 1942

At Nantes, during the night of the 19-20 of October, the German Colonel Holtz, was killed by a shot from a revolver. It was night-time and nobody about in the streets, and the murderer was not caught. It was not even known whether it was a Frenchman or a German who had shot the colonel.

The Germans did not hesitate. Since the man who had killed him was not discovered and did not give himself up, fifty hostages were shot. Twenty-seven of these hostages were chosen from among the 400 prisoners from the camp of Châteaubriant, near Nantes. Who were these prisoners? They were labourers, workmen, shop-keepers, townsfolk, ex-deputies. There were all sorts of people among them, even women, even youngsters. And this is a summary of the account which has come to us from France:

About one o'clock in the afternoon of the 20 October, a German officer arrived to discuss matters with those in charge of the camp. He set about picking out the hostages. About 200 dossiers were brought from the camp to the sub-prefect's senior official, who took them to the Ministry of the Interior in Paris, where the hostages were selected. At the same time, the camp was surrounded by German guards. Nobody was allowed to leave the huts. About nine in the evening, one of the German sentries, thinking he saw someone's shadow, fired at it, and the bullet whistled past the head of a prisoner lying in one of the huts. The German soldiers went away in the morning but came back in the evening.

The 21 prisoners in hut 19 got wind that most of the hostages were bound to be chosen from amongst them. They talked far into the night, unafraid, bravely accepting their fate, only asking "Shall we be guillotined or shot?" Nevertheless, they went to sleep, though their awakening was a gloomy one. At 9 o'clock the prisoners went to the kitchen for coffee. At 10 o'clock, the sub-prefect and two

French officers, Lieutenant Moreau and Lieutenant Tonga, passed in front of the hut and went to look at the gate of the camp, which opened on the main road—to find out, no doubt, whether the German lorries would get in. At midday, the prisoners sat down to table for their last meal. Then most of them wrote to their families. While they were writing, French gendarmes were drawn up on either side of the entrance. Then the Germans made their appearance. All the prisoners stopped writing their letters and rushed to the windows, saying "There they are. It's us they are after."

The Germans set up a machine gun in the middle of the courtyard. The prisoners were shut up in their huts, with a gendarme posted in front of each door.

Lieutenant Tonga entered the main hut, followed by a German officer, saluted and said: "Be ready to go out when your name is called." Then he called out 16 names. The 16 men who were summoned left the hut. The six who were left behind looked at one another, appalled.

The reading out of names went on in the other huts. Here two were taken, here one .... they even took a sick man from the hospital. In hut 10 they only picked out one—the youngest: Guy Moquet, seventeen years old. He answered his name and went out without faltering.

There were 27 of them altogether. They were shut up in a hut and each one was given a sheet of paper and an envelope so that they could write to their families. Eugène Kérival was allowed to say good-bye to his wife who was imprisoned at the same camp.

Some of the hostages were sure that they were going to be executed that same day. One of them finished his rations straight off. Another smoked all his allowance of tobacco. Another was called out just as he was making some tea, without even being able to boil the water.

The priest of Châteaubriant had begged to be excused. It was the priest from Béré who came to the camp. Then the prisoners saw Mme. Kérival, who was allowed to see her husband pass by. At twenty minutes past two the priest left, and five minutes later three German lorries came into sight on the main road. At that moment the sound of singing came from the but where the hostages were imprisoned. The martyrs were singing the Marseillaise. The prisoners in other huts heard them and took up the national hymn in chorus. The whole camp was singing the Marseillaise.

The Gendarmerie lieutenant opened the hostages' door. As his name was called, each man in turn stepped out. The gendarmes searched them, turned out their pockets and tied their hands

together outside the hut. Each lorry held nine hostages. They did not stop singing the Marseillaise and they waved good-bye to the other prisoners looking out of the windows. Dr Ténine said to a German officer: "It is an honour for us Frenchmen to die by a German bullet," and then, pointing at Guy Moquet, he added: "But it's a crime to kill a youngster."

It was a wonderful day. The sky was clear. The milkman's cart arrived at the camp. A gendarme took the horse by the bridle and turned it about. The prisoners' little dog was rolling on the grass in the sunshine in the deserted courtyard. The engines of the lorries were started up. The French gendarmes presented arms. From the lorries the martyrs were still singing the Marseillaise.

Suddenly, just as the lorries were leaving the camp, the doors of the huts flew open and the 400 prisoners burst into the courtyard, singing the Marseillaise. The Gendarmerie Lieutenant Tonga came and talked to them. He told them that their comrades were going to be shot at a quarter past four. The prisoners decided to meet together then and went back into the huts to copy out what the condemned men had written there; the planks that they had walked on, that they had touched, were hidden away like relics.

At a quarter past four, the 400 prisoners assembled once more in the courtyard, with bared heads, in silence. They called out the martyrs' names. After each name, a friend answered 'shot.' Then there was a minute's silence.

Mm. Kérival's calmness amazed the prisoners. When she had come into the condemned men's hut to embrace her husband for the last time, she had been overcome by pity for young Guy Moquet and wanted to take his place. She wanted to die with her husband so as to save the life of the 17-year-old boy. It was refused her. She held herself like that until night when she broke down, but the next morning she was up, full of courage.

At a quarter past four the hostages had been shot. They were shot in a sand-pit, two kilometres from Châteaubriant. As they went through the town in the lorries, they sang the Marseillaise. People came out of their houses and lined their way. In the sandpit the 27 martyrs were shot in three batches of nine. They wanted to go to their deaths with their eyes unbandaged and their hands free.

They cried out: "Long live France!" and one of them, a metal worker, called Timbault, shouted at the Nazi firing squad: "Long live the *German* Communist Party!"

Young Guy Moquet fainted in the pit. He was shot before he came round. He was very big, too big for his coffin. One of the Germans picked up an iron bar, and when the town sexton protested, the German said: "Communist, not Frenchman!"

The gendarmes brought back the watch belonging to one of them, another's ring. The people of the town refused to have the bodies buried in the wretched coffins the Germans had provided. The bodies of the martyrs remained for the night in the castle in the town. They were buried in various cemeteries in the district. There, their families could go to see them; there were no names over the graves—a mark in a register, that was all.

But the people of the district went in pilgrimage to the sandpit. They saw the stakes there, the blood in the sand. The Sunday after the execution, more than

5,000 people filed past and placed wreaths of flowers there .... The same day, the 22 October, 21 other hostages were shot at Nantes.

. . . . .

A description of what the BBC meant to the occupied countries through these dark years was given by a Norwegian who escaped to Britain early in 1942.

THE LISTENING POST

Based on the Experience of an Escaped Norwegian and told
By A. H. Rasmussen. European Service

I stood on the storm-swept headland with a friend—a fisherman. I had been hunted for days by the Gestapo, and he had given me shelter and food at the risk of his life. We had never met before, but such is the brotherhood between loyal Norwegians today.

It was late at night. The stars glittered in the blackness—the storm swept through the pines, and the breakers roared below and filled the shore with a ghastly light.

It is time for the News, the fisherman said, and led the way down to his small skiff. Then we rode off into the storm. The seas smothered us with stinging spray—the little skiff laboured heavily—going was very hard. After nearly an hour we saw a dark hump looming out of the foam ahead, a tiny island.

There was a small cove with several skiffs and we joined them. Muffled voices were heard seemingly coming from the ground. Then we crept through a hole and found ourselves in a deep cave.

A radio set was there, and I could see its green eye and faintly-lit dial—also the dull red glow of several pipes. Apart from that the place was pitch-black. The voices had stopped and the air was tense. The news would be on at any time now.

Then a voice boomed through the silence: "This is the BBC news bulletin in Norwegian."

It was mostly bad news that night—one knock after the other. The green eye of the receiver opened and contracted as if in mortal pain—it looked positively human. The listeners showed no emotion, except that the pipes were puffed a little harder. They could take it, those men. Finally it was over. One of the men said quietly: "Well, thank God for the truth anyway."

It is a good friend who dares tell you the truth when it is bad. Someone lit a pipe, and for the first time I caught a glimpse of my companions. They were strong, weather-beaten, honest faces. Men good to look at, and good to have with you in a tight corner. Then we broke up and rowed off into the storm in different directions towards our distant homes.

. . . . .

Ever since the evacuation from Dunkirk, British soldiers were being trained for the day when they could again set foot on the Continent of Europe. Some of them went through the training of the "battle schools" and became known under the name of "Commandos.' They soon became famous through their raids on the Continent.

One of the most important minor combined operations. carried out during the war was the raid on St. Nazaire in March, 1942. The purpose of this operation was to make the installations in this port unusable to the Germans. St. Nazaire contained one of the largest dry docks west of Singapore and the only one on the north-west coast of Europe capable of taking the German battleship *Tirpitz*.

An Army officer, who took part in the raid, told after the end of the war, when he had returned from captivity in Germany, the story of the operation.

THE RAID ON ST. NAZAIRE

Home Service, June, 1945

I was taken prisoner in the raid on St. Nazaire in March, 1942. I was commanding a small party in the landing craft immediately astern of the destroyer *Campbeltown*. None of us expected to be taken prisoner. We thought we would all get away with it, blow up the docks, and return safely to England, without a casualty. The raid was a success all right, but it didn't turn out quite like that; on the whole we were pretty lucky. Right up to the last moment it looked as if the raid was going to catch the Germans off their guard.

The sea journey took two days and a night and a half. We sailed from Falmouth. We didn't make straight for the French coast. We set a course way out into the Atlantic, so that if we were spotted, the Germans might think we were only a submarine sweep. It was very calm, that was one blessing. No German aircraft came over, and I don't think we were sighted, so at evening on the second day we were feeling pretty optimistic.

We turned in towards the mouth of the river Loire from the south, and took up our assault formation. The destroyer *Campbeltown* was leading. She was an old destroyer converted for this job and she was followed by two flotillas of motor launches. She was stiff with explosive, five tons of it. It was her job to charge the gates of the St. Nazaire dry dock, about six miles up the river, and then she was to blow herself sky-high, and the dock gates were to go up with her. I was in the leading M.L. of the starboard flotilla. I saw our colonel and the naval commander go up and down the line of little ships in their M.G.B.

They hailed us and wished us luck before taking their stations. The escorting destroyers left us, night fell, and soon we saw a light winking at us out of the darkness. The submarine *Sturgeon* had been waiting off the river mouth to give the direction. It was her light we saw. Commander Ryder, V.C., had led the whole convoy and the navigation of Lieutenant Green, his navigating officer, had been so accurate that we met the submarine exactly at the time scheduled. Everything was going very well. She signalled good-bye, good luck and then vanished.

Now we made straight for the entrance to the river Loire. Suddenly two white fringes, like very low clouds, emerged out of the dark ahead, to port and starboard. We went in between them. They were the surf on the French coast, the two banks of the Loire, and I realised now that we had reached the river.

Gradually the river narrowed. We could hear the thud of the RAF bombing and could see the flash of the ack-ack batteries replying on shore. At first, they didn't pay any attention to us and we began to think we were going to get away with it. We were pretty lucky with the tide. The operation had been put forward a night to make the most of the good weather and the tide would have been better for us the night after. I could see the *Campbeltown* outlined just ahead of me, and as far as I could tell she was going along O.K. Her Commander told me afterwards that he felt her jar and in fact she touched the bottom twice going up the river. She just cleared, by a few inches, and went in very steadily with the two flotillas of little ships aft to port and starboard. They were unarmoured and we had come the whole way from England in them, that was a good four hundred miles. The searchlights caught us first. They swung across the black river from both banks and picked us up one by one. Then the coastal batteries opened up—at first uncertainly. After a few minutes everything opened up, and they let us have it. We knew we were for it then. Two searchlights were like the ones at Plymouth Harbour. We had rehearsed the operation there a week before and we never thought it would be quite like that. The *Campbeltown* looked as if she was floodlit for a naval review.

I could see her clearly, just ahead. The troops were lying down at their action stations. Commander Beattie, he received the V.C. for his ship's crew and for his own conduct in this action—Commander Beattie was on the bridge. I could see the shells all over the place, bouncing off every part of the old destroyer. I don't know how she wasn't sunk or crippled: everything in the harbour was focussed on her.

Pretty quickly the searchlights began to pick up the little ships. They swept over my own M.L., and then settled on it. For the last few minutes before we landed, almost the whole convoy was floodlit. The coastal batteries began to bracket us. Shells were rustling overhead and plopping into the water. Many shells and machine gun bullets went straight through the ships, from side to side, killing men assembled below deck. We could see the docks now, our objective, and we could see the outline of jetties and warehouses which we had memorised day after day from maps and air photographs. All of us knew the place by heart. The *Campbeltown* changed course for the last time, and I saw her turn towards the dry dock.

This was the big moment. She put on speed. She was flying the White Ensign as she went in! She opened up with everything she had and charged the boom and the huge dock gates at eighteen knots, head on, with a German battery blazing at point-blank range across her decks. The troops were lying down, firing back with their Brens; the dock was stripped and they hadn't much cover. There was a mass of flame and smoke and gunfire. She went slap into the dock gates, we saw it happen, and lay there dead centre. The gates were thirty-five feet thick and the *Campbeltown* went in with such power that she didn't stick till her bridge was level with them. The *Tirpitz* would think twice now about coming out into the Atlantic to attack our convoys. The battle of the Atlantic wasn't going too well for the Allies then, and we had been told that our attack on St. Nazaire was not just a raid but an important part of Allied strategy. The destroyer had done her job. She crashed the dock at 1.33 a.m., that was three minutes after the time laid down in our orders. At 1.45 the troops were off. At 1.50 the scuttling charges were set off. At 2.00 o'clock she was abandoned and seen to be sinking. The five tons of explosive was concreted in and due to go off some hours later. The troops poured over the sides and knocked out the coastal battery alongside the dock. Another party blew up the pumping station and the station operating the dock gate. There were many wounded on board the doomed *Campbeltown*, and we got them all ashore.

The M.L.s carrying other troops to minor objectives came in behind. The M.T.B. torpedoed the lock gates at the entrance to the U-boat basin and completely scuppered them. Our troops smashed up many installations and killed a good many Germans, but the shore batteries gave us a bad time. We saw ships manoeuvring right under their noses to get into position to knock them out. Our petrol tanks were very vulnerable and many blew up. Just as my M.L. was coming alongside I felt the whole ship shudder. The tanks were hit, she was ablaze and adrift and her steering had gone. No, I didn't know it at the time. The naval commander said 'jump,' so I jumped, swam a bit, and was pulled ashore. Some men were blown into the water and got ashore and reached their objectives. Others I never saw again. Many of our men were last seen in blazing wrecks or swimming away from drifts of burning oil. Some reached shore, but others were too badly wounded.

Our colonel, Colonel Newman, managed to get ashore with what was left of his headquarters. The little area of the dock we had to knock out was under heavy fire. The Germans were pretty hysterical at first. Except in the strong battery positions, many ran away, thinking it was the invasion. Many of our men were in action for the first time. It may seem strange to you, but we had been training so long—and often with live ammunition—that honestly, it was hard to believe, in spite of what was happening, that we were on enemy coast.

So curious things occurred. One man was clearing a house, for example. A German knocked heads with him as he opened the door; first he apologised, then he remembered himself and shot the German.

Most of us knew that the main task of the operation had been achieved, because we could see the destroyer jammed in the dry dock. And we were pretty clear by now that we weren't going to get back to England. When we collected on the Old Mole for our withdrawal and looked back along the river, the water seemed to be on fire. Ships were sinking in flames and streams of fire were pouring from every side. Troops were on rafts, far out in the river, and we heard some of them singing. There was nothing left, nothing to take us home. I don't know how we ever expected that there could be. The coastal batteries were still blazing away, and managed, among other things, to sink one of their own flak ships; and some German destroyers had got out of the dock into the river.

On shore the Germans had been strongly reinforced. They began to close in on us. The colonel organised a small perimeter to hold off the Germans. In this perimeter he issued orders to fight our way through the town into open country. He led the first party himself, crossing the bridge from the docks to the town under heavy fire, and fighting up the streets. He carried out this operation entirely on his own initiative and this helped to bewilder the Germans—they had brought in several armoured vehicles and they still thought it was an invasion. Another party got through a series of German posts by using German phrases we had learnt on training. Some of the ships which came in last did not land. The troops in these ships were disappointed because they had not landed. One of them got several hours clear on the way home. A German destroyer caught up with it and came alongside it in the early morning. The Germans asked if the British Commander of the M.L. wanted to surrender. They asked him in perfect English, through the megaphone. As soon as the troops heard it they opened up, although their ship hadn't a chance, using their Brens against the destroyer with her guns. The destroyer replied, but they refused to surrender. The ship was sunk in the end and many of them were killed.

Most of us on shore were caught in the morning hiding in cellars and boiler rooms, waiting for a chance to get away next night. About 10.30 in the morning we heard the hell of an explosion. The Germans panicked, windows all over the town were smashed, and a huge pillar of flame shot up from the dry dock. The explosive in the *Campbeltown* had gone off, and the huge dock gates and the two merchant ships inside had gone for six. So that was that. It was no good for a year after at least. Some Germans were nosing about aboard the destroyer the moment she went up and went up with her. We were told that some of our lads had taken them aboard, but we never knew which of them had done this. I suppose we shall never know their names.

I suppose we shall never know what happened to many of the men who had been training with us for so long. They'd been expecting something of this kind and hoping for it for many months. We were a very small force, not more than two hundred and eighty soldiers and 350 navy personnel, though the Germans said there were several thousands. Those of us who have survived were very lucky. We have come home now and we would like to pay some tribute to the ones who have not survived. I don't know if we can do better than the French people did, a few days after the raid, and perhaps the families of the men who were killed would like to know what happened.

Many of the French had fought with us on the night and gone on fighting afterwards. Somehow they got to hear of the time when our dead were going to be buried. A huge crowd collected at the hospital to make a procession and the Germans cancelled the funeral service. They tried to keep the new time secret, but the French found out again, and there were many hundreds of them at the cemetery. It was a military funeral, with full honours. The French broke right through the German cordon of guards and heaped flowers on the graves of the men who had been killed. They gave money and food which they really couldn't afford to those of us who were there, and we shall never forget the risk they took. It was thanks to their help that five of our men managed to get to the Spanish frontier and so home by way of Gibraltar. The rest of us were taken into Germany, and while there we found out that the raid had succeeded. Admiral Mountbatten had told us that the loss of all the ships did not matter so long as the dock was smashed, and smashed it was.

. . . . .

Royal Marine Commandos.

All through 1942 the British increased their air offensive against Germany. Two notable operations in the spring were the raid on Lübeck (28 March), and the raids of over 1,100 bombers on Cologne (30-31 May).

The great German writer, Thomas Mann, author of *Buddenbrooks*, and for many years an exile from Germany for his fierce opposition to the Nazi régime, expressed his feelings at the news of the devastating attack on his native town of Lübeck, in a broadcast to the German people.

THOMAS MANN ON RAID ON LÜBECK

European Service, April 11 1942

German Listeners,—

It is the first anniversary of the destruction of Coventry by Goering's airmen, one of the most horrifying deeds with which Hitler's Germany taught the world what total war means and how to conduct it.

It started in Spain, where the robots of death, that race with the blank, inhuman faces, educated in National Socialism, prepared themselves for this war. What sport was it thoughtlessly to divebomb and machine-gun the fleeing masses of civilians who have no chance of defending themselves. Neither will the massacres in Poland ever be forgotten; they can be called a famous landmark in history, and so can Rotterdam, where 30,000 people perished in 20 minutes, thanks to the bravado which is not easily distinguishable from moral insanity.

Did Germany believe she would never have to pay for the crimes which her leap into barbarism allowed her to commit? She is paying already, both over the Channel and in Russia. And what the Royal Air Force has accomplished to date in Cologne, Dusseldorf, Essen, Hamburg and other towns is only a beginning.

During the latest British raid over Hitler's Reich the old city of Lübeck had to suffer. That concerns me, for it is my home town. The attacks were directed against the harbour of Travemuende and the industrial plants there, but fires were started in the town itself, and I would not like to think that the Marienkirche, the beautiful Renaissance town hall of the building of the Schiffer-Gesellschaft were damaged. But I think of Coventry and accept the principle of just retribution. There will be other natives of Lübeck, Hamburg, Cologne and Düsseldorf who likewise have no objection and who, on hearing the drone of the RAF planes over their heads, will wish them success.

It might even be that my sense of justice will be put to a special test by this bombing. Swedish newspapers report that my grandparents' house, the so-called "Buddenbrook House," in the Mengstrasse, has been destroyed during that raid. I do not know whether this information is correct. To many people outside Germany, the town of Lübeck is associated with this house since I wrote my book, *Buddenbrooks*, and they think of it when they hear that Lübeck has been bombed. Of course, in Lübeck itself it is no longer called the "Buddenbrook House." The Nazis, annoyed that visitors to the town were always asking about it, have re-named it "Wullenweber House." These illiterates do not even know that a house, which bears an inscription from the 18th century on its Rococo gable, cannot very well be associated with the bold burgomaster of the 16th century. Juergen Wullenweber did much harm to his town by warring with Denmark. And the people of Lübeck did with him what the Germans might perhaps one day do with those who have led them into this war. They executed him. The occupants of the house which they called "Wullenweber," to obliterate the name of "Buddenbrook" have always, as I can testify, benefited the town. And I have in my own way followed their example. To follow an example in your own way is tradition. The old merchants' house, which is now said to lie in ruins, was to me the symbol of that tradition; but such ruins do not shock those who live for the future as well as for the past. The passing of an epoch need not destroy him who is rooted in it and who grew up in it, nor him who pictured it for you. Hitler's Germany has neither tradition nor future. It can only destroy.

May another Germany rise from its ruins, a Germany which can reflect and hope, which loves the past and the future of mankind. In this way it will win the regard of other nations instead of their bitter hatred.

. . . . .

During May and June, 1942, the back of Japanese sea-power was broken by the American Navy in the gigantic battles of the Coral Sea and Midway. Australia was saved from Japanese invasion. But the submarine sinkings increased and reached dangerous proportions with the German U-boats attacking in new and undefended waters like the Caribbean Sea.

The following is a description from life on board one of the Norwegian tankers which brought aviation petrol from the Caribbean ports to Britain in that terrible summer of 1942.

THE NORWEGIAN TANKERS AND THEIR CREWS

A. H. Rasmussen, Home Service, November, 1942

A few months ago I went out in a convoy. I was in a Norwegian tanker going out in ballast to a Caribbean oil port. I had sailed in these waters before as a youngster in a windjammer, a regular racer—Cardiff to Pernambuco in twenty-eight days, bowling down the north-east trade with our bulwarks awash. Then up through the Caribbean, past St. Vincent, reaching up to high heavens like a monument of jade. And so through Windward Passage, into Laguna del Terminos in the Mexican Gulf. Yes, it was old haunts with many memories. Memories of battles with squalls, tornadoes and electric storms. This time it would be a different kind of battle, for packs of U-boats had made an all-out attempt to sever the Allies' supply lines of oil and petrol, the lifeblood of our war machine. In few theatres of war had the Germans attacked with such savagery and ruthlessness. They expected to paralyse the movements of ships, for they thought no courage could stand up to such slaughter of men and ships. They were wrong and they failed.

I met a jolly Norwegian tanker skipper at a party in the first Caribbean port we called at. He was the life and soul of the party, and I later discovered that he and three companions had landed the previous day after a fifteen hundred miles' trip in a small gig. His ship had been torpedoed and then fought a gun duel with the U-boat. Their third shot hit near the base of the conning tower and the U-boat disappeared. His ship had a gaping hole just below the water-line, but she floated. He trimmed the tanks to lift the damaged plates up a bit and proceeded. The next night another torpedo struck his ship and nearly cut her in halves. They lowered two lifeboats and a fifteen-foot gig under intense machine-gun fire, but only the captain was hit, shot through the arm with a tracer bullet. The boats got separated in the darkness. The gig reached land after fifteen days, and the two lifeboats reached Devil's Island, where the men were interned. After a week they escaped, seized their lifeboats after overpowering the guards, then put out to sea. Eventually they reached one of the Caribbean ports in good heart and none the worse for their adventure. That was fortunately a story with a happy ending, for the ship was carrying heavy oil and did not catch fire.

This skipper was one of the many I met down there. They were a jolly crowd, confident and imperturbable in contrast to the shipping men ashore who were nervous, even frantic. The same was the case in our next port of call, one of the biggest oil centres in the Caribbean. The port lay sweltering in the fierce sun, and the glare from the brightly-painted houses was almost unbearable. Occasionally, the anti-U-boat boom would swing open, and a tanker would come tearing through a narrow gap between the houses, at full speed, and disappear round a sharp bend; or a convoy would go out to sea. Beyond the gap the Caribbean stretched deep blue, and streaked with creamy ripples of the strong trade-wind current. Tiny boats would toss about under minute sails, and occasionally, Caribbean schooners with their rakish rigging and beautiful clipper bows would come in laden with fruit from Venezuela. It all looked so colourful and peaceful, until the roar of some U-boat chasers broke the spell. They were off, out through the gate—British, Dutch and Americans. And soon after you could see them skimming across the blue sea towards the horizon. But somehow the tanker stole the picture.

A few days previously I had come through the gap after a ten days' long trip and two days under escort. We went through the narrow passage, caught a glimpse of the gaily-painted toy town as we flashed past, and then went on further inland. There I saw a new, unexpected and strange world, a world of oil tanks, batteries of chimneys and acres of queer-looking buildings, in a desolate setting of grey lava rock, hoary with age, and just barely supporting a few gaunt sun-scorched thorn trees, aloes and juccas. We moored at a wharf. A monster pipeline was connected up, and soon we had sixteen thousand tons of oil on board. The whole ship trembled and groaned with the strain as if in mortal agony. Then we moved away and made room for another tanker. Our ship was ready for sea almost before I had realised that we had arrived. But her destination had been suddenly altered, and as my work took me in a different direction I had to leave her.

In the eight days I stayed there I got to know something about the men who sail in the tankers, and the cargo. The Norwegian flag seemed to dominate everything, for more than half of the ships were Norwegian, fine modern tankers, which carry a large amount of Britain's oil and petrol. And that splendid fleet has been thrown wholeheartedly into the battle. These ships always fly spotless flags when entering and leaving port, and they are flown proudly like a challenge, and with reason, for they have won many battle honours. The port was full of survivors from torpedoed oil tankers. The men had wonderful tales to tell of their adventures, adrift in the Caribbean on rafts or in lifeboats. They were all looking for ships again; during my daily visits to the Norwegian Consulate I saw them standing in queues waiting for a chance to sign on.

The skippers' rendezvous was in a large room overlooking the gap. There they drank iced beer and talked of anything in the wide world except U-boats. It was there I met Captain A, a Norwegian, and as his ship was going in my direction I asked if he would take me along. He was a massive man with steel-blue eyes that bored right into you, a big, hooked nose, built for cutting through dirty weather, and a chin like the rock of Gibraltar. But he had a delightful twinkle in his eye and his cap was always at a jaunty angle. He gave me a keen look and said: "Do you know I carry aviation petrol?" I said, "Yes, what's wrong with aviation petrol." "Oh, nothing," he replied. "There's nothing wrong with T.N.T. or dynamite either until it goes off." But I was determined to go, and it was soon settled. It was just what I had heard which determined me to go. Here were men taking these appalling risks, trip after trip, silently, and quietly, and I felt it not only a duty but a privilege to share In their life—and get to know something about it to pass on to others. You would hear nothing from them.

It was a strange journey, that three weeks' trip through the danger spots in the Caribbean. The sun poured down until the sea became a steaming cauldron and the sunsets were like searing flames of orange and scarlet. Then the blackness of the night closed in on us suddenly like a lid slammed down. The sea would sparkle with phosphorescence; myriads of tiny glittering specks, like stardust on black velvet. Suddenly the dark sky would flush with pink and a hot red moon rose like a smouldering ball. When it paled, the sea turned to silver and our fleet lay like toy ships of jet with sparkling wakes trailing astern. Then came thunderstorms and deluges, rainbows of incomparable beauty, cool nights with intensely blue skies and glittering stars so clear and near that you could almost touch them. And everywhere lurking U-boats. We had two or three U-boat warnings every day, and the second day out we had distress signals from a lone tanker: "S.S.S.—I am being attacked." There was urgency in their speed: "S.S.S., S.S.S.—" then silence. The following day we received more distress signals, but the convoy steamed on, for the convoys must get through.

Nearly all on board our ship were Norwegians, and for months past they had received broadcast appeals from the German-controlled Oslo radio to come back to their families, or sail their ship into an Axis harbour. They were offered five thousand kroner cash reward, triple wages and special food allowances for their starving families if they would desert. But these men were not for sale. What made them choose exile and their suicidal job rather than German favours? They were honest, loyal, courageous men, and they knew that the only way to deal with the Hun was to smash him. Their cargo meant fuel for the bombers and fighters, and as Norwegian tankers carry a large percentage of Britain's oil and petrol, they were playing a vital part. When a thousand bombers raided Germany, they were responsible for a goodly number of them, and a large percentage of every thousand bombs dropped on Germany came from them.

Against RAF losses of men and aircraft, they put their own heavy losses of men and ships. Above all they were sailors. The freedom of the seas had been challenged, and no sailor has ever failed to accept that challenge. On three or four occasions U-boats were reported right in our track, but the convoy steamed on and dared them to come up and fight it out. The challenge was not accepted. They were after easy prey—lone ships and stragglers. Life on board went on absolutely unruffled by these warnings. Then came a day at sundown when we received a warning of more than usual urgency. Our leading destroyer came tearing up through our columns and warned us by loudspeaker: "Action stations. U-boat very close. Keep your eyes peeled." Darkness fell, suddenly, after that, and I joined the two gunners aft. They were scanning the sea hopefully, for their daily grouse had been that there was nothing to shoot at, and their trigger fingers were itching.

Then suddenly our engines stopped. A tube had broken, and it would require two hours to mend it. Our ship drifted slowly astern of the convoy. We were alone. On the bridge, the second mate, a big jolly chap from Stavanger, whose rollicking laughter used to fill the ship, was peering through the blackness for signs of the U-boat or the track of torpedoes. He carried a gasmask, and I had never seen him with one before. I asked "Why the gasmask?" "Well," he drawled, in his soft, southern dialect, "if we are lucky the torpedoes may hit low, and ten to one the petrol won't catch fire. But the gas will escape, and these masks won't keep out carbon monoxide for more than two or three minutes, worse luck."

"That means you and the other officers have about three minutes to live if that happens?"

"With luck, yes." "Not very long, is it?"

"No," he replied quietly, "but long enough to get the men to jump overboard on the weather side and to lower two lifeboats for them."

"And you?" I asked.

"Oh, if we can manage to do all that before we pass out, we shall be perfectly satisfied."

He smiled and left me thinking in the stillness. Greater love hath no man.

It was late before we caught up with the convoy, and the U-boat did not get us that night, but she torpedoed a lone tanker the following day, and we saw her blazing as we returned from the convoy rendezvous. A pillar of smoke a quarter of a mile wide rose up a couple of thousand feet. The ship was completely hidden except for a moment, when the wind blew the smoke away and her stern was visible for a while. A charred bit of bunting could be seen on the flagstaff. There were no survivors. She carried petrol.

That was the last excitement. Some days later our ship anchored in New York harbour, where I left her. Then she steamed out to sea again, the old veteran of many battles. Her blockhouse was pitted and scarred by machine-gun bullets. She had been "sunk" twice by Gobbels, but since she was "sunk" the last time she had carried thousands of tons of aviation petrol to the RAF. I heard since that she arrived safely in England with another fourteen thousand tons, and that she has gone back for more.

. . . . .

The summer of 1942 saw the supreme efforts of the German armies. In Russia, Hitler's resumed offensive was switched to the south, where the Germans overran the Ukraine and the Crimea and reached Stalingrad and the Caucasus. In North Africa the British Army was driven back to El Alamein.

A memorable occasion in the autumn of 1942 was the visit to London of General Smuts who, three days before the British offensive in Egypt, addressed both Houses of Parliament.

General Smuts' long speech was a survey of the war with a warm tribute to the British people.

The speech was afterwards broadcast by the BBC.

GENERAL SMUTS ON THE BRITISH COMMONWEALTH AND THE WAR

Home Service, October 21 1942

This is a great occasion for me, and I am deeply conscious of the exceptional honour you are doing me. In my experience it is a unique occasion. It is no small thing to be called upon to address the members of this Sovereign Parliament of the United Kingdom, this Mother of Parliaments and free democratic institutions, this Senate of Kings, to use the phrase once applied to the Roman Senate.

I know you have singled me out for this distinction largely because I happen to be the last surviving member still active in high office of the War Cabinet of the last war. I was the youngest and the least of that notable band, and no doubt for these good and sufficient reasons I have been spared, perhaps overlooked, by the subsequent storms and the years. And now that I reappear on this scene after many years you are interested in this somewhat mythical figure and curiosity from the past.

You will allow me to refer to the two leaders in the two supreme crises of our sorely-tried generation.

I am very proud to be honoured by the presence here today of my old leader, Mr Lloyd George, but for whom, who knows what might have happened in the mortal crisis of 25 years ago. Today, in this greater crisis we gratefully remember his imperishable service and thank God for the gift and saving grace of his great historic leadership. He stands out as the supreme architect of victory in the last war.

No less have we been blessed with distinguished leadership in this vaster struggle of today. I sometimes wonder whether people in this country sufficiently realise what Winston Churchill has meant and continues to mean not only to them but also to the Allied peoples, the United Nations and to brave men and women everywhere in the world. His words and foresight, his courage and energy have been an unfailing inspiration to all of us. He remains the embodiment of the spirit of eternal youth and resilience, the spirit of a great, undying nation in one of the greatest moments of history. Let us recognise with gratitude that we have been nobly blessed with wonderful leadership both in the last war and in this.

I have spoken of the two great actors, the two greatest actors in the drama, the continuing drama of our age. I call this a continuing drama because I view this war as a continuation of the last war, and the whole as perhaps another Thirty Years War which began in 1914, was interrupted by an armistice in 1919, improperly called peace, was resumed with greater ferocity in 1939, and may continue—who knows?—till 1944. The intervening armistice was a period of feverish rest or unrest and dreams and illusions.

General Smuts on a visit to troops of 2nd S.A. Infantry Brigade Group in East Africa, July 1940.

I have referred to two great actors in this drama of our age. There is a third and greater actor to be mentioned. I refer to the British people and the spirit that animates them and the young nations around them in the British Commonwealth of Nations. One occasionally hears idle words about the decay of this country, about the approaching break-up of the great world group we form. What folly and ignorance, what misreading of the real signs of the times! In some quarters what wishful thinking!

It is true that this greatest human experiment in political organisation, this proudest political structure of time, this precedent and anticipation of what one hopes may be in store for human society in the years to come, this Commonwealth, is being tested as never before in its history. But is it not standing the test? Is not this free and voluntary association, is not this world-wide human co-operation today holding together the more successfully than ever before under the most searching test?

Knowing the dangers and temptations we have had to face, the stresses and strains imposed on us, nothing has been more remarkable to me than the cohesion of this vast structure under the hardest hammer-blows of fate. We have suffered, we are poorer, we shall be poorer still. We have had heavy set-backs and an exceptional run of bad luck. Is it a wonder that in the fourth year of this war there may sometimes come moments of disappointment, of fatigue, and occasionally even a sense of frustration? But still this great commonwealth remains the heart of the defence against the most terrible onslaught ever made on human rights and liberties. It stands unshaken by the storms and set-backs.

The people of this island are the real heroes of this epic, worldwide drama, and I pay my small tribute to their unbending, unbreakable spirit. I have been absent from this country for almost ten years, and coming back now, I can see for myself the vast change which the trials and sufferings and exertions of the war period have wrought. I remember this smiling land recovered and rebuilt after the last war, where a happy people dwelt securely, busy with the tasks and thoughts of peace. And now I have come back to a country over which the fury of war has swept, a country whose people has had to face in their grimmest mood the most terrible onslaught in its history.

Many of its ancient monuments are damaged or gone for ever. The blitz has passed over cities, ports, churches, temples, humble homes and palaces, Houses of Parliament and law courts. Irreplaceable treasures of a thousand years of almost uninterrupted progress and culture and peaceful civilisation have disappeared for ever. War—the horror people still call war, but in its modern scientific form something very different from what passed under the name before—war has come to this favoured land and attempted its worst. Much has gone which is lost for ever, but one thing is not lost—one thing, the most precious of all, remains and has rather increased. For what will it profit a nation if it wins the world and loses its soul? The soul remains.

Glory has not departed from this land. I speak not of outward glory, of what your Gallic neighbours called "La Gloire" in the past revolutionary fervour. I speak rather of that inward glory, that splendour of the spirit which has shone over this land from the soul of its people and has been a beacon light of the oppressed and downtrodden peoples in this new martyrdom of man.

Let the enemy say "Gott strafe England." "God bless England" has been the response from the victims of this most fiendish onslaught in history. But for this country, the stand it made from 1939 onward, its immeasurable exertions since and up to now, its toil and sweat, its blood and tears, this world of ours might have been lost for a thousand years and another Dark Age might have settled down on the spirit of man. This is its glory—to have stood in the breach and to have kept the way open to man's vast future. And when, after a long absence, I see today this flame of the spirit above the flame of the blitz, I feel that I have come to a greater, prouder, more glorious home of the free than I ever learnt to know in its palmiest days. This is the glory of the spirit which sees and knows no defeat or loss, but increasingly nerves, nourishes and sustains the will to final victory.

. . . . .

"After the war when a man is asked what he did, it will be sufficient for him to say, 'I marched and fought with the Desert Army.'"—WINSTON CHURCHILL.

On 24 October General Montgomery struck at El Alamein. At last the moment had come for the Allies to open the offensive against the German Armies. The beginning of the historic battle was described in a despatch by Godfrey Talbot on the morning of 25 October.

THE BATTLE OF ALAMEIN

Home Service, October 25 1942

As I type this report, duststorms are blowing over the face of the desert, and it's difficult to see far; but up above, very high in the blue sky, our aircraft are going over to gun and bomb the enemy—wave after wave filling the air with the steady, combined roar of the engines. It's almost a procession; sweep after sweep goes over, at frequent and regular intervals, like clockwork. No British land forces have ever had such a powerful air force with them as this.

Last night, when the campaign opened, was dramatic in the extreme. Up to the start, it was, to all appearances, just one of those normal, fairly quiet, desert nights which we have known up here during the past weeks. The full moon shone down brightly; the scene was peaceful. Then, quite suddenly, with a crack and a roar, the barrage opened—our barrage—and in a minute or two, everything was let loose on the enemy. It went on, lifted, and went on again. It was terrific, flashing and roaring almost without pause, for hours. The desert has known nothing like it.

The guns were still going at dawn, and behind it our infantry had moved up, had cleared a gap for our armour to pass forward. So, very early in the morning, the tanks started to move. You couldn't see them just clouds of dust on the stony plain, and a clattering rumble. Enemy guns didn't seem to be making a great reply to ours. Enemy aircraft was kept on the defensive.

The land forces engaged included, of course, a large number of British troops; all our very powerful armoured formations are British: then there is the 44th Division, with Home County units, the 50th Division, troops from the North of England, and also the 51st Highland Division. There are also the Australians, New Zealanders and South Africans, the 4th Indian Division, the Fighting French and the Greeks.

Another report was written by A. L. Curry, of the New Zealand Broadcasting Commission. On the night of the attack he went out with one section of our troops in front of our forward defences, for (as he says)

"This carefully-planned blow was actually launched from no man's land. The troops were assigned two objectives. While one section pushed forward into the hail of enemy fire, the rest remained to leap-frog past them towards the second objective as soon as the first was taken. The fighting was very fierce, as was to be expected against an enemy with fixed lines of defence. But the determination and dash of the attackers carried all before them, and the first phase was completed ahead of schedule. Soon prisoners were beginning to trickle back to our positions.

"All this time the crack of our guns had never ceased as they ranged forward for another barrage against the second objective. As our second infantry elements came towards us to move up to the attack, they were followed by light and heavy armoured forces, passing through to consolidate the initial gain. This was done with perfect timing and co-ordination. The anti-tank guns, too, were. immediately up in support of the infantry. The enemy shelling, which had increased a little, was now dropping behind us, and the crack of our long-range guns continued above the crash of the Germans'. Exactly to time the RAF had joined in the pounding of the enemy positions.

"It was now time for the second, heavier barrage before our further infantry onslaught on the distant objective. Gaps in the minefields were cleared and lighted to ensure the quick and safe passage of supporting armour. The infantry encountered opposition, particularly from machine-gun and mortar fire, but their objective was reached again before schedule."

· · · · ·

Victory in the desert.

On 2 November the battle of Alamein had ended in a decisive British victory. Six days later American and British forces landed in French North Africa.

But the greatest battle of the autumn and winter was the titanic struggle at Stalingrad. This battle, which raged from the beginning of September, 1942, up to the end of January, 1943, was the Verdun of Hitler's war, but ending in the encirclement and destruction of the whole German Stalingrad Army.

After the battle, Alexander Werth gave the following description from the remnants of the great Russian city:

AFTER THE BATTLE OF STALINGRAD

Home Service, February, 1943

I am writing this message to the BBC from a dug-out on the side of a steep cliff overlooking the Volga, two miles from Stalingrad. Everybody in Stalingrad lives in dug-outs because no houses are left. Mine is a small one, which I am sharing with a Russian major and an elderly soldier. Both of them went through the whole Stalingrad battle and both of them frequently comment on the uncanniness of the silence. It is only a week since the encircled Germans in the factory district of Stalingrad surrendered. Until then the firing had continued night and day for nearly six months. U can best convey what some of these days of war meant to the defenders of Stalingrad by quoting the words used by that great soldier, General Zhukov, Commander of Stalingrad's defence when he received me in his dug-out yesterday. Describing the furious German offensive of October 14, launched a few days after Hitler's formal announcement to the Reichstag that Stalingrad would be taken, General Zhukov said: 'It began with a terrible barrage of gun and mortar fire, and during the day there were two thousand Luftwaffe sorties over Stalingrad. Separate explosions could not be heard because there was a continuous roar of explosions. This went on for four or five hours. Inside the dug-outs the vibration broke tumblers into thousands of splinters. That day the Germans advanced one mile, but their losses were so heavy they could not keep it up next day, and so their most overwhelming attempt to break through our defences failed. That was probably the peak of the German offensive against Stalingrad.' But there were many other days when, as one Stalingrad soldier told me, 'Normally, I should have put a bullet through my own head rather than endure this, but I and everybody here knew we must stick it because the whole Russian people and the whole world were expecting it of us.'

And now it's all over. Three hundred and thirty thousand Germans have been lost to Hitler. Thousands have been buried; and many thousands more, dark-skinned, frozen, waxlike corpses, litter the countryside round Stalingrad and Stalingrad itself, and ninety thousand have been lucky enough to be

Winter fighting in Stalingrad.

taken prisoner by the Russians, including twenty-three generals and 2,500 officers.

I have just been outside the dug-out. From the slippery ice path on the slope of the ravine which separates the two cliffs, I saw the vast, wide, snow-covered expanse of the majestic Volga. At the foot of the cliff, a bonfire was burning sending into the cold winter evening air a cloud of white smoke. What was burning was something very familiar to so many of us in England-bomb wreckage. The scene was perfectly peaceful. I could see the road across the Volga ice to the island nearly a mile away—an island with fruit trees, oaks, poplars— that island of several miles length which played so great a part in the defence of Stalingrad. For it was from this island that the Russian batteries which were beyond the reach of the German tanks pounded the German positions and kept the Germans away from the Volga at nearly every point. And where the Germans did break through to the Volga they were under constant fire from the other bank of the river, and so the advantage of having reached the Volga was only a negative one, as long as the main Stalingrad defence continued as it did.

What a story everything tells here. For example, that pleasant road across the Volga with its leisurely traffic tonight: look closely at the river and you see on the other side of the ice road, half frozen into the ice, wrecks of ships and boats hit in the fearful bombing under which thousands of men and women were supplying Stalingrad across the Volga. When I look out from my dug-out in the other direction, what do I see? In the foreground above the cliff are five enormous camouflaged oil tanks, three of them wrecked. Actually all five were burned out in one day. Even by Stalingrad's standards, that was an unforgettable fire. Enormous clouds of black smoke filled the sky, oil poured down the ravines into the Volga and the whole river was ablaze with burning oil. And further along, standing out against the pale blue winter sky, the top of its crest crowned with red sunset, the famous Mamai hill.

Parts of that height, which dominates Stalingrad, changed hands again and again in the ferocious hand-to-hand fighting, but the Russians never fully lost control of it. A large part of it was recaptured on January 10, while the strongest point on the very top of the hill, was not cleared of Germans till little over a week ago. This morning I went up the steep slopes of that hill: it is named after Mamai the Tartar chief who was routed by the Russians in the battle of the Don in the fourteenth century. North from Mamai Hill, I could see stretching in a semi-circle right to the Volga the great industrial area of Stalingrad, with the tractor plant and steel works and the Red October factory. The other day I walked through the acres of ground covered by the Red October factory. Thousands of shells had been fired into it by the Russians and the Germans. The front ran right through the factory grounds. Here among the twisted, mangled skeletons of enormous steel structures with mountains of wreckage all round ran a strange tangle of Russian and German trenches and dug-outs, The earth was riddled with shell craters, and thousands of tons of masonry and steel girders; and among this chaos which no earthquake could have produced, the Russians continued to fight, inch by inch, and finally dislodged the invaders. From the wreckage a frozen hand or leg with a boot protruded, grotesque rather than frightening.

Some of the heaviest fighting in Stalingrad—it was mostly house-to-house fighting, in fact, fighting inside the houses by small units of men armed with Tommy guns and flame-throwers and grenades, and supported by units of sappers, who bored through the ceilings of floors or cellars occupied by the Germans—some of this fighting occurred in the central part of Stalingrad, and it was also here that the final act in the gigantic Stalingrad drama was played. Here the Germans, with Field-Marshal Paulus at their head, were trapped by the Russian ring of artillery and mortars and were forced to surrender.

The German envoy informed the Russians that their Commander-in-Chief wished to see the Russian Commander-in-Chief. A young lieutenant happened to be commanding the nearest unit, and it was he who was received by some of Paulus' generals in the basement of the department store and who agreed with him on the terms of surrender. A youngster whom I saw yesterday in that very room, with sandbagged windows, where he was finally received by Paulus in person, described with a happy boy-like smile how he had caught the Field-Marshal. The oddest thing to him was that the whole basement adjoining the Field-Marshal's room was as tightly packed as a Russian tram during the rush hour. Hundreds of completely demoralised and panic-stricken German soldiers were crowded into the room. And through these men the young Russian lieutenant and his three companions had to push their way to the German generals closeted in their small improvised underground bedrooms.

The Russian army among the ruins.

CHAPTER VI

The Allies on the Offensive

January—December, 1943

> Now all the youth of England are on fire,
> And silken dalliance in the wardrobe lies;
> Now thrive the armourers, and honour's thought
> Reigns solely in the breast of every man:
> They sell the pasture now to buy the horse,
> Following the mirror of all Christian kings,
> With winged heels, as English Mercuries
> For now sits Expectation in the air.
>
> SHAKESPEARE: *Henry V.*

The year 1943 opened with great victories for the Allies. After the successful Allied landings in French North Africa, President Roosevelt and Winston Churchill met in conference at Casablanca. Here the demand for "Unconditional Surrender" was formulated.

While in Russia, the early months of the year saw sweeping advances for the Red Army, in Africa the British forces reached Tripoli on 23 January. In May followed the conquest of Tunisia. The entire Axis force in Africa, 250,000 men, were taken prisoner, and all their material fell into Allied hands. This was a victory as great as that of the Russians at Stalingrad.

At the beginning of June the Allied forces in the Mediterranean launched an attack on the island fortress of Pantellaria, preparatory to the invasion of Sicily.

FALL OF PANTELLARIA

Lieutenant A. H. Rasmussen, European Service, June, 1943

On Thursday, 10 June, the cruisers *Penelope, Orion, Newfoundland* and *Euryalus* steamed out of Malta for the final assault on Pantellaria.

With them went the destroyers which had taken part in the last attack, except the *Paladin* and *Petard*. The last named destroyers were already off the island, giving it a good all-night pasting as a prelude to the big assault.

We were nearing the island the following morning under a dull grey sky over a sombre, oily, lead-coloured sea. The air was clammy and heavy as if oppressed by a foreboding of doom.

At nine we had Divisions on the quarter deck, hymns and a short prayer. After that came P.T.

That we were going into action made no difference to the routine. The band of the Royal Marines played popular tunes, and the stripped, sun-burnt men on the quarter deck, bent, swayed and moved in rhythm.

It takes all sorts to make up the fighting team of a famous fighting ship. There were bearded giants and striplings. Grizzled veterans and youngsters who had only had a few sniffs of gunpowder. Together they are the embodiment of the spirit of the ship and form that intangible something which makes the ship stand out among all others in fame and glory.

The *Penelope* was essentially a ship where you could feel that spirit, which is born in the crucible of the ordeal of battle.

It was born in Malta, when death and destruction was hurtling down in the ship day after day, night after night. And out of the fiery furnace of that ordeal, her indomitable Commanding Officer had pulled a shining sword, where someone less worthy and less beloved might have found only the charred remains of what had once been a good ship's company.

I watched the swinging and swaying men, who were quietly humming the tunes they were keeping time with. Then came the final tune, "Daisy Bell," and the humming changed to a fullthroated chorus which only ended when the bugle sounded "Action Stations" and the men sprinted to their posts.

I went up to the flag deck where the old Chief Yeoman of Signals had the Battle Ensigns ready once more, washed and spotless. Then on to the Pompom deck where I could get an unbroken view without being in the way.

Everyone there was in high spirits, there was a kind of holiday feeling, and all points of vantage were occupied.

It was getting near Zero hour. The sun had broken through a rift in the clouds, the wind had freshened, the sea turned deep blue with tiny white caps.

The destroyers were coming up full speed line ahead, and on their flank three M.T.B.'s with their bows high, came racing along, going great guns.

Then we turned to make the first run towards the target, and as we turned the intercom cracked out, "Hostile Aircraft Sighted"—the bugle sounded the cheerful "Repel Aircraft Stations," and the pompom gunners got busy training on the range and bearing given.

Overhead there was the whining of swift wings as our fighters dived into action, fighters which had previously been soaring like little silver specks, high

up and almost out of sight. Then the air began to growl angrily as the first wave
of bombers came over. Here is the log:—

10.50. J.U. 87's in vicinity.
10.52. First J.U. 87 shot down by our fighters. *Aurora* and a destroyer closing
      shore. Someone is shooting.
10.55. Two groups friendly fighters approaching—Warhawks.
10.56. Hostile aircraft reported ahead. Two more J.U. 87's shot down.
11.00. Enter gun range.
11.02. Aurora opens fire.
11.05. Penelope still closing.
11.06. Invasion craft sighted.
11.07. Penelope opens fire broadsides and keeps on firing.
11.17. Still in range, still firing—no reply.
11.40. Still firing broadsides-six hostile aircraft seven miles north attacking
      landing craft-three shot down by Lightnings.
11.41. Closing range. Destroyers approaching harbour.
11.42. Fifty Fortresses attacking harbour—eleven rounds ack-ack fired.
11.43. Another wave Fortresses attack harbour-seven rounds ack-ack fired—
      Penelope still firing broadsides.
11.44. Third wave Fortresses going in—first wave returning ack-ack
      increases.
11.51. *Penelope* ceases fire, turning towards harbour—first destroyer close in
      firing—lots of shooting—smoke covers half of island.
11.53. Invasion craft closing harbour.
12.00. Still a hell of a lot of shooting. Invasion craft entering harbour and
      disappears in smoke.
12.02. Fighter bombers diving on harbour—Warhawks and Lightnings.
12.07. *Penelope* opens fire.
12.15. Twenty-four Lightnings attack harbour.
12.20. Twenty-nine Marauders bomb. Six rounds ack-ack fired.
12.22. White flag seen on signal tower.

That was Stuart Wood's log, and that was the whole show in a nutshell, and
all that mattered as far as he was concerned. To me it was a fantastic battle, a
battle in which big ships and small, massive formations of bombers and fighters
were used as a boxer uses his fists, to faint, jab and punch with lightning speed
and perfect timing. It was combined operations in its most perfect form, which
blasted all hopes of the defenders to hold out, because they had no defence
against this hurricane from sea and air. Fighters and fighter bombers diving to
low-level attacks, driving the defenders of strong points below ground. On their
tails, heavy bombers, blasting and smothering everything in dust and smoke,
and blinding all shore gun positions. And when the dust had cleared a little, our

M.T.B.'s were right inside the harbour, shooting up everything in sight at point blank range.

Supporting them and covering them were destroyers, also pouring in shells at point blank range, while the cruisers covered both forces with the heaviest fire of all.

The island smoked and rocked, the air was crackling with planes coming and going like flocks of migratory birds in flight. Explosion after explosion came like giant thunderclaps as the bombers unloaded.

My senses were reeling under the impact of this hellish din, but the men on the pompom deck just revelled in it. Cups of hot mulligatawny soup and big slabs of bully sandwiches were passed round.

Most of the men wore their oldest clothes and white anti-flash helmets, for there you got the full blast from the guns, and it will burn your skin off if you are not careful.

I went down to the deserted deck and into the torpedo men's flat amidships.

The gunblast tore in through the entrance and flung the heavy black baffle curtains about as if a full gale was blowing.

I got back to the pompom deck as the invasion fleet was making for the harbour on the heels of the last bomber attacks and the last naval salvoes.

All fire had ceased for a moment and an uncanny silence was suddenly broken by the loud speaker: Padre speaking: "We have just had a signal from the landing party. Harbour seized, practically no opposition. White flags everywhere. Army moving inland after retreating Italians."

The Royal Navy after action.

A cheer broke out and one of the gunners pointed to the signal tower:

"Look, white flag up, as big as a 'ouse." We cheered again, and somebody started a war dance.

Then a big battery on the slope of the second highest peak opened fire. Either they didn't know about the surrender, or they took advantage of the lull to fire their guns. It was the first and last opportunity they had. A big bomber formation, on its way to the harbour, had been stopped by radio when the white flag appeared. It was poised in the air, ready to strike, and was ordered to silence the battery.

The fleet had already opened the bombardment again as the bombers made for the new target.

Then the bombs came down. Where once there bad been a battery the ground was covered by a perfect grey square of smoke, as if drawn with a ruler. And out of this grey square rose a fantastic forest of trees of smoke. Long straight poles and wide-spreading tops, a perfect picture of trees, growing to a giant size in a few moments.

Down near the ground, flickering flames reached the trees, then merged into one big, dull red glow. There was a terrific explosion and the picture blew to bits. The battery had vanished.

The fleet remained off Pantellaria, close in shore until the airfield had been occupied, then we steamed out to sea, bound for Lampedusa.

. . . . .

On 10 July 1943, the Allies landed in Sicily. In the gigantic combined operation no less than 2,000 vessels of all kinds were used, supported by powerful air forces.

SICILIAN LANDING

Lieutenant A. H. Rasmussen, European Service, July, 1943

Darkness fell. The destroyers of Group V quartered the sea like grey ghosts guarding a ghost fleet. And from every port in Tunisia there would be other ghost fleets dashing through the darkness in this gigantic jigsaw puzzle to slip into their respective places at zero hour, 2.45 a.m.

There was a steady droning sound in the air, and we knew that our airborne troops were passing over in droves, high up in the starlit sky. Our ship, the destroyer *Blencathra*, would have the post of honour by leading the landing craft in to a small bay between Cape Passero and Pozallo, and knock out of action a powerful battery overlooking the bay. We were expecting casualties, of course, and preparing for it in the way usually done in small ships. Our dining table was turned into an operating table, with a big, powerful electric light suspended over it, and stacks of instruments were made ready in glittering metal trays.

We had finished by about 11.00, and then had a little sing-song, as I had brought my guitar with me. At twelve I thought I had better take a nap, for when operations started I would probably have a couple of days and nights on deck and on the bridge without sleep or rest. So I lay down on the settee for forty winks. I was suddenly roused by the "Doc" shaking me: "Ras, wake up and see what the wind blew in. Our first patients." I sat up and blinked at eight wet, naked men, with blankets over their shoulders, who were drinking tea and chatting.

They were a fine crowd of men, without a trace of weakness or fear after their terrible ordeal. They had been dropped short from a glider and fell into the sea three miles from shore. After tearing their way through the fabric of the submerged glider, they drifted about for over three hours before we found them. They had then given up hope, as the glider was sinking under them. Four of them were strong swimmers who could have made shore, but they would not leave the others who could not swim. One man had been lost in the crash.

It was getting on towards zero hour, and I had to go up on the bridge. The steward came in and asked: "About your cocoa, Sir. Would you like it before or after action?" It was said so naturally and in such a matter of fact way as if knocking out shore batteries was an every day occurrence in the *Blencathra*. I replied: "Thank you, Steward. I will have it after action. I think it will taste better then." He said: "Very good, Sir," with a puzzled look on his face. To him the cocoa was purely a routine matter and, as such, more important than the action.

As I left the wardroom, Actions Stations was sounded. It was a beautiful starlit night with a waning moon. The *Blencathra* was ripping through the water ahead of the convoy and closing the shore rapidly. Suddenly from the lighthouse at Cape Passcro, the long luminous finger of a searchlight started to probe the darkness. It moved slowly towards us and stopped just short of our position, a long lane of blinding, glaring light, surrounded by pitch blackness. Another move forward of that beam would floodlight the whole invasion fleet for a quarter of an hour too early. I held my breath and watched. Then as suddenly as it had been turned on it was switched off and left us half blinded in the pitch dark. It had been a narrow squeak, for the island fortress Coranti was within rifle shot.

On the bridge, every eye was now turned towards shore, where the massive outline of the fortifications could be picked out against the skyline. We were inside a bay, and it was getting on to zero hour. The gunners were ready to open fire, and the range was being called out in rapidly shortening distances. The moon had by now gone down.

The blackness and silence ashore was suddenly broken by a burst of machine-gun fire and long arcs of white and red tracers. Here and there Verey lights, white and green, cut through the darkness, followed by the sharp rattle of firing. To the eastward, but far away, great fireworks lit up the sea and sky and was followed by the full rumble of heavy gunfire. In the twinkling of an eye the scene had changed from utter silence to a growing pandemonium of sound. One moment the *Blencathra* was alone in the bay. The next, dark shadows were racing for the beaches and the waters were alive with craft and roaring with engines. It was zero hour, and our gunners were on the point of opening fire when the radio crackled and the Army ashore reported: "Situation well in hand. Batteries captured—bombardment unnecessary." The airborne troops had done their job well, and apparently the landing had come as a complete surprise.

We turned to meet the troopers, due to anchor at 3.00, and at 3.00 to the tick I heard the rattle of many anchor chains. Then across the bay towards Pozallo, where a great fleet of supply ships were due at 3.15, and at 3.15 I could see the bow of the first ship coming out of the darkness. The firing to eastward had increased, and the sky was filled with long arcs of red tracers crossed by sprays of white tracers from the shore. Far out to sea the air trembled with the thunder of heavy guns, and the flickering flames of gun flashes made the stars pale.

An arc of flaming guns almost a hundred miles long marked the steel ring of the Royal Navy and the American Navy. A ring of battleships, monitors, cruisers and fleet destroyers were guarding the landing fleet from any naval interference, and pouring a deadly fire into the strong points inland to secure the beachheads. The low, rolling hills shook under the impact of this avalanche of shells and glittered with their explosions.

As dawn broke, the black waters gave up their secrets, and the fleets of shadow ships took shape. Far out, the towering bulk of big fighting ships, and within their protecting ring the sea was black with ships as if all the shipping of London, Southampton and Liverpool had suddenly been assembled off the Sicilian beaches by a magician. There were famous liners and unknown tramps. There were ships from every known shipping company of every allied nation. Destroyers were dashing about here, there and everywhere looking for trouble, like terriers with their hackles up. Close inshore they were shooting up strong points and pillboxes, putting up barrages for advancing troops or blinding enemy gun positions with smoke shells. That was over towards Pozallo where the situation was still a bit sticky. There, some of the destroyers of our Group acted as mobile field artillery in close support of the troops, and did a magnificent job. The *Blencathra* was doing an anti-submarine sweep round the invasion fleet with the rest of Group V.

The sun rose like a big red-hot ember, and across its face moved a stately procession of cruisers, like jet black etchings. The whole bay glowed with the first run rays and the fleet lay in a rosy haze. The air vibrated with sound.

Aircraft swarmed overhead, guns rolled like thunder in the distance and banged off broadsides near the beaches, and in between, hundreds of winches clacked and grated, davit falls crackled as small landing craft were lowered from the troopers and joined the stream towards the beaches. From the Army ashore came this signal: "All operations proceeding as planned. Forts and airfields captured."

And now it was also possible to see how the land lay. To eastward the long low tongue of Cape Passero reached out into the sea with wide stretches of golden beaches. To the north a wide half-moon bay backed by low grey foothills, stippled with dull, dusty green of olive groves and orchards. Small villages of cream-coloured houses nestled in the dips and down by the beaches. Dominating this were the squat, massive fortifications and barracks on the rising ground above the bay. At the western end of the bay I could see Pozallo town and fortifications where a battle was in full swing. Further inland and beyond the nearest ridges nothing could be seen except clouds of yellow dust from the heavy shells of the big ships.

The bay itself was alive with craft, coming and going, and the beach itself was already a vast storehouse of supplies, crawling with men, tanks, trucks and Bren carriers in orderly converging streams. The beach roads were packed with convoys racing towards the front line just beyond the first ridge of hills where our field artillery and tanks were already in action.

Out to seaward were new fleets coming in, the vanguard of the ferry service between North Africa and Sicily. More landing craft, more supply ships, more special equipment, each wave carrying special gear, supplies and men required for the successive stages of the operations. There seemed to be a bridge of ships between the landing beaches and North Africa.

It was while we were pumping shells into Pozallo that the first air attack on the invasion fleet came. But that fleet could take care of itself. A solid sheet of flame shot skyward, like a volcano in eruption, as every ship went into action. No aircraft could face that barrage, and the attack soon fizzled out after two planes had come hurtling down in flames. All the bombs fell wide. We kept on bombarding at regular intervals all through the night. It was essential to knock out opposition there, because Pozallo was the junction between the Canadians and the Highland Division.

All Sunday morning, the 11th, the bombardment continued, when suddenly at 13.18, HMS *Brissenden* signalled: "The town of Pozallo wishes to surrender." The Senior Officer signalled back: "Proceed in and accept surrender." Later on the Senior Officer signalled to the *Brissenden*: "Hand over Pozallo to Army now approaching." Pozallo was ours; the rest was now plain sailing, and the *Blencathra* returned to her 'ack-ack' duties with the invasion fleet.

· · · · ·

The re-conquest of the Mediterranean was the great achievement of the Allies in 1943. On 24 July, Mussolini was overthrown. On 8 September Italy formally surrendered to the Allies. On September to the Italian battle fleet surrendered to the British Navy at Malta, the George Cross island, whose resistance had saved the British Armies in the Middle East. The historic scene of the surrender was described by an eye-witness.

THE SURRENDER OF THE ITALIAN NAVY

European Service, September 13 1943

Moving along in an impressive array towards Malta, were ships forming the backbone of the Italian Navy—two battleships, five cruisers, and four destroyers which had sailed out of their anchorage at Spezia following the course prescribed in the armistice terms. The Italian warships were accompanied by the British battleships, the *Warspite* and the *Valiant*, with a screen of six destroyers ahead and six on either side.

As we approached Valetta harbour, a British cruiser, carrying on board General Eisenhower, Admiral Cunningham and other high naval officers, came out across the sunlit waters to review the two fleets. Admiral Cunningham stood on the bridge of the cruiser, all smiling, obviously hugely pleased by the events which removed virtually all menace to shipping in the Mediterranean. "This is a great day for us," said Admiral Cunningham. "I always thought it might end something like this though," he added, with a humorous smile, "we would have been glad to see the ships at any time during the last three years."

A few minutes later our cruiser broke formation, and going full steam ahead, passed the two Italian battleships to go into harbour. As we went by, the Italian crews stood to attention along the decks. It was a nice gesture, and the Italian sailors were evidently behaving with great dignity and admirable discipline. The attitude of the sailors on board our ship was that it was a really tragic sight. But they respected the Italian sailors for the way they had carried out the terms of the armistice.

As we steamed into Valetta harbour, I turned round and gave one more look at these magnificent ships, with guns pointing from turrets, and the crews lined up an the decks, all silhouetted jet black against the wide, red path of the quivering light thrown into the Mediterranean from the setting sun.

Thus ended one of the greatest days in the history of the British Navy: the surrender of the Italian Fleet at Malta.

. . . . .

Later in the year, on Trafalgar Day, Admiral Stark, Commander of the United States' naval forces in Europe, paid the following tribute to the Royal Navy.

ADMIRAL STARK ON THE ROYAL NAVY

Home Service, October 21 1943

Today is Trafalgar Day. One hundred and thirty-eight years ago a little man, in an Admiral's uniform, sat at his cabin desk in HMS *Victory* and brought his diary up to date.

He wrote: "Monday, October 21st, 1805. At daylight, saw the Enemy's Combined Fleet; made the signal for Order of Sailing and to prepare for battle."

Battle was no new thing for the Admiral. He had lost an eye in Corsica, an arm at Tenerife, been wounded at Cape St. Vincent, and again at the battle of the Nile. A man of 47, he had served in the Royal Navy since he was a boy of twelve. Now, with twenty-seven ships of the line he faced a combined force of thirty-three. The outcome might well decide whether British sea power could save England from the tyrant, who then dominated the continent of Europe.

During the long morning the two Fleets manoeuvred. Shortly before noon they met. By late afternoon the British forces were victorious. But in the moment of victory, the little Admiral had received a fifth and fatal wound.

Admiral Lord Nelson was dead. England was saved.

I know that no one in these islands can look back on the day of Trafalgar without a quickening of the pulse.

It may seem strange to you that an American should be speaking on an occasion which is so essentially British, but the memory of Lord Nelson lives in every Navy in the world; and after all, about seventy million of our population are of British stock, or over half as many as you have in the British Isles. We, too, can be proud of Nelson.

His memory lives as a symbol of that intangible element that you will not find in lists of ships, or estimates of fire power: that intangible element which enabled Nelson to carry twenty-seven ships to victory over thirty-three: the element which means the difference between victory and defeat: the fighting spirit-the will to win.

Attack—love of battle—were ever the key notes of Nelson's actions. Although he attacked against odds, it was not in a vain spirit of rashness, but in the calm confidence that the superior training and morale of his men would more than offset the odds,—bold and daring, yes,—but also an infinite capacity for taking pains.

He studied French tactics and how best to beat them. The clearness of his Trafalgar memorandum is perhaps best illustrated by the remark of Admiral

A Royal Navy aircraft carrier at sea.

Collingwood, his Second in Command. When Collingwood saw the flags of Nelson's famous signal begin to flutter, he said, "I wish Nelson would stop making signals, we all know what to do." That was a great tribute to the thoroughness with which Nelson had indoctrinated his command.

Nelson, himself, never made it clear just what he meant by "The Nelson Touch." But to those who have come after him, the Nelson Touch stands for that combination of fighting spirit, and long and efficient preparation, which are the keys to victory.

Nelson lived in an age of great Admirals: Hawke, Howe, Hood, St. Vincent— their very names evoke the Golden Age of naval warfare under sail. Yet compared with Nelson, all of them remain to the average man but portraits, hanging on the wall of history.

Some have called Nelson a genius; perhaps, but genius in his case can be summed up in one word: Leadership.

It was no accident that Nelson described his captains as a band of brothers. His warm, human traits, combined with a fervent devotion to his country and a great offensive spirit, won for him the respect and affection of the men with whom he served.

He inspired them with that same offensive spirit which was part and parcel of himself, establishing more firmly than ever that offensive tradition which has been the crowning glory of the British Navy to the present day.

Although Nelson died almost a century and a half ago, his spirit, in a very real and true sense has survived, and lives in the present. I can say this with some assurance because during the two great wars our generation has witnessed, I have been in a position where I could observe not only the work of the Royal Navy, but also the heart and soul of this country.

I have seen, both in the past war and in this present struggle, the spirit of Nelson continually animating the British people and leading them once again, just as it did off Cape Trafalgar, to final victory.

The world will ever marvel at the fortitude of a people who fought on after Dunkirk. Gone were most of your weapons of war: guns, tanks, vehicles. Little else was left but pitchforks, broomsticks, and the will to fight. Food was scarce. The U-boat roamed the Atlantic, gravely threatening your life line. The Luftwaffe swept over your skies devastating your cities.

Yet you fought on. In those perilous days Nelson's famous signal, "England expects every man this day to do his duty," did not go unheeded. Men and women worked by day, and fought fires by night.

Your Air Force fought constantly against vastly superior numbers. Your Navy was hard put to it to protect the sea lanes where your merchant ships struggled against heavy odds to bring in the supplies that enabled you to continue the fight.

Your First Sea Lord, Admiral Sir Andrew Cunningham, speaking of the war at sea in the Mediterranean in those early days said: "We started very weak at sea, and even more so in the air. However, because of the very fact of our weakness, our policy had obviously to be one of aggressiveness, and it paid handsome dividends."

Admiral Cunningham also said: "It may be said with some truth that Greece and Crete were reverses—perhaps—but I count it my greatest pride to have been privileged to command those men in that time of adversity."

Those words might have been spoken by Nelson himself. Nelson's spirit is roaming the seas today just as truly as it did over a hundred years ago.

It was Nelson's spirit which inspired that immortal trio, the *Exeter, Ajax* and *Achilles* to hang on to the *Graf Spee* like grim death. It was the Nelson spirit that has repeatedly disregarded heavy odds in the Mediterranean, where notable victories have been won, and of which Matapan is a shining example. It was the Nelson spirit which sent those midget submarines through the intricate defences of the Alten Fjord, to put their deadly torpedoes into the *Tirpitz*. It is the Nelson spirit which night after night sends your coastal forces out across the Channel to attack the enemy convoys which creep stealthily along the coast of France. The Nelson spirit transcends the Royal Navy and the Merchant Navy. And above all, it is the spirit of the British people themselves, who stood unfalteringly, alone, in the greatest crisis of British history, resolute, firm, and completely ignoring the possibility of defeat, thereby making defeat impossible.

It may be a far cry from Nelson's old wooden ships of the Nile to the tremendous battleships and deadly aircraft, which make up the striking power of modern navies. Yet today, as on the first Trafalgar Day, one element retains its supreme and basic importance—the fighting man.

That is the great lesson from Trafalgar. This is the lesson which all who seek to survive must learn; for if the average man should ever lose the fighting edge, and become soft. Greatness will pass.

I began this talk with a quotation from Nelson's diary. I did not finish the quotation. I should like to do so now, because his words would he fitting for any Commander, before battle, anywhere, any time.

The last entry in his diary concludes in this way: "May the great God Whom I worship, grant to my country, and for the benefit of Europe in general, a great and glorious victory; and may no misconduct in anyone tarnish it; and may humanity after victory, be the predominant feature in the British Fleet. For myself, individually, I commit my life to Him Who made me, and may His blessing light upon my endeavours for serving my country faithfully. To Him I resign myself and the just cause which is entrusted to me to defend. Amen."

Pigeons feed quietly in Trafalgar Square. Sailors, soldiers and airmen of many nations sit there under the shadow of Nelson. High overhead his statue looks up Whitehall to that famous grey old building, housing the Admiralty. A great naval officer lived there for the past five years, working day and night, quietly, effectively—undaunted and determined. He faced naval problems, perhaps more difficult and complex than any First Sea Lord ever faced before him. By clear and straight thinking, and by tireless devotion to duty he successfully met the multitude of tasks which confronted him. Truly it may be said of Admiral Sir Dudley Pound, "Well done." Truly he typifies Nelson's saying that "Duty is the great business of an officer. All private considerations must give way to it, however painful it may be."

And now Admiral Sir Andrew Cunningham takes up these tasks. You may rest assured Nelson's spirit lives, and will carry on.

. . . . .

With the Allies advancing first through Sicily, then up the Italian peninsula, and with the tremendous Russian victories on the eastern front, resistance was spreading in all the occupied countries. More and more this resistance took practical forms, such as sabotage of German war production. This secret war was, in the great majority of the occupied countries, carried out in close collaboration with Britain. The training of saboteurs in Britain was described in a talk after the war by a British secret agent.

A SCHOOL OF SABOTAGE

Home Service, June, 1945

Can you imagine a Whitehall Government Department—you know, all respectability and red tape—teaching you to be a gangster? That is what happened to me. Remember the awful boredom of army life in 1941 and '42? Everyone, everywhere browned off. I certainly was until—well, if you ever read

Part II Orders on the Orderly Room notice board during that time you may remember seeing a notice: Officers and men having a knowledge of France, Belgium, Holland—all the occupied countries—and able to speak the language fluently, should report to the C.O.

"What a hope," you probably said, and thought no more about it. But as a result of these notices, a tiny trickle of men from all over the country were sent up to an office in London. They came up on their own. A nice change. No waiting in a queue, as at sick parade. You would just go to an address; find it was a block of flats. You would ask for Major So-and-So, and be taken up in a lift, and shown straight into an office, where Major So-and-So was waiting to receive you and looking as though he was pleased to see you. He would talk to you for an hour, half in French (if French was your language) and half in English. He would find out a lot about your past life, and he would make notes about it. He asked you if you were ready to be transferred to a kind of work which might mean action against the enemy in the near future. If you said 'Yes,' and looked as though you meant it, he would say: 'Go back to your unit and wait.' You hadn't the faintest idea what it was all about. You might wait a week, you might wait a month, you might even give up hope of hearing from the major at all. And then one day the Orderly Room would send for you, tell you to be at the station with all your kit the next day, and to report to the Major at another London address.

That is what happened to me. At this second interview I was told even less than before about what I was going to do. All I learned was that I was going to be sent off to what he called a school in the south of England. We were packed into an eight-seater shooting brake and were driven out of London. And after an hour's drive through country lanes, well away from the main roads, we drew up in front of some imposing gates. Here we were in our first 'school'. When we got out I looked around and tried to size up my companions. They were a motley lot. A FrenchCanadian lieutenant, a timber merchant in civil life; a Parisian street vendor whose father had been a British Tommy in the last war; a café-keeper from Nice; a student of French from London University (he was very shy); an aristocratic young man from Mauritius. There were about a dozen of us from all parts of the world and from all sorts of jobs. The C.O. was a magnificent Guards Major who treated each one of us as an honoured guest at his country house.

In the entrance hall there was a time-table up on the board. A pretty full time-table. P.T. every morning for half an hour before breakfast. Weapon training. Grenade throwing. Explosives—theory and practice. Learning to send and receive morse signals on a buzzer. And on our first afternoon we had a talk, from someone we had thought was one of us, on what he called Security. He went through all the training with us. He warned us of the terrible crime of talking about our training or our identities to anyone outside the school, and to tell nothing to our families or friends; also we learned our outgoing mail would be censored. Rather obviously, we nicknamed this harmless individual 'Gestapo'. It was a hard month, but grand fun. Then we were sent up (first-class reserved seats) to the wilds of Scotland—a desolate shooting lodge in a glen. In the middle of this Highland scenery, it was odd to see a mass of rusting industrial machinery and twisted girders. These were the toys we were to practise blowing up—before we left school for occupied Europe.

Our next move was to the parachute school. Where was it? I've still remembered enough of my security training not to want to tell you. We had a sergeant-instructor—he was a great character. Hundreds of us who jumped into occupied Europe from Warsaw to Bordeaux, from Oslo to Athens, remember his perpetual saying: 'You lucky people'; and his most serious assurance that if your parachute did not open he himself, though he was a poor man, would pay for a new one for you. Of course, our parachutes did open.

All this training was only a preliminary, but it was obvious while it was going on that the high-ups had formed their opinion of you, based on reports of instructors and C.O.s and the Gestapo Boy. And they had made up their minds more or less where they wanted to send you and in what capacity. If you were to be a radio operator, you would be sent for six weeks to the Wireless School. There you would not only do so much morse that you dreamt in dots and dashes, but you learned about the theory of radio and the inside of a set. You were sent out with your set to the house of some respectable family in the provinces who had agreed to put up an allied soldier. They were told you were practising with a new form of radio equipment, still secret; they usually cottoned on to the real truth of the thing, but they didn't talk about it. The radio operator had to send and receive two or three messages, lasting an hour each, every twenty-four hours. At the same time, he might be followed, he might be stopped in the street and questioned, he might have his room visited and searched. He had to meet men in pubs by appointment, and take messages to transmit back to headquarters. All this business was stage-managed by the people nicknamed Gestapo Boys, wearing civvy clothes.

If you weren't much good at morse—and you were lucky if you weren't, because a radio operator was surely the most dangerous job of the war—you would be sent to a special Security School. Here, smart young officers, who had read all the reports, and a lot of books, would tell you what life was like in the occupied countries, and put you up to the numerous tricks and dodges that might be useful to you in your every-day life under the Germans. They taught you the use of codes, disguises and secret inks, all of which almost everybody forgot straight away. You were taught how to pick locks, how to live like a poacher off the land. Then you would be sent out to some provincial town to contact some individual you didn't know, a bank manager, or a trades union leader—it might be anyone. You had to get into conversation with him and give him the first half of a password—he was supposed to provide the second half. If he did, you knew he was the right man and he would help you. All this time, you were still being watched: you would probably end up by being arrested by the local police and they would tell you where you had slipped up, or where you had done well.

After this school, you might be sent to a place where they specialised in industrial sabotage; after a few days of lectures you would know the weak spots in an industrial system. After that you would go visiting factories, railway depots and power stations, and at the end of it you would know the exact spots on the machines, and the transformers and railway engines, the exact spot to place an explosive charge to do the kind of damage most awkward to repair. You had a strange outlook on life when you left this school. Everything you looked at outside in the ordered humming activity of war-time England, you looked at wondering how you could best stop it working. It was a shockingly destructive attitude, but there was a compensating feeling: we knew that in using half-a-pound of explosive successfully and intelligently somewhere in occupied Europe, we should be saving the RAF the job of making perhaps an expensive raid, and we should be saving the lives of hundreds of allied European civilians, who might otherwise have been killed or maimed under the rubble of their own homes.

At another school there were RAF instructors. They gave you the 'gen', for guiding an aircraft flying over occupied territory to the exact field where you were waiting for it, either to come in and drop supplies, or to drop two or three people by parachute. The RAF, of course, didn't call us 'Secret Agents.' We were just known as 'bodies', Joes', or just 'bods'. In England we could practise these operations, a group of six or seven of us, driven out in a fast army car to a large field near an aerodrome, placing our lights in a special pattern, waiting for the aircraft, hearing it in the distance and seeing its great mass circling over us; then packing up in the cars again, and going back to a late supper and safe and comfortable beds. It was not very realistic. Then in the later stages of the war they brought out electrical gadgets, kind of cumbersome wireless sets, which you set up in the field, switched on and then, even without the aid of lights, the aeroplane would be guided towards you from perhaps twenty miles away. Later still when I was in France we had similar sets, which we could use as a telephone to the pilot, or to anyone in the 'plane who might fly out from the London office to give us direct instructions. Once in occupied France, when a friend of mine was using one of these, he heard the 'plane approaching, and the voice of the rear gunner: 'Bloody awful lights he's got. His morse is pretty ropey, too.' 'So would yours be, mate,' my friend shot back, 'if you'd just been chased off the field by a Jerry patrol. You're six miles south of the field you should have come to.'

Well, all these schools were the sort of training we had to go through. But besides the schools there were endless interviews and appointments, as the time drew near for you to be sent away—to go 'into the field,' to use the official language. There was the tailor who made you a couple of civilian suits, and a whole outfit of clothes with no markings on, not even laundry marks. There was the thin, intellectual officer who made up a phoney life-history for you, and issued you with corresponding identity papers and false ration cards. There was the prim and smiling officer who decided what codes you would use, making a note of the key words of your code in a ledger. Then there was the briefing officer—a business-like major, who made you feel that his whole undertaking was nothing more than an efficient travel agency. He would tell you about the towns you were going to, the three-star factories you should not miss, and perhaps give you the name and address of the local agent. Finally, there was the officer who saw you off at the aerodrome. His job was to search all pockets for English money, London bus tickets, stamps or family letters. When we were all ready to go off, we were sent up to what was known as 'the departure school,' another enormous country house with a beautiful park, an orchard, a walled garden and a tennis court. There was almost nothing to do except eat, drink, play tennis and wait. Sometimes you would wait a fortnight there, during the period when the moon was over half full, and then be sent back home to say goodbye all over again. I said good-bye three separate times to my wife before I finally left.

And often this sort of thing would happen—we would fly over France, and inside the aircraft we would get ourselves all worked up, preparing to jump. The despatcher (that's the man who tells you when to jump, and, if necessary, pushes you out) would open the huge hole in the floor of the aircraft through which you would have to leave British territory. You would look down over the fields and villages sweeping past in the moonlight, the aircraft would twist and bank, searching for the line of lights flashing the agreed signal—and wouldn't find them. Then a few hours later you would step out of the aircraft, on to your home aerodrome. And when, finally, on your last trip, the hole was opened and you were told to get ready to jump, you couldn't believe that this time you wouldn't be making the return journey. You sat with your feet in the hole. The pin-point of red light went on behind you (the 'be prepared' signal to the despatcher); then all at the same time it seemed, the green light flashed on, there was a raucous shout from the despatcher, and his hand, which he had been holding a yard in front of your eyes, shot down like a railway signal—you gave a push with your hands, slipping your behind off the floor of the aircraft, and let go. Tossed into the slip-stream you felt a slight jerk—that was the static line, the wire rope attached to the aircraft which was ripping the envelope off your parachute, your last link with England was snapped, and there you were floating down over the friendly fields of France, friendly fields occupied by the not-so-friendly Germans.

. . . . .

What the war meant to one of the small peoples, Norway, and the very close friendship that grew up between Norway and Britain, was described in a broadcast by the former Mayor of Narvik, Theodor Brock, who escaped to England.

NORWAY AND ENGLAND

Home Service, December, 1943

By the time it ends this war should have taught us much, among other things that we can benefit by mistakes, if they are big enough, and if they are our own mistakes. And where mistakes are concerned I should not think that by now any of us can complain of lack of opportunities. We of the occupied countries, at least, have paid the price in full. I admit that whether we can make good use of that experience still remains to be seen. But one thing is certain: we have all had a shock which will affect our outlook for the rest of our lives.

I can still remember the strange stunned feeling when out of the fog came foreign warships and blew our former existence to pieces. We had not expected it. We thought our land was so far away. My own little town, Narvik, lay hidden beyond the Arctic Circle. Through our streets, in long strings of lorries, the iron ore had flowed so steadily up till then, down from the mountains to the harbour, to be carried by ships out into the world—we didn't know where; we didn't bother where. Well that night in April, we got some of that iron in return, refined, as they say.

We called ourselves neutral. That was not because we were indifferent to wrong and violence in other countries. We followed what went on in the world. We were interested, but as a small powerless nation, we thought we had no responsibility for it all. We trusted in our neutrality as a young woman trusts in her innocence. That was our background. It could hardly have been otherwise. The only war we had known was the struggle for existence against a hard and brutal nature. We felt we were winning that fight; we felt we had our destiny in our own hands. Perhaps the common picture of the Norwegian standard of living was a little exaggerated. But it was true that life had become easier for us all in Norway during the last generation. Still, there was much to be done. The fishermen in the north, the forestry workers and the small farmers on their meagre hill farms presented us with many problems that we still had to solve. But at least we were aware of them. We felt the country belonged to the people and we were learning to enjoy that.

What had all this to do with our neutrality? All this was our neutrality. There were less than three million of us in a country larger than Great Britain and Ireland. We did not feel that we were answerable for the rest of the world. It had been hard enough for us to make something out of our country. Foreigners—we thought they could hardly want anything from us, except to visit us; and they were welcome. Then one day a stranger came to dinner. He took not only the food, but the table and the whole house as well. The only thing we had left was our pride in refusing to put up with it. We have refused, you know. And for our attitude we have paid in ruined towns, and a whole population in a concentration camp.

We don't regret what has happened. I believe we should all say now that it will have been worth the price. We shall get our country back, stripped and plundered, and more naked than it has ever been before. But we shall get it back without having a feeling that we have haggled over it. And we shall get it back with an enormous sense of opportunity.

What shall we do with our opportunity? What shall we do when we have cleared up the worst of the mess and can straighten our backs? I do not want to try and speak politics; I can only tell you but it is what I want to tell you, what the ordinary young Norwegian over here thinks we shall believe in when we go home. We know that in some ways we have changed. Probably those who will have stayed at home during the whole of the occupation will have changed still more. Friends who arrive over here now keep on saying: "You'll be surprised." The people are different in Norway already, they say: they are Norwegians still, of course, more Norwegian than they were before, but in another way. Then they try to explain, but it's not easy. People in Norway are hardened, they say, and yet warmer than they used to be. Things are black or white in Norway now—important or else not worth mentioning. Money doesn't count; possessions don't count; clever talk doesn't count; but character counts. Young people have grown up to be leaders. A new loyalty has grown up, a readiness to serve without asking questions. "You'll be surprised," they say.

And we say, of course, over here, that we think we can understand. We had some experience of the war ourselves and the first part of the occupation. But we were more isolated then; we were one town without means of communicating with the next The rapidly moving front broke up any administration. I remember how isolated we felt when the telephone in our city hall didn't work any more. Rumours came. Our allies were leaving. The isolation seemed complete. Then we began to escape, in small groups, those who could. I myself happened to come out through Russia and Siberia. Since then our people back home have learned to organise—the technique of the underground. What they have done we have followed here. But however much we sympathise with them it is not the same as being there ourselves. Their experience is not ours, and it may be that these few years may already have created barriers between us which it will take time to overcome. It seems to me certain that there will be greater differences still between the occupied countries and the rest of the world. I am not speaking about the enemy; they will not count for a while in this connection. I am thinking of our allies to whom we owe our liberty and everything. You, for instance, in particular, will have to be patient with us. I don't suppose that we ourselves will be in a mood to be patient: we shall have too much to do quickly.

On the other hand I do think we all recognise now that we have a responsibility beyond the frontiers of our own country. It may still be too early to speak about a feeling of world citizenship or even a feeling of European citizenship, but I think we can say that there is at least a tendency in this direction. British friends, often ask us if we have noticed any development of such a broader outlook here in Great Britain. Our reply is "Yes." We don't say that merely in order to be polite, nor on the other hand do we say it because we so often hear complaints that there is so little of it. One doesn't become a citizen of the world in one jump. To become a good man it isn't enough to have a bad conscience. But it may be the beginning. There are people who say that world citizenship is impossible. The same ideas have been thought before. Every time soldiers come back from wars they have always been disappointed. New wars have come, and always bigger wars, until they now embrace the whole world.

Perhaps exactly this will be our salvation. We are so many this time. It seems to me that this time it's not going to be only a political problem for statesmen; it's going to be a moral question for every one of us. For many years now we have marched together, and some heavy hills are still certainly ahead. We are united now because we have the same aim. After the war different interests will arise. This will make it hard for us to understand each other. Take us Norwegians, and you, for example. You have your country intact. We shall have to start from scratch. People from Norway might be lucky to live in barracks and tents when the Huns have withdrawn. If they can't find their old officials somewhere in Germany they will have to find new ones. Doctors, hospitals, schools, all may be gone. We who go back might meet our countrymen on the scorched earth of our homeland as once the settlers met on the virgin prairies with only a pattern of a free society in their hearts.

Physical things are not the most important. I have talked about the loss of homes and property, but it is the consequence of loss and not the loss itself which makes the difference. My own cottage was still standing when I left it. It had been taken over by enemy officers. They brought German girls there. I was told they had used my books as fuel, but that they had repaired the house. I was not interested. So many of us had lost everything, and made the discovery, which you do make, that personal property and privileges do not mean so much after all. We discovered that the things we owned collectively were worth more to us than the things we owned alone. I wonder if I am able to make you see what I mean. I am trying to take the emphasis off physical things. We know, for instance, that after the occupation, food will be brought over to us until we can start to produce it for ourselves. We are not afraid that we shall starve. The difference in conditions between us and you will not be so important in itself, but it will create another outlook for us. Not that we will swear to any special social or political system. I do not think that we shall swear to any doctrine at all. We might try new methods anyway. I think we shall probably go further in social experiments than will seem necessary to you from inside your more stable society. I think we are likely to put up claims that you will think extreme. Claims like "Live and let live" should not mean that the bad and evil should be allowed to live too. As a nation with a new start we might be stubborn. We might be impatient.

It will be good that not all of us will need to start from the beginning. You will be the fixed point in Europe with old connections all over the world. You will have your traditions unbroken. The hooks which have been burned on the Continent we shall be able to find in Britain. We shall use your firms to deal with and to consult. It will be from Britain that the new system of communications will have to be built up. We shall need each other badly. And yet there will be such big differences in our outlook. That's perhaps where we who came out can be of some help. For many years now London has been the free capital for many European countries. Those of us who have come to you from abroad have been treated well. We think you have treated us as one of the family. We think we are going to leave you pretty soon now. We are keen to leave: you understand why. But we shall be just as anxious presently to come back to take up our family connections again. And we shall want you to come and see us, more, much more than you did before. You have soldiers and sailors buried on our soil. When you come, we will show you graves which during the years of occupation were covered with forbidden flowers. And when you stand looking at them you may find that not only our pasts but our futures too are tied together. I hope you will.

. . . . .

In the Pacific the Allies had passed to the offensive and were gradually driving the Japanese back from one group of islands to the other. The following is a description from General MacArthur's campaign in New Guinea by William Courtenay.

FIGHTING IN NEW GUINEA

Home Service, November 25 1943

General MacArthur's campaign in the last islands of the Solomons group and in New Guinea is moving along very nicely to its ultimate objective, the expulsion of the Japanese from all of these islands between the Australian mainland and Truk—where the Jap navy is skulking. Here you are looking at a combined operation where sea, land and air forces are blended and where good staff work, marvellous timing and gallantry of all involved enable an amphibious operation to succeed.

Now the pattern for these operations, the really classic instance where they have brought great victory, was laid down at the Huon Gulf on the north-east of New Guinea. I was there, as a matter of fact. I had marched with the Australians through the rain, forests, and over the razor backs of the Owen Stanley Mountains from the pretty little township of Wau, set amid the hills in the heart of the New Guinea goldfields, to Salamaua at the coast. So I am going to start the story for you in the third week of August last.

We had arrived just two or three miles from Salamaua. The Japs occupied the last high features; they are well defended with pill-boxes and many machine-guns, and they had their backs to the sea. It would have been easy, of course, for General MacArthur and General Sir Thomas Blamey, the Australian Commander, to bound forward and seize Salamaua, but they were after bigger fish. To have gone straight for Salamaua, you see, would simply have alarmed the Jap High Command, who would have taken extra precautions to save Lae, which lies just north of Salamaua in the bend of the Huon Gulf, under the mouth of the mighty Markham river. General MacArthur was really anxious to seize Lae and Salamaua, and to the north-east, Finchhafen, and the whole of that Huon Gulf peninsula. He desired actually at one stroke to cut the remnants of the Jap force, which had been operating there all year against us. Let me tell you how I watched him set about it.

First of all, through the latter half of August, he mustered all his air power to smash the Jap air bases. They had a number of airfields along that north New Guinea coast. They have still got four at Rabaul on the northerly tip of New Britain, and several on the south coast of that island just across the straits which separate New Guinea from New Britain. From all these, Jap airplanes could converge to attack our troops or upset the amphibious plan. So MacArthur set upon them with all his resources. On one day alone in August I remember he caught nearly 900 aircraft on the ground, at the airfields at Wewack, destroyed them all in a midnight to dawn attack of great intensity and slew some 1,500 skilled personnel who were all lined up waiting to take off.

These attacks reached their highest intensity on the night of September 3rd, the anniversary of the war's outbreak. On that night, all of these airfields were attacked at once to deprive the Jap of his eyes, when the grand manoeuvre for encircling the whale Jap force was to commence. At 6.30 a.m. on that Saturday, September 4th, while General Sir Thomas Blamey was describing to some of us in the jungles of New Guinea details of the plan, it had already started. Australians of the famous 9th Division had moved along the north New Guinea coast in barges, protected by air cover and by the United States Navy. Their task was to land at two beaches above Lae. One part of this force marched along the coast and cut the Jap supply line. The other part turned in the opposite direction along the beaches towards Lae. These landings were protected by a smoke screen, laid by the American warships in the Huon Gulf. The Japs didn't have wind of the plot for half-an-hour, which is a very long time in amphibious operations.

Now MacArthur hoped that when he halted his troops in front of Salamaua, the Japs would be tempted to believe they still had a sporting prospect of holding it, and that they would bring the defences of Lae to send men to Salamaua to reinforce it, and this was precisely what happened, just what the doctor had ordered! It made Lae an easier target, and of course once Lae fell, you'll see that Salamaua must automatically go, because its sole supply line came through Lae.

But the attack on Lae still gave the Japs one avenue of escape. That was to move inland from the coast. Now this was just what MacArthur and Blamey desired to avoid, for if the Japs escaped into the interior of New Guinea, we should have to face more of these heartbreak marches next year. So the plan for the encirclement included a daring parachute exercise; American paratroops were to descend behind the enemy's lines, just a few miles inland from Lae, along the Markham river to seal the backdoor to Lae, and prevent an escape along the river. This paratroop exercise was designed to take place on Sunday morning, September 5th, just 24 hours or so after the Australians had successfully landed on the beaches above Lae.

But there was also a third exercise. Another Australian force had been secretly landed at an advanced airfield in the mountains. They had 800 New Guinea boys with them carrying pontoon bridge equipment. This force commenced marching actually on September 1st, marching northwards along the course of the snakelike Wampit river, towards the lower bank of the Markham river, which they were due to reach by dawn on September 5th. This was the most gruelling of all the razor-back marches of this war, because the forest-clothed mountains reared their ridges in solid ranks, the gradients were almost one in two. In fact the trail along the creek bed dare not be followed because of the risks of detection from the air. The Australians were without a supply line or any staging camps, crawling with heavy packs on their hands and knees over these mountains in the green ghostlike tunnels, which they carved as they marched. Each man had got to carry his five days' rations. Each one, in fact, was told there would be no turning back, even the wounded had to march onward until the Markham was reached. And at the Markham river they were to hide in the jungle awaiting their cue to cross.

That cue was to be the spectacle of the American paratroops descending. I spent Saturday, September 4th, among the American paratroops in New Guinea, attended their final briefing. I met and talked with General MacArthur, and that night under flitting storm lanterns amid the ghost gums and eucalyptus, I saw the officers being given their final instructions. We all turned in by ten, you see it takes several hours to move a parachute unit; so by two-thirty next morning the stillness of the jungle was rent with the sound of bugles calling us from our blanket-rolls. The birds of paradise uttered shrill protest at this indecent disturbance of their rest. Hot breakfast was served to us at three-fifteen, and by the play of torchlights, looking very much like fireflies in the trees. I remember, the Captains assembled their men in the ghostly jungle, called the rolls and marched them to their waiting lorries.

I should explain that each of the Douglas planes holds 21 men, so each lorry held the same number. Each lorry and each aircraft were given identical numbers. We were all seated in these vehicles by four-thirty, and by four-thirty-five in the morning, before dawn, a long procession of lorries moved out of its jungle hide to the main road. I was to fly in the last of the troop carriers, so was given a seat in the last lorry. We commenced to move by ten past five. By six we were due at the air strip, just as dawn was breaking in the Owen Stanley Mountains. Zero hour was to be at any time over seven, but now we had to wait upon weather reports. Our route was to take us for 300 miles above the wild headhunters' lands, and to 10,000 feet over the Bismarck ranges, and it was essential to have good weather. Not until 8.30 was the signal given to start. So for an hour-and-a-half the paratroops had to face the ordeal of self-discipline sitting in those transport planes all waiting to go, keyed up after eighteen months' training.

Well, the transport lined up in a long line on the taxi-way. Just like taxi-cabs at a railway station, and when the signal to start comes at last, all the propellers start whirring together. The long line, nose to tail, moves forward, turns into the runway at the end of the taxi-way and the aircraft take off at thirty-second intervals, close together. Within a few minutes a vast armada of troop-carrying aircraft are in the sky. At the end of the taxi-way at the end of the jungle I saw a lone figure. It was General MacArthur; he, too, had risen at 2.30 that morning to salute his men as they started. Then I saw him jump into a Fortress bomber, which led the host into battle. He was first over the battle line, last to leave, and he spent seven hours in the air that morning. The great adventure had begun. We were now joined by bombers which were to hammer the Lae defences up to sixty seconds prior to the drop; by Bostons which were to drop a smoke-screen sixty seconds before this event, and by a cloud of fighters stepped up to thirty thousand feet. The whole armada met above a razor-back to rendezvous and then we all turned on course. Then we commenced the 300-mile flight high over the mountains, maintaining radio silence, every man tense. All were wondering if we would see any Jap Zeros, and how far secrecy and supplies were with us. Soon after ten we crossed the mighty Bismarcks, and then commenced the great wheeling movement over the beautiful Markham Valley within full view of the foe at Lae, which we could see so clearly only a few miles away at the coast. We had to descend to within a few hundred feet of the dropping area. The glorious valley looked very green and English this warm Sunday morning; the folds of the hills gentle and velvety, reminded me of Sussex Downs. But this, of course, was the dangerous period and not an enemy aircraft was in sight. At ten-past-ten, a green light appeared over the doorway of my Douglas plane. The 21 paratroops silently rise, blacken their faces, adjust their 'chutes, and form up in line, just as if they are in an omnibus which has reached its terminus. I shook hands with the Lieutenant in command; the officers, of course always jump first. At ten-twenty the green light changes to red. Without looking over his shoulder, the Lieutenant calls out, "Follow me, men," and hurls himself through the open doorway. One by one the twenty men follow as the jump master calls, out the signal—Go-Go-Go to each of them in turn. Within two minutes all of the hundreds of paratroops had left their aircraft. I could see the great mass of men floating down to earth. A smokescreen between us and the enemy was laid to time as six Bostons flashed past underneath me, and everybody dropped and disappeared into twelve-foot high jungle grass, which, of course, hid each man from his neighbour—secrecy and supplies had been maintained to the end. The Japs were trapped and encircled. The Australians waiting at the lower bank of the river, bridged the 800 yards-wide Markham and rushed across. The two armies met and embraced upon the airfield.

Next day seventy air transports flying more Australians landed at an air strip which the Aussies, who had marched so far, had cleared of its jungle grasses. Within 24 hours it had become one of the busiest airports in the world, after it had lain hidden for eighteen months in silence beneath its tall jungle coverage. So falls Salamaua, Lae, Finchhafen, and the whole Huon peninsula.

· · · · ·

At the end of the year, which brought the Russians from Stalingrad beyond the industrial Ukraine past Kiev, and which had seen the re-opening of the Mediterranean, with Italy as a co-belligerent of the Allies, Winston Churchill, President Roosevelt and Marshal Stalin met for a conference at Teheran to plan the final defeat of Germany.

THE TEHERAN CONFERENCE

Home Service, December 6 1943

Their four-day conference at Teheran, which ended on the night of December 1 signed the following declaration:—

"We, the President of the United States of America, the Prime Minister of Great Britain, and the Premier of the Soviet Union, Marshal Stalin, President Roosevelt, and Mr Churchill, after have met these four days past in this capital of our ally, Iran, and have shaped and confirmed our common policy.

"We expressed our determination that our nations shall work together in war and in the peace that will follow.

"As to war, our military staffs have joined in our round-table discussions, and we have concerted our plans for the destruction of the German forces.

"We have reached complete agreement as to the scope and timing of the operations which will be undertaken from the east, west and south. The common understanding which we have here reached guarantees that victory will be ours.

"And as to peace, we are sure that our concord will make it an enduring peace. We recognise fully the supreme responsibility resting upon us and all the United Nations to make a peace which will command the goodwill of the overwhelming masses of the peoples of the world and banish the scourge and terror of war for many generations.

With our diplomatic advisers we have surveyed the problems of the future. We shall seek the co-operation and the active participation of all nations, large and small, whose peoples in heart and mind are dedicated, as are our peoples, to the elimination of tyranny and slavery, oppression and intolerance. We will welcome them as they may choose to come into a world family of democratic nations.

"No power on earth can prevent our destroying the German armies by land, their U-boats by sea, and their war plants from the air. Our attacks will be relentless and increasing.

"From these friendly conferences we look with confidence to the day when all peoples of the world may live free lives, untouched by tyranny and according to their varying desires and their own consciences.

"We came here with hope and determination. We leave here, friends in fact, in spirit, and in purpose."

Signed at Teheran, December 1 1943.

Roosevelt, Stalin, Churchill.

Roosevelt and Stalin joke about Churchill's karacul hat at Tehran. The hat was a gift from the British Press Unit.

. . . . .

And now for the background picture of these historic meetings in Teheran. Here is a description by Kenneth Matthews:

"I will try to pass on to you something of the story brought back from British and American delegates from Teheran. It was a conference between three great national leaders, who put all pomp and ceremony aside and lived and worked together for four days, not only as equals but like old and well-tried friends. The main conference meetings took place in the Soviet Embassy at Teheran, where President Roosevelt was staying as Stalin's guest. Mr Churchill stayed at the British Legation just opposite the road. Both buildings stand within high-walled parks and by means of screens thrown across the road they were joined into a single conference headquarters. The setting was like one of those old Persian pictures. There were weeping willows in the gardens and cypresses and ornamental ponds, and the roses were in bloom. "President Roosevelt went first to the American Legation when he arrived on the Saturday, and moved over to the Soviet Embassy just before three o'clock on the following afternoon. A few minutes later came the historic, first meeting between the Premier of the Soviet Union and the President of the United States. And no one else was present except the interpreters. But several of the American party saw Marshal Stalin arrive. He came striding down the gravel path, a stocky, iron-grey figure in a superb dark blue Marshal's greatcoat. He was followed by Mr Molotov and a group of Soviet officers. Mr Hopkins drew Mr Molotov aside to one of the adjoining rooms and left Stalin and Roosevelt together. They were talking for about an hour, and then Mr Churchill arrived, and the three-power conference began.

"The conference ran Sunday, Monday, Tuesday and Wednesday—four days. The first three days were military days; one big meeting took place from about 4.30 till about 7.30 each afternoon, and those who attended were the Big Three, the two Foreign Ministers, and Mr Hopkins, the three Chiefs of Staff-Marshal Voroshiloff acted as Soviet Chief of Staff—and occasionally Ambassador Clark-Kerr and Ambassador Harriman from Moscow. On the fourth day, the military chiefs left Teheran, and Mr Churchill, President Roosevelt Marshal Stalin, Mr Eden, Mr Molotov, Mr Hopkins and Mr Harriman had a meeting lasting over lunch, all through the afternoon, through dinner, until half-past ten at night, planning the post-war world. That was the conference proper.

"But there were two not unimportant events. One was on the Monday afternoon, when Mr Churchill presented Marshal Stalin with the Sword of Stalingrad. 'I have the command of His Majesty,' said Mr Churchill, 'to present to you, for transmission to the city of Stalingrad, this Sword of Honour.' And Stalin, with grave face, and a few low-spoken words of thanks, took the sword, kissed it and passed it to Marshal Voroshiloff, who had twice before stood at his side in dark hours when the city of Stalingrad was in deadly danger. The three full delegations were present at this solemn, little twenty minute ceremony.

"And then the day after, came Churchill's sixty-ninth birthday dinner. Thirty-four guests were fitted somehow round the Legation table; toasts were drunk to His Majesty King George VI, to President Kalinin and to President Roosevelt; Mr Churchill toasted 'Stalin the Great'; and Stalin toasted 'My fighting friend Churchill and my fighting friend Roosevelt'—and, in fact, as the evening wore on, Stalin was so carried away by the spirit of the occasion that he several times left his seat at Mr Churchill's left hand in order to clink glasses with some of the other guests. Stalin also paid a great tribute to American war production. He is reported to have said that without American machines, the United Nations could never have won the war.

"The decisions of this great Teheran Conference are recorded in the official communiqué. One point stands out, and that is the whole-hearted agreement about the time and place of the Second Front. I imagine this communique must be unique for the emphasis it places upon friendship as a motive force in international affairs. Here are three statesmen, leaders of three mighty and victorious nations, who publicly declare their belief in friendship as a power capable of winning the war and rebuilding the world. Friendship between Governments and mutual confidence in the innermost councils of state, that is the example which has been set for posterity by the Conference at Teheran. If I had to name the Conference. I would borrow Stalin's phrase and call it 'The Conference of Fighting Friendship'."

CHAPTER VII

Preparing and Waiting for the Invasion

December, 1943—June, 1944

After the Teheran Conference followed months of intense preparation and of growing air attacks on Germany. The U-boats had gradually been mastered during the latter half of 1943, and immense supplies reached Great Britain from America, and Russia from America and Britain.

About the middle of November the Royal Air Force started its big offensive against Berlin, dropping no less than 22,000 tons over the German capital during the next three months.

THE RAF OFFENSIVE AGAINST BERLIN

Squadron Leader John Strachey, Home Service, December 16 1943

Bomber Command's assault upon Berlin marks the highest point yet reached in the air offensive.

It is not too much to say that the bomber offensive is today the joint product of the brains, the courage and the grinding hard work of this entire nation. The very success which has been achieved may tend to make some people think that the bomber offensive has just been a matter of building a sufficient number of bombers, flying them over Germany, dropping the bombs and coming home again. The fact is that the bomber offensive has only been carried forward by keeping one step ahead of the enemy's continually improving defences. It would have been fatal even to pause. The counter-measure—the new method of fighter attack against the new form of bomber defence—has never been long in coming. We have had to be ready with the counter-counter-measure; and we have been. If, for example, we were to attack Berlin today with the same aircraft, using the same methods which we employed only two years ago, our bomber force would be massacred in one or two operations. But equally, if today our Lancasters, Halifaxes, Stirlings had to meet no more than the defences which existed in

Twilight at an RAF base somewhere in England.

1942 they could destroy every industrial centre in Germany with negligible losses to themselves.

Recently we have been given an account of the work of our Pathfinder force. The need for someone to find the path to the target is obvious—for naturally that same darkness which hides the bomber from the defending fighter also tends to hide the target from the bomber. You will have noticed that the moonlit nights are not now the only ones upon which the main force goes out; rather the contrary in fact. Again you will have noticed that several of the recent major attacks on Berlin were made through thick cloud. None of this could have been possible without the Pathfinders. The Pathfinders mark out the target for the main force which follows on their heels. They mark it with target-indicators which hang low over the city or actually lie burning upon the ground. And they mark it by flares, hanging high in the air upon parachutes, which show, in the way buoys at sea show a sandbank below the water, the area of the sky within which the bombs must be released in order to hit the target. The need for these high, sky-marking flares arises when there is such thick cloud over the target that the ground-markers would disappear into the clouds and the main force of bombers would lose sight of them. In weather conditions when there would have been not the slightest hope of a successful attack even a year ago, the Pathfinders are marking the target so that intensely concentrated bombing is being achieved. For Germany that is perhaps the most ominous development of all. For it is the concentration in both time and space that counts: the tons, per minute, per acre.

You can imagine the productive effort which the bomber offensive has called for from the men and women of the aircraft industry, and of all the other industries which stand behind the aircraft industry. It has been a gigantic and sustained effort. Everything depends upon the output of aircraft—above all, of heavy bombers and of everything that goes into them. Everything depends upon our output reaching, or surpassing, the high totals which have been set for it. It will not be easy. This is not the first but the fifth winter of the war. We have all been working for a goodish time and without much break. But do yon remember the answer given by Marshal Foch in 1918, when they told him that the British and French armies were too exhausted for the general offensive into which he was about to order them? "Wars," said Foch, "are only won by exhausted armies." He ordered them to attack, and the war was won in three months. Today we are very far from exhausted, for we have not had to bear anything like the severity of fighting which our armies sustained in the last war. But we have put forward a vast productive effort, above all, perhaps, in the aircraft industry. The bomber offensive has been, up to the present, our major effort.

Into it has been poured the courage, the industrial power and the scientific genius of this country. Upon it our hopes of an early victory which shall not be too dearly bought must mainly depend.

. . . . .

In Russia, January, 1944, saw the raising of the siege of Leningrad.

THE SIEGE OF LENINGRAD

Henry Shapiro, Home Service, January 30 1944

It is an incredible story—a tale of suffering, and of triumph over suffering, such as no big city in this war can surpass. In Leningrad everybody worked and everybody fought unceasingly against the Germans—and against the cold. And not only the soldiers and the people of the factories. Writers, artists, professors and priests learned how to throw hand grenades and handle machineguns.

In the factories—unheated factories—men and women worked on night and day in the bitterest weather while shells from enemy guns dropped on them. Each morning children used to collect fragments of German shells. By night those fragments became Russian shell casings.

Once, factory workers marched from their benches straight to the front line; they beat off a German attack; and then they marched straight back to work.

There were firemen—firemen who had nothing left with which to fight fires but snow and dynamite. The snow they threw on the small fires. The dynamite they used to blast a path in front of the great advancing flames so that their progress could he stayed.

Those, in outline, are a few of the chapters of the story of Leningrad. Very many people died in the city—died from fire, bombs, shells, hunger and cold. But there was no thought of giving in, neither to the Germans nor to the appalling weather. Germans were round the city on one side, Finns were on the other. But privations and a threatening military situation made no difference. Leningrad stood it all. Moreover, they achieved what they did—lacking fuel, electricity, water and transport; they had only four ounces of black bread a day; they were shelled all the time.

The Germans dropped leaflets saying, "Gentlemen workers, what are you fighting for? Lay down your arms and we promise you life and liberty." To that the workers, through Marshal Voroshilov, replied briefly: "We did not build beautiful Leningrad far Nazi bandits." When the Germans nearly broke through, the workers of Leningrad drove the tanks they had made from the assembly line to the battle front and there fought in them until the push was held.

Meanwhile, cold gripped the city. Intense cold. Birds dropped dead from the trees, frozen. Wooden houses were chopped down by the hundred to provide fuel. All dogs and cats disappeared: they were eaten.

I walked through the streets of the city during the siege and marvelled that human beings could have stood so much. The men were not like men. They were ghosts with green sunken cheeks. The people lived in houses whose rooms were festooned with icicles. From those rooms they trudged long miles through the frozen streets to their offices and factories.

When things were worst some relief came; sailors of the Baltic Fleet built a good road across Lake Ladoga, and supplies began to trickle in. By the spring, 300,000 Leningrad people were able to start cleaning up debris, bury their dead, and cheer the first tram as it started from its sheds, and went through the battered streets. It was then that almost every inch of Leningrad's soil, even up to the very kerbstones, was used to grow vegetables. The city became a garden of greens.

All the time the people of Leningrad never stopped working. They knew that they themselves had to make the weapons, the tanks, the guns to beat back the Germans. They made them; the Germans were thrown back; and today Leningrad is free.

. . . . .

The following are three descriptions from Occupied Europe. One by a Polish officer of the Underground Army, who came to Britain on a mission, one by a Dutch officer, and the third by a Danish clergyman.

WHAT "FRIENDSHIP" MEANS IN POLAND

Home Service, February, 1944

For a few weeks now I have been surrounded by decency and respect in London. For a few weeks now I have dismissed with a smile the sudden palpitation of my heart when I have seen a policeman. I have almost got used to the feeling that tomorrow also I will have all the food I want. At night the persistent nightmare of the Gestapo is beginning to stop waking me in a cold sweat. But...

I hope I will not hurt the feelings of all those who have been so very kind to me over here, but I don't feel altogether happy. There is something, among all these luxuries and comforts, which urges me all the time to go back to Poland, to go back to the hungry and anxious misery of my occupied country. I know this may sound fantastic to you, and I must tell you before I go any further that I am anything but a "killer," I am not even a born "fighter." If I could tell you what my pre-war job was, you would easily understand that executing German brutes, dynamiting bridges or setting fire to fuel dumps does not fit with my likings. These are duties which I have performed, and, I hope, always will perform well as befits a Pole, but I assure you it isn't the thrill of pressing a well-aimed trigger which makes me want to go back.

The truth is simply that we have something over there in Poland which is so very dear, that nothing can replace or make up for it. It's our unique friendship, the friendship of the Underground. How many friends does a man have in the ordinary way? How many have you: three, five, or perhaps seven friends? If you are a popular and likeable fellow there may perhaps be a hundred people all told willing to do a lot for you. But I—the same as each of us—have got thousands of friends, that is to say people for whom I am prepared to die, the same as they are, and have been, willing to die for me. Were this not so I shouldn't be here now. Two in particular have directly given their lives for me.

Some time ago, information vital for my further security was to be passed on to me at a pre-arranged spot. The first messenger was caught. I was already on my way to the spot and could no longer be reached and stopped, so a second messenger was sent. He also fell into the hands of the Gestapo. Neither of them knew me personally, nor did I know them, but a few words would have been enough to betray me. One died while being tortured: the other a few days after. But I, the unknown companion. I was saved.

Most inhuman tortures wait for us if we are caught, and they are the supreme test of friendship. If a soldier falls in the field, for him the fight is over, but if any of us is caught, the most dreadful fight of our lives begins: the fight against one's own weakness for the sake of one's friends. Yes, when I say that in Poland today a new meaning has been given to the word "friendship"—I really mean it. I would like to tell you about Rys, for instance, though that, of course, is not his real name.

Over eighteen months ago now, I was looking for a man to take on an exceptionally risky and difficult job. In the Underground Army we do not like overstatements, so you can take it for granted that the job called for very much skill and courage. It was then, for the first time, that I came across this man nicknamed Rys. He had an excellent reputation. When I had been told about his achievements and exploits, I decided that this was the man I needed, and I fixed an appointment with him. At the set time I noticed a small, rather child-looking fellow walking merrily down the empty street, obviously enjoying the loud clatter of his wooden soles, but I did not pay much attention to him. I glanced at my watch and was bracing myself to give Rys a "ticking off," for in the Underground punctuality is a sacred thing, when the little fellow came to a standstill in front of me. He looked down at my shoes and exclaimed, "Hey, misterl Why don't you wear these? It's grand fun." And he followed that up with a peculiar version of tap dance on the pavement.

This was the famous Rys. He was the son of a miner. He had the most fascinating eyes I have ever seen. They could plead and laugh as well as threaten and hate. He soon became my closest associate and teacher. For Rys knew all the answers. He was always on the go; he never had enough work, never enough risks.

His wife Kasia was a housemaid. Many's the time I have waited with her all through the night for the return of Rys, who was to bring me some important materials. At every approaching footstep she used to brighten up with a smile of triumph, and as they passed she found a comforting explanation. When the light came and there was still no Rys, she would be the one to say, "Don't worry, mister, my Rys is all right. Remember, transport is not what it used to be." When Rys, as he sometimes was, would be a few days late in returning, God only knows what was going on in that little woman's heart. But she never complained, and when the time came round again for him to go off on a new mission, it was always she who would pack his bundle, knowing perfectly well that what she had to pack would be the death sentence of her man if he was caught.

Then, another lad Wladek was caught. When the Gestapo realised that no tortures would make him speak, they seized his father and tortured him in his presence. The old man died in front of his eyes, but Wladek was still silent. It was only when his mother was brought in to be tortured that he couldn't stand it any longer. And he told them the place of one of our mutual hideaways. A week later Rys walked into a trap set there by the Gestapo. After the first day of torture he returned to the cell and unscrewed the electric bulb to "do away" with himself by swallowing broken glass, but his fellow prisoners stopped him in time. After the second day he declared that he could "take it." He was then confronted with Wladek who by that time was half mad and did not even recognise him. The first thing Rys did, however, though flogged by the guards, was to walk up to Wladek and shake his hand in silence. I would not venture to describe my feelings when I learnt about Rys's capture on my return from a mission. I do not think I would have been more moved if it had been my own father or sister. Rys knew a large sector of the Underground. He knew workers, soldiers, couriers, officers and commanders. He knew hundreds of them and they all realised that once he was caught and tortured, their lives depended entirely on him. Still, not a single one of them even changed his address or hideaway. That shows you what they thought of Rys.

The first thing to do was to get Kasia and their baby into safety, but on the other hand we all knew that the Gestapo was just waiting for any of us who would appear there. Jozek, who volunteered to investigate never came back. Still, after a few days I was able to send this message to Rys in prison: "Your family is safe. What is your escape plan?" Meantime, I enlisted the experience and advice of old-time burglars, who many a time already had proved their value to the Underground on such occasions. But once again I had miscalculated Rys. Knowing now that his wife and child would not suffer for it, half-dead himself after his tortures, he and three others made their escape unaided. I do not remember ever feeling so happy as when a breathless lad ran into my room to report: "Rys is out; he is safe here in the neighbourhood."

I immediately went there. I was so moved that I could not utter a word. I could not even shake his hand because ... but I must spare you those details. His swollen face was changed, but the glow in his eyes was the same. He spoke first. After what he had seen, he was asking to be transferred to another more dangerous job, the one of rescuing prisoners. That's Rys for you, and that's the spirit in which we live and fight with our eyes set on London. For us over there the word London is synonymous with our leaders, who work here and direct our activities in Poland; it is synonymous with Poland's freedom of thought and action. To us London is also a symbol. So much so that I often catch myself now on a feeling of astonishment, seeing that, after all, London is only a town. Let me tell you one more thing. I am twenty-nine, and though the last four years in Poland have noticeably advanced my age, I feel young. My mind is set on the future, on the future of Poland in particular, and I must say that I feel confident. I am looking forward to that "tomorrow" of Poland. The other evening I was tidying the clothes in which I travelled from Poland. A small unexpected lump attracted my attention. I ripped the lining and found a folded piece of paper carefully stitched to the seam. A few typewritten words on it: "God bless. You will find me the same when you return." I don't know who put it there, perhaps my girlfriend, perhaps a comrade. I don't know, and I don't care, for those words are true of all of them. They will not change. This great friendship of the Underground, this anonymous friendship prepared for every sacrifice, this great friendship taking in all classes, creeds and beliefs, this friendship of all for all, this friendship will not change. Born in torture, hunger and oppression this great friendship will survive to shape and inspire the Poland of tomorrow, the Poland I want to see.

. . . . .

HOLLAND UNDER GERMAN OCCUPATION

Home Service, February 13 1944

When Dives was in Hell, he wanted Lazarus to be allowed to go and tell his relations how bad Hell really was, and how they would be bound to land there themselves unless they changed their ways. Do you remember what Dives was told? That his relations would not be persuaded even though one rose from the dead. Those of us who get back from Nazi Europe are not unlike people risen from the dead. Are you going to believe us? We all say the same thing about the Germans. But it does not seem to make much difference. Maybe telling is not enough. The last ten years of European history certainly make it look like that. The free peoples, as long as they are free, could not realise what Nazi rule implied. It is as if nothing short of actually experiencing it will do.

In Holland, up to May, 1940, we were not guessing any better than you were what might be coming to us from the German conception of life. The French might have known better. They had the Germans in France in 1870. The Belgians had them in Belgium in the last war. It was different with us. For longer than anybody remembered Holland had been independent, rich, free, peace-loving. We did not dream any more than you, how bad things might become. If you asked a Dutchman before the war, what he thought of the Germans, he would have said something very much like what you would have said, and unfortunately some still say here: that the Germans he had met had seemed to be quite decent fellows, rather given to ordering each other about, but wasn't that their own affair?

And now let me tell you something. When I either read or hear a story of German cruelty I do not feel even the slightest inclination to doubt it. Why not? Because I have seen for myself now how the Germans behave. They talk about Herrenvolk and Kultur, but it is precisely in human culture that Germany has stood still or even gone backwards for a hundred years. No one denies them, of course, their first-class achievements in music, philosophy and science. Unfortunately, however, their qualities in these fields do not rule out their lack in others. What the Germans so terribly lack is humanity. They lack what the rest of the world calls "culture."

In some moods, we most of us know, the Germans are sentimental. In others they are incredibly arrogant. But in all moods they are absolutely incapable of understanding other people's rights and traditions. And that is why every country they go into resists them, even after military defeat. The different countries develop their own particular way of resistance according to their national character and their geographical situation. Norway, for instance, has its sparse population, its long coastline, its hundreds of miles of mountain and forest, its remote fjords: that gives Norwegians all sorts of opportunities which Dutchmen have not got. Holland is very thickly populated. It has neither mountains nor forests. We could not, like the Yugoslavs, or like the Greeks or the Savoyards, organise guerrilla warfare. We have to resist as civilians, with a stubbornness of character which is, I think, anyway a natural Dutch characteristic. Like you, we have a profound sense of freedom and justice, and we seem to have been incapable of taking the Nazi political creed seriously. It is not the first time the Dutch have had to wear out an invader. We wore out Spain, once, in a life-and-death struggle which lasted eighty years. Thank God this isn't going to take so long! Remember, when you think of Holland now, that, like the Norwegians, but unlike the French and the Belgians, the Nazis, in addition to military occupation, have organised their own civil administration of Holland. And a very ruthless administration it is. If the Germans had gone about it differently (who knows?) they might, conceivably, have induced the occupied countries to remain passive even if they had not won them over to their side. Everywhere they went I suppose they tried. Certainly when they just arrived they showed us, just as they showed everyone else, always excepting the Poles and the Russians, their famous "correct" behaviour. But when it failed to bring them their magical reward of being accepted as supermen, when it left the Dutch, as it did, distant and contemptuous, their mood turned to uncontrollable fury. The word "correct" is now altogether banned from our vocabulary. The fact is, I think, that the Germans could not have gone about it differently. They were beaten by their own vices and their own inability to understand other people.

We used to wish in Holland, that you knew a little more than you seemed to about what we were doing. The fact is that neither news nor people can get out of Holland at all easily. But we were much disappointed when our national strike took place in April last year that you did not hear more about it. It put the wind up the Germans all right and more than twelve hundred Dutchmen were shot.

In Holland we shall not think the war over, any more than you, when Germany capitulates. We mean to have back our traditions and our liberties and Her Majesty the Queen, who is a symbol of all we love and stand for. But then we have to fight our way back with you to the Netherlands East Indies and the overthrow of Japan. And now let me tell you one story. In 1940, after the capitulation of France, when things were going well for Hitler and very badly for Britain, a collection of loudspeakers appeared outside our Peace Palace in the Hague ready for the announcement that Britain had been conquered. We could not help remembering Foch's railway carriage. Hitler and Goebbels have a taste, as we all know, for dramatic stage settings. Well, these German loudspeakers hung outside our Peace Palace for a very long time. And then one night they disappeared. It seemed that Britain wasn't, after all, going to be dictated to.

. . . . .

FROM DENMARK UNDER GERMAN OCCUPATION

The Rev. Paul Borchsenius, European Service, March, 1944

One Sunday, shortly before Christmas, I stood as usual in my pulpit. Little did I know that it was to be for the last time for a long while. The text was that of the ten virgins, the five wise virgins who had oil in their lamps and the five foolish ones who had forgotten the oil. I started my sermon from the saying of the virgins when the bridegroom arrived: "Our lamps are going out."

Without knowing how truly this was going to apply to myself who, two days later, slipped out of my house at the last moment and went to Sweden, I began by telling how, during these war years. I had often stood on the blacked-out shores of the Sound looking towards the Swedish towns where the lights were shining through the darkness. I often thought of what it would be like to stand in Malmo or Landskrona looking towards the shores of Zealand. The Swedes who were used to seeing the light from Copenhagen reflected on the night clouds must have found it strange now to seeing everything dark over there. It could truly be said of Denmark: Our lights are going out.

But in Randers, where I was vicar, there were lamps that had been extinguished just before that Sunday. Five young men had sacrificed their lives in the struggle against the oppressors of Denmark.

We were at war with Germany and we took an active part in the struggle. In Jutland the slogan was: "No through traffic to Norway." And so the explosions thundered on the railway lines night after night, and the climax was reached at the end of November, when the three great bridges across the Guden river, near Langaa, were blown to pieces.

A few days later it became obvious that the Gestapo was on our trail. Informers had been out. Four young saboteurs were caught and taken to Aarhus. When the great German razzias of the Jutland towns began, the Danish authorities there received orders to empty the prison. The Danes asked the Germans where all the prisoners, thieves, forgers and pimps were to be put, but received no answer. But now the prison was tilled with Danish patriots, and among them four young men from Randers. They behaved like brave saboteurs and told only what the Gestapo knew already. When the German Criminal Council asked one of them if he would consider volunteering for the Eastern Front to save his life, the young man replied: "If I get out, I shall continue the sabotage." It is not strange that the German officer who saw his mother out of the prison, after she had said farewell to her boy, said, "Your son does you credit, Madame; I wish he were mine." The four young men were hanged in the cellar of the oil refineries in Aarhus. Their corpses were taken to Rostock.

On the top of the hill in Randers lived a young teacher from Randers State School, Kay Hoff. He was surprised early one morning and the case was clear. Both revolvers and explosives were found in his flat. He was taken to a barracks and placed near a very hot stove in a corner of a room. He was ordered to stand with his face to the stove with both hands above his head while two German soldiers stood behind him with their guns at the ready. When he had been in this position for an hour and a half he could stand it no more and began to lower his hands. He heard the soldiers cock their rifles and lifted his hands again, but suddenly turned round and jumped with lightning speed at one of the soldiers. They tumbled on the floor in a fight to the death until the other soldier shot him through the back. The bullet perforated his liver—a deadly wound. Nevertheless, Hoff managed to jump on the window sill and tried to fling open the window so as to escape, but he was shot in the back of his head and fell dead to the floor.

Strangely enough, we were allowed to bury him in Randers Cemetery on condition that we did it by night and that nothing was said. It was a cold dark night, when half a dozen Danish policemen and Cemetery employees carried him to the grave. We had a few civil defence lanterns with us and an uncertain light fell on the immediate surroundings. In a flash one saw the corner of the railings round the grave, a monument or a yew tree. Suddenly the light fell on a helmet and I saw a German soldier with steel helmet and gun. My attention was quickened and I peered into the darkness round me and lo and behold: the cemetery was full of German soldiers, while their patrols rattled past in the street. We reached the grave and lowered the coffin.

Then we sang: "Be always tranquil when you walk the path of God"—that song that though a hymn has become one of Denmark's national songs during these years of war. Never have I heard the third verse sung so defiantly and strongly as by that little handful of men standing around the open grave in which was placed the dust of a young man who had lived up to that verse. And through the darkness towards the German soldiers floated the words: "Fight for all that you hold dear, die if the need arises; to live is not then so hard nor to die."

The following morning the grave was covered by a thick layer of red and white flowers, and that made the Germans appear on the spot at once. Three large soldiers in steel helmets, carrying rifles, with hand grenades dangling from their belts, were placed as guards by the grave. There is something fitting in that picture: three German soldiers looking after one dead Dane. But on the grave one of the wreaths carried long red and white streamers on which was printed another line of the same song: "Never fear the power of Darkness."

Our lamps are going out. There were young people whose lives were extinguished far too early but we remember the words of a Norwegian mother: "If my country is to live there must be some who know how to die." Therefore we believe that the lights will again be kindled in Denmark and we shall win a liberty that will be ours, because it was not presented to us as a gift from outside, but because we won it with our own blood and our own strength.

· · · · ·

In May, 1944. the Prime Ministers of the British Dominions came to London for an Imperial Conference. The Prime Minister of Australia, John Curtin, made a broadcast to the British people, and the Canadian Prime Minister, Mr Mackenzie King, addressed both Houses of Parliament in a speech which, like that of General Smuts in 1942, was also broadcast by the BBC.

JOHN CURTIN: AUSTRALIA AND THE WAR

Home Service, May 7 1944

I speak to the people of Britain on behalf of seven million Australians. Australia is the greatest land-mass south of the Equator held by the British race. Along with two million white people in South Africa and a million and a half in New Zealand, we are the bastion of British institutions, the British way of life and the system of democratic government in the southern world.

I suppose that the average citizen of the British Isles has some conception of Australia and Australians, whether it is because of the A.I.F. in the first world war, or Don Bradman's performance at Lord's, or the kangaroo and the koala bear. Many, no doubt, have relatives who made their home in Australia. But that conception must have been enlarged enormously when Japan came into the war and Australia was faced with extinction as a free nation. Then you must have realised that if Japan's onward march south engulfed Australia and New Zealand, all vestige of British freedom and liberty would have disappeared from the South Pacific. The Australian people stood firmly in the path of the aggressor because they knew that their most precious possession—their liberty—was at stake in the struggle. But they also stood as the trustees for you—the people of Britain—for everything for which British people everywhere stand. Today, I can say with just pride, that that trusteeship has been carried out honourably and successfully. What we did, we did to preserve our British way of life. We did it, too, for the United Nations. We did it for civilisation itself against a barbaric, ruthless and fanatical enemy.

Let me tell you how we did it; how Australians undertook to marshal the maximum strength of which they were capable so as to meet an entirely transformed position in the Pacific. That was a task suddenly thrust on Australia after she had sent three A.I.F. divisions to the Middle East; another division to Malaya; maintained the flow of Australian air crews for the Battle of Britain, and garrisoned numerous islands around Australia. No country—not even this gallant little island—faced a greater danger with less resources than did Australia, and the threat of invasion became such a grave possibility that the absolute priority of the fighting forces and their requirements became paramount over every other consideration. That threat has now been removed because of four main factors. These are the gallantry of our own and the

American forces; the skill of the commanders; the aid given by the United States; and the splendid effort of the Australian people themselves. While Britain's resources have been committed in other theatres, we are grateful for the assistance you have extended to Australia. I can tell you that when the fact that British Spitfires had been in action against the Japanese was made known, a great thrill ran through the Australian people.

Australia is now grappling with a task of no less magnitude. That is to maintain Australian combat forces; to feed and service Australian and Allied forces; to feed and maintain the Australian civil population and to produce vital food for Britain. All that imposes a terrific strain on Australia's manpower pool. Of the total male labour force, 40 per cent are serving in the forces, or are engaged in direct war work, while 60 per cent are engaged in providing food, clothing and other services for the Allied forces, in maintaining the civil population, and in providing food for Britain. Seventy-two per cent of Australian manpower is engaged in the fighting forces, in munitions-making and other essential industry. The corresponding figure for Britain is 75 per cent.

Since Pearl Harbor, Australia has been almost completely preoccupied with the war against Japan. But our airmen and our sailors have continued their fight, side by side with you, against the European enemy. Australian fighting men have given a new birth to the Anzac tradition established in the first world war. They have pushed the Japanese back from the very coast of Australia until the Allied retreat of 1942 has been turned into an Allied re-conquest of 1944. Our men have fought under conditions worse than any army in any war anywhere in the world has suffered since the beginning of human combat. I make it clear that Australia's preoccupation with the war against Japan involves more than Australia. The interests at stake concern the whole British Commonwealth, the whole of the democratic nations throughout the world. The issue in the Pacific, as in Europe, is between slavery and freedom. We, like you, have stood and fought for freedom; we, like you, do not mean to see the freedom we have helped to win for all people everywhere in the world diminished when peace comes.

There is one thing more for me to say to the people of Britain. We Australians are proud to be of the stock which populates the British Isles. Our forebears were your forebears; our sons and daughters are as your sons and daughters. What has been done in the past four years in this fighting fortress of Britain will ring through the halls of fame for ever. When Britain alone stood against Hitler we are proud that we had the honour to be with you.

What has to be done in the future is in the hands of the peoples of the British Commonwealth and of men and women of goodwill elsewhere who subscribe to very much the same ideas and ideals. Our generation will have left its mark. Before we hand on the torch to our sons and daughters our remaining task is to think and plan so that their world may in truth be a new world. There can be no going back to the 'good old days.' They were not good days and they have truly become old. We have to point the way to better days. The responsibility is a grave one. In one of the Allied Nations the other day it was said that 'the British Commonwealth may well be studied as an object lesson in free association.' The important word in that comment was 'association.' The partners in that association have a primary responsibility to each other, jointly and individually. By their behaviour in the future they may very well present to the world the blueprint for future happiness for all mankind. If they fail to do that, then they fail not only themselves, but they may precipitate more misery, unhappiness and degradation into this suffering world. So I say to the people of my own country: we inherited something priceless, we have enhanced that heritage; let us be sure it is handed on untarnished.

. . . . .

MACKENZIE KING TO BOTH HOUSES OF PARLIAMENT ON CANADA AND THE WAR

Home Service, May 12 1944

Perhaps I may be allowed to convey a special message from the Parliament and people of Canada to the people of Britain. No memory of happiness in the past is more cherished than the recollection of the visit of their Majesties the King and Queen. In Canada as, in Britain, the years of war have heightened the admiration and increased the affection felt by men and women everywhere for our King and Queen. We have been inspired by, their courage and devotion in sharing the dangers and sorrows of the people. In all the nations of the Commonwealth, their example has deepened the meaning and significance of our common allegiance to the Crown.

The heroic endurance of the people of Britain is ever present in our minds. Clearly the maintenance of human freedom has depended upon the preservation of the freedom of Britain. It is our greatest pride, as it is the greatest pride of other British nations, represented here, that when for long a time you alone bore the brunt of the attack, we stood with you in arms against the might of Nazi Germany. The free nations of the world can never forget that it was the indomitable resistance of the people of Britain that bought the precious time for the mobilisation of the forces of freedom around the globe.

It is, however, not of Britain but of Canada that I am expected to speak on this occasion.

I place first the aspect I regard as most significant. Canada's war effort is a voluntary effort. It is the free expression of a free people. Like the other nations of the Commonwealth at war today we entered the war on our own free will, and not as the result of any formal obligation.

Canada's population numbers 11,500,000. Three-quarters of a million of our finest young men are serving in the armed forces. This military demand on our manpower resources has not prevented our country from doubling its pre-war production. Thanks to the skill and devotion of our men and women, Canada is a granary, an arsenal, an aerodrome, and a shipyard of freedom. Our country has become increasingly proud of the fact that every fighting man from Canada serving across the sea, and in the air is a volunteer. We can say in very truth, that Canada's war effort in this war is a voluntary effort.

Canada's decision to enter the war was an immediate decision. When, in 1939, the last hopes of peace were fading from the world, I announced that if Britain took up arms in the defence of freedom, our Government would ask Parliament to place Canada at Britain's side. When war came there was no hesitation. As soon as Parliament could act Canada was at war.

From the beginning our war effort was so planned and organised that we might reach, as rapidly as possible, the maximum effort our people could sustain during a long war. We expanded our Navy as fast as we could build or acquire the ships and train the men. We expanded our Army to the highest strength we believed we could maintain in a long war. We expanded our Air Force to the limit of our capacity to secure the needed equipment and to train personnel. The British Commonwealth Air Training Plan was expedited and expanded beyond all anticipations. The 100,000th fighting airman has just completed his training. The co-operative training in Canada has vastly increased the joint strength in the air of the United Nations.

In fighting men, in weapons and munitions, in food and in finance, we are seeking as a people to make our utmost contribution to the fight for world freedom. For more than two years our country, alone in the Americas, was at war. In more ways than one our effort has been a pioneering effort.

Canada's contribution to the present war has been the greater because we live side by side with the United States. Without the harmony and reciprocity which exist between our two countries, neither could have achieved so much in the common cause. The ability of both Canada and the United States to defend the North American Continent, and to fight abroad, has been greatly increased by our arrangements for joint defence, and by the pooling of resources.

Under our system of mutual aid war materials have for the past year been supplied without payment to the United Nations, in accordance with strategic need. Canada is now supplying mutual aid to Britain, Australia, the Soviet Union, China and the French Committee of National Liberation.

As the war has progressed our effort has become more and more a worldwide effort. Canadian-made machines and munitions of war have been used on all the fighting fronts. Canadian sailors and merchant seamen have served on all oceans. Our airmen have fought in the battle of the skies around the globe. From the early days of the war our soldiers have helped to guard this island. They have seen active service in the Pacific area, as well as at Dieppe and in the Italian campaign.

Today our army awaits the word of command to join with their comrades in the liberation of Europe. The morrow will witness Canadian forces taking part in a final assault upon Japan. Canada's effort has truly become a worldwide effort.

I have spoken of the war effort of Canada. May I hasten to say again that a like spirit has animated the war efforts of each of the other nations of the Commonwealth? With due allowances for varying conditions, the several aspects of Canada's war effort have been paralleled in Australia, New Zealand and South Africa.

The war efforts of the nations of the Commonwealth owe their inspiration to a common source. That source is the love of freedom and the sense of justice, which, through generations, have been nurtured and cherished in Britain as nowhere else in the world.

The terrible events of 1940 revealed how great was the menace to freedom, and how suddenly freedom might be lost. So long as freedom endures, free men everywhere will owe to the people of Britain a debt they can never repay. So long as Britain continues to maintain the spirit of freedom and to defend the freedom of other nations, she need never doubt her own pre-eminence through-out the world. So long as we all share that spirit we need never fear for the strength or unity of the Commonwealth. The voluntary decisions by Britain, by Canada, by Australia, by New Zealand, and by South Africa, are a supreme evidence of the unifying force of freedom.

We are approaching in the European theatre the supreme crisis of this long and terrible struggle.

Our first duty is to win the war. But to win the war we must keep the vision of a better future. We must never cease to strive for its fulfilment. No lesser vision will suffice to gain the victory over those who seek world domination and human enslavement. No lesser vision will enable us fittingly to honour the memory of the men and women who are giving their all for freedom and justice. In the realisation of this vision, the Governments and peoples who owe a common allegiance to the Crown may well find the new meaning and significance of the British Commonwealth and Empire. It is for us to make of our association of free British nations "a model of what we hope the whole world will some day become."

· · · · ·

All the time, every day, year after year under the German occupation in Europe thousands of people were dying in German concentration camps. Millions of Jews were being deported and systematically exterminated in Poland, killed in gas chambers and cremated in furnaces. Those are the darkest pages in the history of mankind.

Here is the story of a French prisoner who escaped from the Alexander Platz prison in Berlin. It may stand as something symbolic of these years when

nearly all Europe had been turned into a Nazi prison—until the thunder of
liberation should be heard.

IN GERMAN PRISON

Told by a French prisoner and reported by Norman Macdonald
in Home Service, March 13 1945

The Alexander Platz prison is normally used by Nazis to lodge political
prisoners awaiting trial, but for the majority of its inmates it has become an
eternal prison, because the Nazis have not put their prisoners on trial, if trial
it could be called. Most of us were kept in solitary confinement in dark, damp
cells, although some prisoners were packed as many as fifteen or twenty in one
small cell, packed so tightly that they had to take turns to lie down.

I never once had a light in my cell, which, like the whole prison, was filled
with vermin which swarmed everywhere. The food was so bad that I lost
forty pounds during the first three months in my cell, and many among by
fellow-prisoners died daily, owing to the complete lack of medical attention.
We weren't allowed to do any work; all we could do was to just sit and stare
into the darkness or at the bleak walls of our cells, when we could see them.
Sometimes the Gestapo would give us permission to read, having first made
certain that it was impossible for us to do so.

During my time in the Alexander Platz prison we had three different kinds of
guards. At first we had professional prison warders, who thought their treatment
of us was mild, although we thought it quite bad enough. They eventually
disappeared during one of the man-power drives for the Army and for war
industries, and their places were taken by men who had had special training in
how to deal with political prisoners. After a time these men disappeared too,
most of them being sent to the occupied countries. Their successors were even
worse, if that were possible. They were so utterly brutal that they didn't seem
human, and that wasn't surprising because the more brutal each of these men
was, the better qualified he was thought to be for his job.

These guards kicked us and beat us with cudgels whenever the mood took
them; it was terrible. I am sure no kind of cruelty can exist that I didn't see
practised in the Alexander Platz prison by these men. I myself luckily escaped
most of their more refined tortures or I would not be alive today, but even so, I've
been tortured and beaten and kicked again and again until I thought I would die.

I don't even want to describe some of the tortures these brutes inflicted on
many of my fellow prisoners, especially those accused of sabotage in factories
or of plotting against the Nazis. I just could not recognise them after they had
been questioned by the Gestapo; they would lie on the floor semi-conscious,
moaning for somebody to kill them, and so end their misery. More than once,

these luckless men succeeded in killing themselves, rather than face more Gestapo torture to make them reveal the names of their accomplices.

There were women guards, too, in the Alexander Platz prison. If possible they were even more sadistic than the men. Some of the punishments they inflicted on women prisoners, many of them Germans, are unprintable. I have seen small girls grow old and haggard overnight. I've seen these women guards kick their helpless charges into insensibility, and then laugh about it.

When the Allies made air attacks on Berlin our prison guards—men as well as women—completely lost control of themselves and ran about hysterically firing revolvers at random. In such circumstances, many prisoners naturally tried to escape, but they never did. I saw a 13 year-old Polish girl cruelly beaten because she'd succeeded in getting out of her cell during an air raid. She'd not only attempted to escape, but she had stolen some blankets from the Guard Room— a double offence, for which she was beaten into insensibility. Fortunately for her she died quickly, for she'd broken her back when she fell from a window while trying to escape. She'd been brought to Berlin from Warsaw, and sentenced to imprisonment for the duration of the war just because she'd offered cigarettes to Polish soldiers taken prisoner by the Germans.

But it was the Russians in the prison who suffered the most brutal reprisals if they tried to escape. For them the guards had what the Gestapo considered to be quite a simple punishment. They just took away all their clothes and pushed them, stark naked, into unheated, damp cells, handcuffed together. They were left until they went mad and died, or just died. Those who became most violently mad were taken out and shot. Once, during an Allied air raid in which some bombs hit the prison itself, I remember how eight Russian prisoners managed to get out of their cells and reach the top floor of the building. There, they had a terrific battle with the guards, fighting like the mad animals that life in that prison had made them. It's not difficult to guess what happened to those Russians when they'd been overpowered. After suffering every brutality known to the guards, they all became insane, and screamingly implored the guards to shoot them. But the Gestapo shot only one; the remaining seven they continued to torture, stopping every so often to allow them to recover; then, they'd start again, and that went on until the seven died too.

. . . . .

PLANES GOING OUT FROM BRITAIN

Pat Smithers, Home Service, May 5 1944

If you live in Sussex or Kent nowadays (or I suppose in a good many other counties besides), you know before getting out of bed and pulling aside the black-out if it's a nice day. A clear dawn has a new clarion—the deep and throbbing roar of hundreds of planes, outward bound. They may be sailing high towards the coast, flashing or shining in the light of the sun that's not yet up over the horizon. Sometimes they look white and as graceful as gulls against the blue; at others they look black and sinister as they come and go between the clouds. But the impressive thing—the thing that makes land-girls pause in their stringing of the hopfields and makes conductors of country buses lean out and look up from their platforms—the impressive thing is the numbers. Never in the Battle of Britain, in the days when the Luftwaffe was beaten over these fields and woods, did the Germans send over such vast fleets. Never were their bombers four-engined monsters, such as these of the Americans which go out in their scores and hundreds. Sometimes you will see one big formation coming, say from the north, others from the north-east, others from the west, all heading for a common rendezvous. Their courses often converge, and a stranger to the scene might hold his breath seeing the approach of disaster as the formations close in. At the moment when it looks as if they must collide, he sees with relief, that they're at different heights; and they make a brief, fascinating cross-over pattern and sail on as easily as an express train flies over complicated points. As their roar fades with them, another rises until things on the kitchen mantelshelf tinkle and rattle as they catch the vibration. Up over the beechwoods on the hill, the leading formation of a second wave of heavies appears, followed by others and still others. Some days it will go on like this pretty well all day—not all heavies, of course, but twin-engined bombers of various kinds, fighterbombers and fighters. There are always lots of Marauders, packed together, flying very fast-reminding one of those sudden clouds of migrating birds which appear from nowhere and as quickly vanish. They have an appointment abroad, and they're keeping it.

Quite often I have noticed that some time after the heavies have gone out, fighters will follow them, flashing across the sky, seeming to leave their noise behind them. I always imagine that they're the escort, whose pilots might still have been having breakfast long after the heavies took off, knowing that with their much greater speed, they'd be there at the rendezvous in plenty of time.

On some of the really big days, you'll see the first of the raiders coming home, still in formation, as others are going out, and it will be more or less like that till well after sundown.

I remember how thrilled people were—and how they even stood in the streets and fields and cheered—as German planes were shot out of the sky over this part of England in the Battle of Britain.

Now, all this time later, you find people looking up and counting the homecoming Allied bombers. I went into our little village shop the other morning just as one big formation was coming back. The old lady behind the counter said, "I wonder if they're all there?" and made her way out of the shop to shade her eyes, look up and count. "Twelve there," she said, "twelve there, twelve there, and twelve there. Oh dear, only eleven here. Another twelve, another twelve. That's one missing. I do hope he's all right." We went back into the shop and chatted for a few minutes about what it must be like on the other side. The roar of the heavies had died away. But there was one single plane somewhere around. We strolled across to the door again and looked up. "Oh good," said the old lady, "it's the missing one." She was probably right, too. It was a Fortress with a hole in its tail and one engine stopped, flying much lower than usual, but getting home just the same.

. . . . .

The first of the three offensives of the summer came from the South. After slow and laborious progress in Italy, the big Allied offensive opened on 12 May, and Rome, the first European capital to be liberated by the Allies, was entered on 4 June 1944.

THE LIBERATION OF ROME

Professor Betts, European Service, June 4 1944

The hearts of civilised men everywhere will be strangely moved by the news that the army of liberation is in Rome, and that the army of destruction has fled. It is not only that the capital city of one of the two great powers which made war on Europe has been won by a brilliant feat of arms. This is also one of the great moments in the history of civilisation. The liberation of Rome from Fascist and Nazi barbarism means that the catastrophe which threatened to destroy the achievement of two thousand years has been decisively averted.

Rome and civilisation have been synonymous ever since Western Europe emerged from barbarism. It was Rome which first gave order to the West; it was Rome which first reconciled liberty with order by establishing the rule of law, that same law which still provides the basis of society from Amsterdam to Capetown. It was Rome which took over from Greece the art of politics, the art of living together in society. The Greeks had taught men how to live in a city; the Romans taught them how to live in an orderly society that embraced in a single whole all the nations between the Atlantic and the Euphrates. From the Greeks, too, Rome took the torch of learning and literature. and handed it on to the nations of the West.

Even when the Teutonic barbarians destroyed the Roman Empire, Rome itself was not effaced. Christian Rome took upon itself the burden of civilisation; the missionaries it sent out to Britain and Germany, to Poland and Hungary, taught the old Roman gospel of order and unity and law to the barbarians. Pope Leo

The liberation of Rome.

III, Bishop of Rome, restored the warring tribes of Western Europe to unity by crowning Charlemagne in the basilica of St. Peter's.

In the struggle for 'civilitas' Rome has ever had to fight and suffer. Since the Visigoths of Alaric sacked the city at the beginning of the fifth century until the day, fifteen hundred years later, when its Fascist tyrant handed it over to the latter-day vandals of the Third Reich, Rome has been many times besieged, assaulted and sacked; by the Saracens in the ninth century, and the Normans in the eleventh; it suffered fearfully from the mercenary German army of Charles the Fifth in 1527. But never was it so basely surrendered to so barbarous a foe as when Mussolini last year opened its gates to the Wehrmacht and S.S.

The whole free world is indebted to Rome: the whole free world is participating in its liberation. First, and fittingly, the people of Italy and Rome have played an invaluable part, by resistance, by sabotage, by armed revolt. The children of Rome—Frenchmen, Poles and Britons—have had the privilege, on the grim battlefields from Salerno to Valmontone, of repaying part of the debt that Europe owes to Rome. From the ends of the earth New Zealanders and Americans have came to fight under the walls of Rome for that civilisation to which they, too, are heirs.

The birthplace of Europe's civilisation has been delivered; that is the inspiration with which the forces of Freedom will go forward to complete their task by destroying barbarism in its inner fortress.

CHAPTER VIII

Invasion

June—October, 1944

At 9.30 on 6 June, the following communiqué was issued from the Supreme Headquarters of the Allied Expeditionary Force:

"Under the command of General Eisenhower, Allied naval forces, supported by strong air forces, began landing armies this morning on the Northern coast of France."

In a broadcast to Europe, following the communiqué, General Eisenhower said:

"People of Western Europe: A landing was made this morning on the coast of France by troops of the Allied Expeditionary Force. This landing is part of the concerted United Nations plan for the liberation of Europe, made in conjunction with our great Russian Allies.

"I have this message for all of you: Although the initial assault may not have been made in your own country, the hour of your liberation is approaching. All patriots—men and women, young and old—have a part to play in the achievement of final victory.

"To members of resistance movements, whether led by nationals or by outside leaders, I say: Follow the instructions you have received. To patriots who are not members of organised resistance groups I say: Continue your passive resistance. Do not needlessly endanger your lives. Wait until I give you the signal to rise and strike the enemy. The day will come when I shall need your united strength. Until that day I call on you for the hard task of discipline and restraint"

The following Order of the Day had been issued by General Eisenhower to each individual of the Allied Expeditionary Force:

"Soldiers, sailors, and airmen of the Allied Expeditionary Force. You are about to embark upon the great crusade toward which we have striven these many

Operation Neptune — the landing phase of Operation Overlord, 6 June 1944.

months. The eyes of the world are upon you. The hopes and prayers of liberty—loving people everywhere march with you.

"In company with our brave Allies and brothers-in-arms on other fronts, you will bring about the destruction of the German war machine, the elimination of Nazi tyranny over the oppressed peoples of Europe, and security for ourselves in a free world.

"Your task will not be an easy one. Your enemy is well trained, well equipped, and battle-hardened. He will fight savagely.

"But this is the year 1944. Much has happened since the Nazi triumphs of 1940-41. The United Nations have inflicted upon the Germans great defeats in open battle man to man. Our air offensive has seriously reduced their strength in the air and their capacity to wage war on the ground. Our home fronts have given us an overwhelming superiority in weapons and munitions of war and placed at our disposal great reserves of trained fighting men. The tide has turned. The free men of the world are marching together to victory.

"I have full confidence in your courage, devotion to duty, and skill in battle. We will accept nothing less than full victory.

"Good luck! And let us all beseech the blessings of Almighty God upon this great and noble undertaking."

This order was distributed to assault elements after their embarkation. It was read by commanders to all other troops in the Allied Expeditionary Force.

. . . . .

In the afternoon General De Gaulle spoke to the French people.

GENERAL DE GAULLE TO FRANCE

European Service, June 6 1944

The greatest of all battles has been joined. After so much fighting, violence and grief, the decisive blow, so eagerly awaited, has been struck.

This is the battle of France, yes, but it is also France's battle. Immense attacking forces—which means for us immense liberating forces—have begun to flow from the shores of old England. This final bastion of Western Europe which not long since halted the tide of German oppression is today the forward base for the offensive of freedom.

France, four years submerged, but never subjugated, never vanquished, France is on her feet today ready to play her part. The simple sacred duty of the sons of France—whoever and wherever they may be—is to fight with all the means in their power. The enemy is to be destroyed; the enemy who bruises and soils our country, the hated and dishonoured enemy. He will do all he can to escape his fate, he will fight desperately to retain his hold on our soil as long as possible. But for some time now he has been only a beast in flight. From Stalingrad to Tarnopol, from the banks of the Nile to Bizerta, from Tunis to Rome, he has made a habit of defeat.

France will wage this battle with fury and in good order. We have won our victories in this way for 1,500 years and thus shall we win again—in good order. For the Army, the Navy and the Air Force this presents no problem. Never were they more eager, more skilled, better disciplined. Africa, Italy, the ocean and the sky have seen their strength and glory reborn. Tomorrow their native land will see them. For the nation which fights, bound and gagged, against the oppressor armed to the teeth, good order in battle is dependent upon the fulfilment of several conditions: the first is that the instructions given by the French Government and by the French leaders whom the Government has authorised to give orders locally, must be strictly obeyed. The second is that the struggle carried on by you behind the enemy lines must be co-ordinated as closely as possible with the battles fought by the Allied and French Armies. Further, everyone must realise that the Armies have a long and hard task before them. This means that the effort of the Resistance Forces must be sustained and gradually increased until the Germans are routed.

The third condition is that anyone who is capable of action, under arms, by sabotage, by intelligence work, by refusing to do work useful to the enemy, must avoid at all costs being taken prisoner. Get away beforehand whatever the difficulties, escape the menace of prison bars or deportation—anything is better than to be put out of action before battle.

The Battle of France has begun. In the nation, in the empire and in the armed forces there is now but one purpose, one desire.

Look upward. There, where the burden of our blood and tears lay like a lowering cloud upon us—there the light of our greatness is shining through.

. . . . .

Chester Wilmot, who was with the soldiers before the big operation began, gave the following description of the Invasion eve; and Guy Byam—later killed in action—described how the Allied paratroops first went into battle.

INVASION EVE

Home Service, June 6 1944

Somewhere in Britain on the eve of Invasion. This is from one of the many airfields from which the first wave of invasion is being launched tonight. Within a very short time the airborne forces —the spearhead of the Allied assault—will be heading for France. They'll land by parachute and glider behind the German coastal defences and they'll carry the battle well into enemy territory before the seaborne attack comes in. If all goes well, the airborne forces will make considerably easier the task of those who'll attack from the sea some hours after we land.

More than a week ago the airborne troops were moved from training camps to marshalling areas near the 'dromes from which they'll fly. When they left camp they were nominally on an exercise, but when they reached here they knew it was the real thing. They were issued with live ammunition, boxes of concentrated battle rations, paint for camouflage webbing and equipment; they got field dressings and phials of morphia, and then to leave no doubt—they drew French money and a booklet about France, which began with these words: "A new B.E.F., which includes you, is going to France. You are to assist personally in pushing the Germans out of France and back where they belong."

This was the occasion that these troops have been training and planning for ever since Dunkirk—just four years ago last week. Now—fit, eager, determined, there'd be no holding them. This was quite evident when their general spoke to his men in this camp last week. He gave them the broad outline of his plan and their task, told them how much depended on their success. He didn't belittle their task—in fact he ended by saying this: "I don't think the Hun'll expect us to land where we're going to land. He's obstructed the whole area so thoroughly that no doubt he thinks no one but a bloody fool would try to go there; but I'm going." The general stepped down from his rostrum; a thousand soldiers rose as a man, whipped off their red berets and cheered.

I saw the same eagerness when the troops were fitting their parachutes and making up their battle kit-bags yesterday. They had crammed so much ammunition into their pouches and pockets, so many weapons into their webbing, that they could barely struggle into their parachute harnesses. But they'll be ready to go into action the moment they hit the ground. Grenades were festooned around them, hanging from any spare inch of webbing. No man was carrying less than 85 lbs.—some had more than a hundred. And yet they had trained themselves to move and fight with loads like these. I talked to one section of men that had marched in training—ten miles in two and a half hours—fully laden. With endurance like that, these walking human arsenals will lead the attack tonight. But they won't have to rely wholly on the arms and ammunition they bring down. Heavier arms, medical supplies, explosives for making demolitions and other stores will come down in containers on parachutes or else in gliders. I've watched them packing the gliders these last few days. They're crammed to capacity and they carry an amazing tonnage. Jeeps and guns specially designed to fit in gliders will be towed out in the same way.

The troops haven't had many spare moments since they came to the marshalling areas. Four or five hours a day they have been poring over maps, aerial photographs, models of the ground on which they'll land. They've been most fully briefed in the whole operation until they know the exact plan for the force and their part in it.

On the beach.

The last few days of waiting have been long-drawn out. As the sky clouded over and a gusty wind whipped across the airfield during the weekend, the troops' faces lengthened. The day they thought was the day came and went, and this morning dawned blustery as before. But about noon the word came through, and long faces broke into broad smiles.

Now the troops, aircrews, glider pilots have had their final briefing. After these many months of training it's difficult for them to believe that this at last is the day. This morning I heard one paratroop say to another: "Think of it— tonight we'll really be in France—fighting."

. . . . .

Here is a report from a quayside in Britain from which troops were embarking for the invasion.

EMBARKING FOR THE INVASION

Colin Wills, Home Service, June 6 1944

Across the quayside moves a stream of men. These particular troops embarking here are British. Ahead of them lies Europe. Behind them lies Britain. Many of them glance back as they march, for a last glimpse of their own country. Some of them shout farewells, some of them sing. Some are silent. Some of them laugh, some smile, some look thoughtful, some look grim.

One thing is common to all of them—an unmistakable air of purpose and resolve. They count it a high honour to be chosen for this job. They will do that job well. They look superbly fit, high-spirited and dedicated to their task.

I talked with them as they waited their turn to embark. Two things were in all their minds—the job that lay ahead, and the homes they left behind.

You will now hear some of them calling out, whatever they like to call out:—

"Hallo Betty, darling—how're you getting on? Back soon when it's all over— don't get worried, George."

"Cheerio, mother—keep smiling. Up John Smith." "Hello, some public house. Save us a pint!" "We're off on a little trip. Love to you all—Frank."

"Hallo, Mum and Dad. This is Derek speaking. All the best. We're going to give Jerry all he gave us at Dunkirk, and, boy, we're going to give it to him strong."

. . . . .

WITH ALLIED PARATROOPS TO FRANCE

Guy Byam, Home Service, June 7 1944

Just after midnight I jumped into action with Allied paratroops. It started on an airfield where the paratroops knelt round their padre in prayer before emplaning. With bent heads and on one knee the men with their equipment and camouflaged faces look like some strange creatures from another world.

And darkness comes over the airfield and the men sling their explosives and weapons round them, get their parachutes and emplane.

In the plane we stand back to breast. I am jumping last but one of my stick. And as we stand in the plane—for there is no room to sit down—we feel the tremendous vibration of the four motors as we start down the runway. And all around in the coming darkness are the great planes and row upon row of gliders.

Then the plane is airborne and in the crowded fuselage all you see in the pale light of an orange bulb is the man next to you.

And you fly out over the Channel and the minutes go by and the stock commander says that the pilot has told him we are over a great armada of naval ships. And then it is something else he says—something that gives you a dry feeling in your mouth—flak—and the word is passed from man to man. The machine starts to rock and jump with it. Ahead of us—a comforting thought—Lancasters are going for the flak, and a coastal battery is one of the objectives.

We're over the coast now and the run in has started—one minute—30 seconds. Red light—green and out—get on out—out—out fast into the cool night air out over France—and we know that the dropping zone is obstructed. We're jumping into fields covered with poles. And I hit my parachute and lower my harness. And then the ground comes up to hit me. And I find myself in the middle of a cornfield. I look around and even with compass I can't be sure where I am—and overhead hundreds of parachutes and containers are coming down.

The whole sky is a fantastic chimera of lights and flak and one plane gets hit and disintegrates wholesale in the sky, sprinkling a myriad of burning pieces all over the sky.

The job of the unit with which I jumped was to occupy the area and prepare the way for gliders—we were to rendezvous near a copse, but I could not find it. It's a tricky business this moving about the countryside at night. But we are well in hand and at the most I shall only meet my own patrols. I find the unit after having been sniped at once and challenged a number of times. They are assembling under a hedge. And things are happening all around and it's difficult to guess what exactly is happening. The sky is crossed and recrossed by tracer, and the distinctive splutter of a light machine-gun is quite near us.

Like a tentacle into the air was the radio set aerial, and the major was signalling, and the radio messages cross the fields—Allied soldiers talking to each other through the night.

Things are going well for our troops; at this early hour they have deployed and infested the whole area around the dropping zone. A tremendous bombardment has started now on the coast defences from the sky, and hundreds of Lancasters are raining their blockbusters down on the coast. It's an awe-inspiring sight, for in another few hours or so the navy will bring the men to the beaches.

Meanwhile on the dropping zone, shock paratroop engineers are finishing blowing the poles that obstruct the dropping zone, and soon the gliders come in scores, coming out of the sky like a sign.

And the night wears on, and soon it is light and to the northwest the cannonade begins on the beaches. While our paratroop unit fights a terrific battle over the bridges, actually repelling an attack by a panzer formation—paratroops able to deal with the panzers. I think that one surprised the German High Command. These airborne units fight magnificently with terrific morale and vigour.

The people are pleased to see us. We apologise for the bringing of war to their homes. But in little ways they show they are glad to see us, A dead paratroop is laid out on a bed in the best bedroom covered from head to foot with local flowers.

· · · · ·

Over 4,000 ships were employed, together with several thousand smaller craft, and the forces were backed by 11,000 aircraft. A war correspondent, Gordon Hodman, on board HMS *Hilary*, gave a description of the ships on the way to the Continent.

OFF THE INVASION BEACHES

Home Service, June 6 1944

We have gone in. British, Canadian and American troops are now scrambling over the rubble of the West Wall and pouring into Hitler's European fortress.

The breach has been made by sea, air and land attack.

Before dawn broke on this historic June morning I watched the first battering of the wall in the sectors chosen for the assault. It came from the air and had been going on for most of the night.

As we headed steadily towards the French coast through a night more reminiscent of December than June, we strained our eyes towards the land. Presently we were sure that our eyes were not playing tricks—there were dull flashes breaking the darkness in the far distance.

Our objectives lie in the broad bay of the Seine, from Le Havre to the Cherbourg Peninsula.

Many hours ago—during yesterday, Monday, the first vessels of the great Armada of ships in this invasion fleet were on their way. I watched a long snake of flat-bottomed craft wind their way between a mass of shipping, which, during the day, gradually dissolved until only comparatively few big ships remained.

Before we left our anchorage many hundreds of ships were well on their way to France.

Sea conditions were far from ideal, but the Navy was confident. Admiral Ramsay, Supreme Naval Commander of the Invasion Fleets, paid a flying visit to this ship and there could be no doubting his confident outlook. As he went down the gangway to board a motor torpedo-boat, he said, with a broad smile, "Good luck—good luck to you all."

Then, with the wind whistling in no uncertain manner through the rigging, we were on our way.

The Navy's task was to take a great striking force many, many miles to the enemy coast and land it according to the most complicated schedule on precise beaches.

In addition, with the large-scale co-operation of the United States Navy and the naval forces of a number of our allies, it had to put in a smashing attack on the Nazi defences.

British, American and Canadian soldiers are fighting side by side on the beaches, and it is imperative that objectives well inland should be in their hands before this unforgettable day-long awaited D-Day—is over.

Royal Naval beach commandos near Courseilles directing traffic by loud hailer.

There is one word that can be applied to our passage—uneventful. Apart from a measure of anxiety caused by the heavy weather conditions, we suffered in no way. There was neither attack from the air nor from the sea.

The conveying of this huge and novel force proved a great triumph for the sea forces. Proceeding at various speeds and to different destinations, the ships passed through a fantastic Clapham junction in mid-Channel. Forces crossed and re-crossed each other and then went straight in as if they were following railway lines.

Only many months of planning and calculating made this possible.

It was thought that for practically half of our journey there was danger from the wide enemy mine belts. But the little minesweepers had gone before, marking the channels for us to follow.

As daylight came, the dull glow of fires started by the night bombers faded from the sky, and only the flash of guns and the shooting of tracers could be seen.

Ships appeared to port and starboard in uncountable numbers. The French coast came up clearly on the horizon although visibility was not particularly good.

And then, as the little ships, the infantry landing craft, the tank-landing craft, the flat-bottomed vessels taking in the Sappers whose task was to clear the German beach obstacles before the fighting troops arrived, and many other vessels prepared to make the assault, the Navy showed its hand.

For more than an hour the bombardment forces, which included battleships, monitors, cruisers and many destroyers, subjected the enemy coastal positions to a massive attack.

From this ship one looked at an almost complete circle of fire. Starting slowly, almost lazily, it seemed, the naval guns rumbled into a continuous roar which sang in the ears while the great flashes of flame dazzled the eyes. Although the ships were very close inshore and their shells were falling even further away, the blast came back across the sea in an unbroken wave.

Away towards Havre huge flashes indicated where one or more of the capital ships, hidden in the mist and protected perhaps, by a smoke screen, smashed fifteen or sixteen inch salvoes into the heavy German batteries on shore.

In the other direction, where the land runs up towards Cherbourg, constant spurts of flame indicated the impressive support being given by naval forces to the American landing forces.

Six hundred guns, firing as fast as their expert crews could load them, were pulverising the German positions on shore. Two thousand tons of high explosive were dropping on the beaches and pillboxes every ten minutes.

Overhead the night bombers had gone back only to be replaced by a mighty fleet of medium bombers. The soldiers going in to the assault, looked up and cheered as the planes went over, blackening the sky.

Spitfires winged their way backwards and forwards over the mass of shipping and, out of sight, in the higher heavens Thunderbolts droned in constant watchfulness.

But up to two hours after the Invasion army had set foot in Europe not one enemy aircraft had been sighted.

The day bombers, Fortresses and Liberators, came in with a deep roar of engines, although they were flying too high to be seen. They added something in the region of 3,000 tons of bombs to the carnage on the beaches. Assault craft stretched from the shore right out of sight when the Canadians went in to attack the sector immediately in front of us. Fortress tanks waddled on to the beaches and sat there firing solidly at anything that remained after the greatest bombardment ever carried out on shore positions.

Obstacles more than a hundred yards deep had to be dealt with by the sappers and special naval units.

Now the infantry are ashore in strength. The tanks are rumbling in. In many places German opposition in the forward areas has been completely wiped out. The paratroops have achieved spectacular success, not only gaining the high ground they were sent in to capture but striking with such speed that vital bridges are now in their hands intact.

There may be critical moments ahead but we have made a magnificent start and nobody is looking back.

. . . . .

Breakwater of the concrete caissons of the Mulberry Harbour.

The impressions of German soldiers entrenched on the Normandy coast and taken prisoner on the first day of fighting, were later described by themselves in the German programme of the BBC.

A GERMAN PRIVATE SPEAKS

European Service, June 17 1944

On that night of the sixth of June none of us expected the invasion any more. There was a strong wind, thick cloud cover, and the enemy aircraft had not bothered us more that day than usual. But then—in the night—the air was full of innumerable 'planes. We thought: "What are they demolishing tonight?" But then it started. I was at the wireless set myself. One message followed the other. "Parachutists landed here—gliders reported there" and finally "Landing craft approaching." Some of our guns fired as best they could. In the morning a huge naval force was sighted—that was the last report our advanced observation posts could send us, before they were overwhelmed. And it was the last report we received about the situation. It was no longer possible to get an idea of what was happening. Wireless communications were jammed, the cables cut and our officers had lost grasp of the situation. Infantrymen who were streaming back told us that their positions on the coast had been overrun or that the few 'bunkers' in our sector had either been shot up or blown to pieces.

Right in the middle of all this turmoil I got orders to go with my car for a reconnaissance towards the coast. With a few infantrymen I reported to a Lieutenant. His orders were to re-take a village nearby. While he was still talking to me to explain the position, a British tank came rolling towards us from behind, from a direction in which we had not even suspected the presence of the enemy. The enemy tank immediately opened fire on us. Resistance was out of the question. I saw how a group of Polish infantrymen went over to the enemy—carrying their machineguns and waving their arms. The officer and myself hid in the brush. When we tried to get through to our lines in the evening British paratroops caught us.

At first I was rather depressed, of course. I, an old soldier, a prisoner of war after a few hours of invasion. But when I saw the material behind the enemy front, I could only say: "Old man, how lucky you have been!"

And when the sun rose the next morning, I saw the invasion fleet lying off the shore. Ship beside ship. And without a break, troops, weapons, tanks, munitions and vehicles were being unloaded in a steady stream.

A GERMAN CORPORAL SPEAKS

I was at Quineville when the invasion started. The number of ships, aircraft, and tanks thrown in against us defies any description. The guns of the Allied warships pulverised one position after another. Planes overhead reported on the accuracy of the guns, quite undisturbed and with uncanny precision. Every moment we expected our own fighters to appear. The whole sky was darkened by planes, but they were Marauders, Typhoons, Liberators, Flying Fortresses and Mustangs, attacking our posts, our machine-gun nests and artillery positions with their bombs and guns. As far I could see, there was no anti-aircraft, fire with the exception of a few two-centimetre rifles. Defenceless we lay there pressed to the ground in our positions. It was here in the West that the fate of Europe was going to be decided. Had they not always explained the absence of the Luftwaffe to us by saying that the machines had to be kept in reserve for the decisive moment; then they would inflict a fatal blow on the enemy. Even at this moment reports came through from our Divisional Headquarters that a thousand planes were going straight into action: "Stuka squadrons are approaching. The fighters may be expected at any moment." So they said. With what burning expectation we imagined the moment when our machines would arrive. But hour after hour passed by while we scanned the sky.

No help came. We felt completely abandoned.

. . . . .

On 14 July Marshal Stalin made the following statement on the Allied invasion of Normandy:

"One cannot but acknowledge that the history of wars knows no other undertaking similar as regards breadth of design, vastness of scale and high skill of execution.

"As is known, the 'invincible' Napoleon, in his time, failed in his plan of forcing the Channel and capturing the British Isles. The hysterical Hitler, who for two years boasted that he would effect the forcing of the Channel, did not even venture to make an attempt to carry out his threat.

"Only the British and American troops succeeded in carrying out with credit the vast plan of forcing the Channel and effecting the mass landing of troops. History will record this deed as an achievement of the highest order."

The liberating armies, after consolidating their bridgeheads, advanced inland, and the cathedral town of Bayeux was captured intact.

THE LIBERATED POPULATION

Home Service, June, 1944

One of the correspondents, Leonard Mosley, tells of his impressions on the way back from the front line:

As I drove back I could see seaborne invaders putting in an attack on our flank. It was quite a distance away, but through glasses you could see the infantry advancing up the slope under cover of a smoke-screen and hear the rattle of small-arms fire.

Most of the villages on the way were damaged by shells or bombs, but the inhabitants seemed to be carrying on as usual. They showed their appreciation in substantial ways, and any Tommy who looked thirsty was called over and handed a tumbler of good dry Normandy cider. Almost every child you talked with was gleefully sucking sweets, and they were probably the first sweets they had seen in years.

When I stopped to talk with little groups of people, they looked me over, and when their eyes lit on my thick, strong, brown boots, they exclaimed: *"C'est magnifique ça."* They said it as if they had never seen good leather before. They took me into their house and pressed me to cider and calvados and cognac, and it was very hard to refuse and impossible to pay once you had accepted. "But I insist," said one French woman. "You are the soldiers of liberation."

A French officer, who for the past four years had addressed the French people by radio from London, first as the official spokesman of Fighting France and later of the French National Committee, entered Bayeux on the first day of Allied landings and afterwards told French listeners of his visit.

"I did not expect this triumphal march. This sea of flags, these Crosses of Lorraine appearing everywhere! This fire of enthusiasm which a few kilometres from the front line has already consumed the very memory of four years' martyrdom.

"It was in the midst of the battlefield that on June 6, the first day of the great crusade, I fell into the arms of the first Frenchman, who had been attracted from a distance by the shape of my helmet. He led me to my first village. And since then, without interruption, I have been carried aloft, upraised, submerged. The Normans are said to be calm folk. What in heaven would it be like if they were excitable?

"I am writing from beneath the shadow of Bayeux Cathedral, where for three years the organiser of local resistance has directed his sector of the French front. Around me there are his fifteen chief lieutenants, who but a moment ago, did not know each other. I should have liked you to see a canon of the Cathedral and an old hardened anti-clerical, bitter opponents for thirty years, falling into each other's arms, now they know that for months past they have both been part of the same secret army; two schoolteachers, decorating their comrades with tricolour armlets, bearing the Cross of Lorraine, which they had made up secretly two years ago. Two young men asked me calmly when de Gaulle is coming to clothe them in uniform, and how long it will take to learn to use the new arms. Outside, an immense crowd, the whole town, swarms by, acclaiming the liberators, hanging flags at every window.

"That is Bayeux today, and it is you tomorrow, all of you!"

. . . . .

Twelve days after landing, the Allies had reached the Western coast of the Cherbourg peninsula. On 26 June they captured Cherbourg.

A vivid record of how the invasion appeared to the German High Command was given in a despatch from Matthew Halton.

THE GERMAN GENERALS AND THE INVASION

Home Service, September 22 1944

"I saw a captured transcript of the telephone conversations between the German Generals during the first month of the invasion of Europe.

"It is a fascinating record, first of confidence, and then doubt and fear, and finally despair. The first conversation is on the morning of June 6th, two hours after the Allied landings had begun. General Marx is speaking to the Chief of Staff. He says,

'I urgently request mobile reserves for the area west of Caen.' A few hours later the Chief of Staff of the Western Command is speaking to General Marx. He strongly emphasises the desire of the Supreme Command, of Hitler himself, to have the enemy in the bridgehead completely annihilated by the night of 6 June. 'This is imperative,' he says, 'because there is danger of additional sea and airborne landings in other areas; the beachhead must be cleaned up not later than tonight.' The reply comes 'I'm afraid that is impossible.' Repeatedly on that first day there are frantic demands for air support. On the morning of 7 June, Rommel is speaking, 'The counter-attack today,' he says, 'must succeed without fail.' This seems to have been the counter-attack against the British and Canadians by the First S.S. Panzer Corps. The Commander replies that he cannot attack, because his men are pinned down by Allied air attacks. Rommel interrupts harshly, and says, 'Attack at once, on the left, using all three divisions.'

"The next day Rommel is talking again. 'At all costs the enemy must be prevented from getting Cherbourg and from connecting his bridgeheads.'

Rommel himself was deeply anxious because, to use his own words, 'He expected larger landings in the Calais-Boulogne area in a few days.' He thought our landings in Normandy were perhaps no more than a feint. Powerful German reserves were held in the Calais area until it was too late. Time after time in these talks, day after day, till they become monotonous, there are demands for air support and demands for reserves. The commander in the field calls for reserves: the higher command saves the reserves in case of new landings, and so the battle is lost.

"Hitler enters the picture several times a week. He always says the same thing, there must be no retreat, every man must fight and fall where he stands rather than give an inch of ground.

"Day after day some German general complains that movement of troops are paralysed by Allied fighter bombers or Typhoons, and there are signs of rigidity in the German mentality. One general complains in the critical days near Vildieux, that there are many navy and air force troops in Brittany who are not being used. The reply comes, 'They are not under my jurisdiction.' As the Americans begin their breakthrough, the Commander-in-Chief in the west telephones to Supreme Headquarters. He describes the seriousness of the situation with impressive eloquence. He says morale is suffering heavily, that French Maquis in the rear are growing bolder every day, that his signals are knocked out, and that orderly command is difficult. But always Hitler replies, angry and stubborn, 'Every man must die where he stands'."

Hitler shortly after the failed assassination bomb attempt, 20 July 1944. From left to right: Wilhelm Keitel, Hermann Goering, Adolf Hitler and Martin Bormann.

. . . . .

A vital help for the liberation of France were the fearlessly and masterly executed operations of the Maquis.

THE MAP OF THE MAQUIS

Pierre Lefévre, Home Service, July 5 1944

I have just seen staff officers, British and French, poring over a map. A map of France. Of the whole of France. A map of the Maquis. On it are marked whole areas in grey or in black with the legend reading: "Area under patriot control," or else "Particularly heavy fighting." Arrows lead from certain towns, certain main railway lines, or from the grid power cables. In the margin of the, map, at the point of these arrows one can read: "All railways out of Paris cut on"—such a date, or else "All railways cut"—in another region—"majority of cuts being maintained," "trains of 30 tanks derailed."

A Panzer division now in the line in Normandy is shown on this map as having been delayed for a whole week between the town of X and the town of Y, by railway cuts. Elsewhere is a date with the simple words: "No trains Paris-Bordeaux or Paris-Toulouse." Further along: "Paris-Toulouse line cut each night by the Maquis." In the Alps a railway bridge is marked as demolished. "Line blocked indefinitely," one can read. One zone is marked: "Two German divisions engaged, 1,000 casualties both sides." Another place is marked: "Evacuated by Maquis forces after an attack by 10,000 Germans using artillery support and mortars. Patriot losses over 1,000" But elsewhere one reads: "2,400 Germans defeated, 300 prisoners taken," or 560 Germans killed in this region, own losses less than 300." And better still, just below the most hated place-name of the whole of France—Vichy—the laconic mention: "Geissler, Gestapo chief, executed by patriots, 23 June."

. . . . .

From the middle of June, part of the Royal Air Force had far a while to turn aside and fight a new battle of London. For eighty days the Germans aimed their flying bombs at London, and during those eighty days the fighter pilots of the RAF shot down 1,900. Squadron-Leader Berry brought down 60 before he died in action. This is the account he wrote.

CHASING THE FLYING BOMBS

Home Service

The "Doodle Bug" doesn't go down easily. It will take a lot of punishment, and you have to aim at the propulsion unit—that's the long stove-pipe, as we call it, on the tail. If your range and aim are dead on, you can see pieces flying off the stove-pipe. The big white flame at the end goes out, and down goes the bomb. Sometimes it dives straight to earth, but at other times it goes crazy and gives a wizard display of acrobatics before finally crashing.

Sometimes the bomb explodes in mid-air, and the flash is so blinding that you cannot see a thing for about ten seconds. You hope to be the right way up when you are able to see again, because the explosion often throws the fighter about and sometimes turns it upside down.

. . . . .

The flying bombs were followed by the V2's. For eight months British and American aircraft bombed the German launching sites.

All over Europe the invasion of the Allies inspired the occupied countries with a new hope and courage. A remarkable instance of the growing resistance against the hated Germans was the general strike in Copenhagen at the beginning of July.

THE GENERAL STRIKE IN COPENHAGEN

Sten Gudme, European Service, July 6 1944

After a crisis lasting a fortnight, and culminating in a five days' general strike, the citizens of Copenhagen have inflicted a decisive defeat on the German forces of occupation. There is no question of this being a carefully planned revolt, to be carried out when it would hit the Germans hardest. It all happened quite spontaneously. Started, probably, by irritation at the imposition of a curfew, it gathered force, and, suddenly, on the introduction of German counter-measures—and the Germans spared no effort—it finished as a real popular rising, as 22 Danish towns followed the lead of Copenhagen.

Twice during the crisis the Germans tried to quiet the storm which they themselves had provoked, by making partial concessions to the Danish demands, and each time their offers were rejected. Finally, on Monday, July 3, fearing that the whole country would join in the general strike, the Germans gave in and surrendered unconditionally. The despicable Schalburg corps of

Danish traitors, criminals and mentally deficients, the dregs of society which was used by the Germans to murder Kaj Munk and a number of other good Danes, was driven from the streets of Copenhagen by the Germans at the order of the inhabitants.

The last week of June, so important for the great European war, became thus a great and decisive victory also in the history of the occupation of Denmark. Ever since D-Day it has obviously been the aim of the Danish patriots to bring to a complete standstill those essential industries which were working for the German war machine. In Denmark this involves about 16 concerns, each employing anything from four or five hundred men up to several thousand. Even before D-Day eleven of them had either partly or completely been put out of action, but one of the biggest was working day and night for the Germans. This was Denmark's only big arms factory, situated in the free port area of Copenhagen, producing machine guns and automatic rifles for the Germans. On June 22, Danish partisans, arriving in four lorries, stormed this strongly-defended factory, and with four high explosive charges razed it to the ground. There won't be any more of that factory during this war.

This great blow was the culmination of the whole sabotage offensive against the Germans in the early summer. The reply of the enemy was swift and brutal. Among Danish patriots imprisoned and charged with entirely different offences, 16 were executed in one week; eight of them came from a small village in Jutland of barely a hundred inhabitants.

But the executions were not all. The Germans also introduced courts-martial, so that this cruel punishment might be promptly carried out. And then they made the move which was to lead to the great trial of strength; they introduced a curfew in Copenhagen. Nobody was allowed in the streets after eight p.m. In the light summer evenings the citizens of Copenhagen could not go to their allotments or walk about the streets.

The thousands of workers of the B. & W. factory were the first to react. On the very first day of the curfew they downed tools at one o'clock and sent a protest to the German Commissary in Denmark, Dr Best, in which they emphasised that at such a time, when the food situation was so difficult, they could not manage without working their allotments. On the following day the workers at nearly all the big factories in Copenhagen followed the example of those of B. & W. and went home at 1 p.m., and the employers of the big stores, the shops and the offices followed suit. Copenhagen had embarked on an "Early Closing Campaign"—a daily half-day strike.

In the evenings, too, the people went out into the streets after eight o'clock; and they did one thing which must have greatly irritated the Germans: they lit bonfires by hundreds. On one single night more than a thousand. The Germans had made yet one more psychological blunder. After the sabotage of the arms factory, they had forbidden the citizens to celebrate mid-summer eve with bonfires along the coast. In return, the Freedom Council arranged a giant bonfire on the square in front of the town hall, just outside the Gestapo Headquarters, where hundreds of rockets shot up into the sky. This fire, which was meant also as a gentle ironical imitation of Hitler's flying bombs, was repeated on a small scale evening after evening in the streets of Copenhagen.

The German patrol cars turned out, of course, in order to disperse the crowds and put out the fires, but the Copenhageners were now in a fighting mood. They built barricades of overturned trams and buses, and of material from the air-raid shelters which were being constructed throughout Copenhagen. Some of these barricades even reached up to the second floors of buildings. The Germans then sent low-flying aeroplanes over the streets, firing at the crowds with machine guns, and on certain open places they put light artillery in position. The casualty lists, not yet complete, show that 87 Copenhageners were killed and 650 wounded during this week of conflict.

Dr Best had reckoned that approximately 200,000 work hours were lost during the first three days of the disturbances; and then made his first concession, which was to cancel three hours of the curfew; but what do a few hours curfew more or less matter when the very feeling of justice has been violated, by the turning loose of the Schalburg corps against the people of Copenhagen? The strike was not called off. On the other hand, between 300,000 and 400,000 of the citizens of Copenhagen declared a general strike on the following day, Friday, June 30. Factories, Government offices, shops—all were closed. This general strike began quite spontaneously, without consultation with the Trade Union leaders, without the sanction of the Freedom Council, although naturally these quickly concurred and supported the powerful patriotic front.

Dr Best thereupon adopted a method which no nation or army had ever descended to employ. He cut off supplies of gas, electricity and water, as well as all transport to Copenhagen, which resulted in no food reaching the capital. In Berlin, a Wilhelmstrasse spokesman expressed his contempt for the Copenhageners, stating that these typical "Petits Bourgois" would soon come to their senses when they could no longer obtain their "beef-steak." The people of Copenhagen were to be starved into surrender. At the same time, considerable German troop contingents were sent to Copenhagen, and the city was declared to be in a state of siege. The great trial of strength had begun.

Berlin was not too pleased with Dr Best's activities in Denmark. After three days of the general strike, Dr Best's second set of concessions were announced: he would restore light, gas and water as well as food supplies, provided the Copenhageners would return to work the following day. By that time the people in the capital were seriously threatened with starvation; for three days there had been no bread, in fact no supplies had arrived in the city at all; nevertheless the workers of Copenhagen refused to resume their work.

On the same day the Danish Freedom Council in Copenhagen formulated the demands of the citizens. Apart from the re-opening of the public works, which had already taken place, the Council demanded the interning or deportation of the Schalburg Corps, a pledge that no reprisals would be undertaken against the leaders of the strike, and a complete cancellation of the curfew.

The Underground front had spoken. We are not able to say who had carried through the negotiations with the Germans, but we do know the result. On the following day, Monday, July 3, when the general strike spread from Copenhagen out to the larger Danish provincial towns, in fact no less than 22 towns in all, the Germans saw no other way out than unconditional capitulation. On July 4, work was resumed. Three times the Germans had been defeated. Three times had the population, faced with starvation and executions, scorned any and every compromise.

. . . . .

At the end of June the Russians launched their big summer offensive with tremendous advances on the Eastern front. In five weeks Vitebesk, Miytsk, Vilna, Livov, Stanislavov, Bralystok, Przemysl, and Brest-Litovsk all fell to the Russian armies.

THE RUSSIAN SUMMER OFFENSIVE

Alexander Werth, Home Service, July, 1944

In Moscow today all hearts are filled with joy. Every night, sometimes once, sometimes twice, sometimes even three times, a familiar deep male voice, speaking like a man giving orders to soldiers, announces a new major victory, and then ten minutes later guns boom and thousands of coloured rockets light up the night and the summer sky. It is always much the same spectacle, but it remains equally thrilling. The new places now being captured by the Russians are in distant Lithuania or in western Byelo-Russia. And every night, in millions of Russian houses, little paper flags and pieces of coloured string and red pencils mark off more large slices of Soviet territory liberated from the enemy.

The present debacle is the biggest disaster the Germans have suffered since Stalingrad. Their casualties are mounting up and are approaching the half-million mark. Division after division has been encircled and wiped out, hundreds of thousands killed and about a hundred thousand taken prisoner. The score of the generals captured is about twenty-five.

Of these hundred thousand or more prisoners, fifty-seven thousand were paraded through the streets of Moscow with their generals at their head. They had been concentrated on the race course for a couple of days; they were given plenty of food and drink and even a concert of music. Then they were taken to the railway stations in a number of groups, ten or fifteen thousand in each. The wide sunny avenues of the outer ring of Moscow's boulevards, with their ten- or twelve-storey blocks of flats, were lined with hundreds of thousands of people who had come to see the Fritzes. It was a bright, almost cheerful-looking crowd: girls in light, usually white summer dresses, young fellows in white open-necked shirts and light trousers, and everywhere children swarming about, many of them perched on lamp-posts or on top of cars and stationary trolley-buses. Many of them had got on to the roofs of the smaller houses. Moscow was looking its brightest and sunniest, and in its wide, modern avenues there was not the slightest sign of bomb damage. When the Germans were thinking of their own capital it must have annoyed them considerably.

The Moscow crowd was remarkably disciplined. They watched these Germans walk, or rather shuffle past, in their dirty green-grey uniforms—this green-grey mould which, as somebody remarked, had rotted away half of European Russia and was still rotting a great part of Europe. Most of the Germans shuffled along with a hang-dog look. Others, the younger ones, seemed surprised and startled at the sight of Moscow, which they had imagined would look quite different. They were startled at the clean, cheerful, and well-fed appearance of the crowds on either side of the street. A few of the Germans glared. The Moscow people looked on quietly without booing or hissing, and only a few youngsters could be heard shouting, "Hey, look at the Fritzes, look at their ugly snouts." But people only exchanged remarks in soft voices. I heard a little girl perched on her mother's shoulder say, "Mummy, are these the people who killed Daddy?" And the mother hugged the child and wept.

People looked at the Germans with loathing and distaste, but said very little. Most of the comments were on their dirty, shabby appearance. One Russian officer in the crowd near me said: "The German officers keep themselves in good shape, but the German soldiers seldom wash, especially in winter, and are extraordinarily filthy in their habits." And a Russian literary man I met during the German parade said to me: "This is truly an historic occasion. I bet you after the war, many novels will be written with this parade as the last chapter. And these novels may be written not only here but also in Germany." I confess it gave me some satisfaction watching these Huns. I remembered those endless torchlight processions of the Nazi Storm Troops in Berlin before the war, bawling the Horstwessel song and uttering raucous animal cries, and the current Berlin joke then was that old Hindenburg, looking from a window, remarked in a moment of absentmindedness, "Good heavens, where have all these Russian war prisoners come from?"

Immense planning for post-war reconstruction is going ahead in Russia in all fields. Plans have been drawn up and in some cases approved for the restoration of the devastated cities such as Stalingrad, Voronezh, Rostov, Kalinin, and also of the ancient city of Novgorod.

. . . . .

A turning point in the operations on the Western front came when the Americans broke out from the Cherbourg peninsula. Early in August the remnants of the German army fled over the Seine, Paris sprang into revolt, and at the same time Allied forces were landed in the South of France.

> Cette ville,   Des toits frêles,
> Aux longs cris,   Cent tourelles,
> Qui profile,   Clochers grêles,
> Son front gris,   C'est Paris!
>
> Victor Hugo.

LIBERATED PARIS

Jean Oberlé, European Service, August 23 1944

The Allied Armies are nearing Paris. The whole world has been waiting for their entry into the capital. The fate of Paris has hung in the balance while people waited for each new edition of the newspapers, every new despatch. They're at Rambouillet, they're at Versailles, they'll be entering Paris any minute now.

And then once again Paris amazed the world. Paris rose in revolt, recapturing the spirit of the great days of revolution in the same eternal places where the heart of Paris has always beaten. Once again the fate of Paris has been decided in the Place de Motel de Ville in the shadow of Notre Dame—that same Town Hall square, the old strikers' meeting place, where the history of France has always found its renewal. The Place de Motel de Ville of the great days of revolution from La Fayette to Lamartine. And the city, where the heart of Paris beats, and the University, the heritage of the people; the whole world knows now that Paris will soon have freed herself, though the firing has not ceased yet in the streets of its suburbs and twenty districts.

Paris saw the Allied Armies reach the surrounding hills and decided to anticipate them. She wanted to emulate a century old tradition and make her pavements, so often barricaded, speak with a voice of thunder. She wanted to show the world that the last battle would be her battle. Last Saturday morning the loyal Parisians decided to revolt. Armed and unarmed they flung themselves into the struggle. On the eighteenth, fighting bad already broken out on the Boulevard Bonne Nouvelle and rifle fire echoed in the Rue de Rivoli, where German lorries opened fire on the citizens. At mid-day the Post Office employees, who had gone on strike, were demonstrating in front of the Town Hall, unfurling the Tricolor and singing the Marseillaise. The marvellous railwaymen were lying on the railway tracks and disconnecting the lines. The students of the training schools were out in the streets, whilst the police, who had also gone on strike, barricaded themselves inside the Central Police Station

The Paris uprising, 19-23 August 1944.

and the barracks on the Ile de la Cite, converting the island into a fortress which beat off all German attacks.

After four days—four glorious days of fighting—the enemy was beaten. He still held out in some places, but Paris had conquered. The wonderful city, the city of gaiety, happiness and elegance, had once again become the city of courage, heroism and sacrifice. From the 19th to the 22nd August she fought as she fought in the gravest crises of her history, as in 1789, 1830, 1848 and 1871. She wanted to prove to France and the world that she is still the heart and soul of France. The Paris of beauty has suddenly become the Paris of heroism; and the world stands still before this beautiful city, as the Allied Armies did when they reached the hills outside and saw her steeples and towers silhouetted against her lovely sky-line. And the world and our Allies see in the action of Paris the symbol of four years of struggle, four years of planned underground resistance by the Maquis and the patriot forces, who have freed towns and villages and have now added the crowning glory to the list—the liberation of their capital.

Great Paris, beautiful and dear Paris, your walls have often been scarred by bullets, your people have often risen when freedom was threatened; once more the wind of freedom and love for your country has swept through you from Notre Dame to the Hotel de Ville, from the Bastille to the Republique, from the Montagne St. Genevieve to the Invalides. After the humiliation of four years of occupation you have shaken off the vermin which defiled you. You have proved to the world, who sometimes doubted you and thought you too happy, that you have always remained the citadel of liberty and the capital of a great people.

. . . . .

The following is a tribute to Paris and France by the well-known BBC commentator, "The Man in the Street:"

"THE MAN IN THE STREET" ON THE LIBERATION OF PARIS

European Service

I speak tonight as one of millions of ordinary British citizens, with a full heart and a quickening pulse at the news that Paris is again rid of the defilement of German occupation. While that lasted, it was iron in the soul of all of us who had been brought up to recognise France as our natural friend and ally.

For me at least there have been two moments in this war when I felt sick at heart and had to grit my teeth to regain my faith that civilisation would conquer in the end. One was when we heard that our great battleships *Repulse* and *Prince of Wales* had been sunk. The other was when Paris fell. That the Japanese should have been able to strike so shattering a blow at Britain's naval power and that Hitler and his garish gang of barbarians should be able to strut as conquerors through the gracious streets of Paris struck at the very foundations of our world.

But we took these blows without quailing because we knew that the everlasting greatness of British sea-power and of France would triumph over these grievous disasters.

Not one of us could think for a moment that the day would not dawn when Paris would once more belong, not to the tasteless and uncouth plunderers from beyond the Rhine, but to the nation which built it and made it great and to the civilised world which recognises it as the fountainhead of its inspiration and the chief shrine of its culture.

And now that day has dawned. Paris is free and herself again; a stifling weight has been lifted from our minds, and the sickness has left our hearts. Now we realise again with a sharp pang how much Paris has always meant to us.

Tonight we British vow that never again shall there be allowed to arise the slightest risk that Paris could be seized and violated by the invader from the cast. The inviolability of the capital city of France shall be a charge upon the British as well as the French people. Paris shall be made as impregnable as London has been. Never again shall she suffer the bitter humiliation of foreign conquest.

Paris liberated, 25 August 1944.

The Paris that we loved only a little less than the people to whom she belongs, will be herself again—only more beautiful and glorious than ever and much more secure. Purged and purified of the evil and rotten elements which marred but could not destroy her loveliness, Paris today enters upon the most brilliant era which she has known even in her long and dazzling history.

It has been the lot of Paris to make history, and her liberation today is indeed a historic milestone in the downfall of the Third Reich, the Reich which reached the pinnacle of its murky fame when Paris fell to its goose-stepping hordes four years ago. It is a milestone, but not the end of the road, the road which leads all the way to Berlin. For a moment we pause to hail the liberation of Paris, but only for a moment. Stern tasks are ahead before the power of that monstrous machine which for so long threatened to throttle the life and soul out of Paris and all that for which she stood, is finally shattered.

We go forward with a new zest to those tasks, side by side with the resurrected French nation in all its pristine greatness.

The French Army is in the battle line again, and France's allies will fight all the better for the knowledge of it, and for the knowledge that the heart of France is once more beating freely and steadily and pumping the life-blood into the great people without whom this civilisation of ours could never be restored. Paris is free, French, and fighting again. The thought of it is a bugle call and a banner to all our fighting and working people.

. . . . .

Sight-seeing in Paris.

The following are two accounts from Luxembourg and Belgium of their resistance to the enemy.

LUXEMBOURG

Jean Oberlé, European Service, September 6 1944

Allied troops have entered the Grand Duchy of Luxembourg. Fighting as they retreat through the valley of the Moselle, the Germans are evacuating the smallest of the countries they occupied for four years. This little country is an example in miniature of what the Germans would have done everywhere if they had won the war. They simply annexed it.

Between the Maginot Line and the Siegfried Line, Luxembourg had managed to maintain a prosperous neutrality. This little country comes seventh on the list of the world's steel producers. The Germans were well aware of it and counted on a good dividend from their occupation. When the German avalanche had rolled over Luxembourg and beyond, Hitler sent one of his personal friends—a certain Gustav Simon—there as Gauleiter. This grotesque little individual decided quite simply to abolish the name of the Grand Duchy which was at once incorporated in the Moselgau, which is the Nazi province of Moselle. The headquarters of the 'gau' was in Coblenz. Having crossed Luxembourg off the map, the Gauleiter set about the population. He abolished the constitution, dissolved the Chamber of Deputies and forbade the use of the French language which he elegantly styled 'the mumbo-jumbo of a half-breed people.' The citizens of Luxembourg were warned that every time they uttered a word of French in public they would be liable to a fine of ten marks. "Bonjour Madame" meant twenty marks. And the children of the Hitler Youth movement were entrusted with the espionage and policing of speech. The same system was applied to telephone calls; as soon as a word of French had been spoken the line went dead and the defaulter was traced.

Names were Germanised, too. It was rather a tall order. Brincourt translated literally into German was Kurzhalm. Christian names went the same way—and when there was no equivalent in German the Latin equivalent was adopted, so that René became Renatus. Absurdity in fact was added to hatefulness.

The Luxembourg population reacted like all the occupied countries to this Nazi civil occupation. The country is small but thickly populated; it has 300,000 inhabitants, and resistance showed itself at once. At least five clandestine papers started to circulate.

The Germans increased their pressure. They put the young men and women of Luxembourg into uniform and sent them to work in forced labour camps in Germany and even in Poland. At the end of August, 1942, the Germans set up compulsory military service. They distributed memorandum forms—like a sort of census—on which everyone had to state that he admitted to being German by birth and tongue. The population decided unanimously to write 'Luxemburger' on the form. The Germans yielded. They did not wait to declare the results of the census, but simply declared that 'the registration was useless since the Luxemburgers were quite obviously German.' The German demands at this time led to a general strike throughout the Grand Duchy. If was the first strike of its kind on the Continent. Everything stopped completely, from farm to factory, all work, all production immediately ceased. The Germans replied in their usual manner with firing squads and imprisonment. The concentration camp and the prison did not satisfy them; they deported the Luxemburgers at five hours' notice and installed Germans from the Ruhr, whose houses had been destroyed by the RAF, in their homes. One in every seven people in the Grand Duchy of Luxembourg went to a concentration camp or prison. So the young Luxemburgers joined the Maquis in the Ardennes forest, or became members of the Belgian resistance or the French Forces of the Interior.

Luxembourg today sees the German army sweep back over her soil in retreat. Grim battles are being fought in the Moselle valley. The Prince Consort and the Crown Prince are with the little Luxembourg army which is fighting by the side of its Allies.

But Luxembourg will soon be free. The refugee Luxembourg Government in London will soon return to its native land and the Grand Duchess will return to her Duchy. Adolf Hitler Street will once again be called Freedom Street.

. . . . .

THE LIBERATION OF BELGIUM

Home Service, September, 1944

A Flying Officer of the Royal Canadian Air Force met one of those Belgian families who have helped hundreds of British, American, Canadian and Allied fliers to get out from behind the enemy lines through the Belgian underground. They knew perfectly well that death was the price for anyone who was discovered.

Madame told me her part in the great underground effort was 'nothing.' I know that mothers in many allied nations will think otherwise. She took us to meet her husband, a soldier with four rows of medals on his tunic-one of the key men in the Belgian secret army. He showed me the facts and figures on paper, a record of which Belgium can be proud. More than nine hundred and fifty Allied airmen who had parachuted behind enemy lines were passed along the underground line to safety; this is one sector which was one of five.

And when the signal came from Britain on D-Day, a wave of sabotage spread through Belgium—59 bridges destroyed; hundreds of railway lines cut; 63 trains derailed; hundreds of locomotives and freight cars blasted; seven lock gates destroyed; and 26 telephone exchanges put out of commission by the Belgian secret army. In addition, ten thousand prisoners, including three generals were taken. But these are only cold statistics. Here is the story; his daughter rode her bicycle and carried messages to the officers of the secret army. Sometimes she rode 30 miles a day right under the noses of the Germans. My husband told me to move to our country house. I never asked any questions.

"Our house in the country was headquarters for a section of the secret Army. Many fliers were brought in to be kept in hiding by Belgian families until the word came that they could be sent along to the next point. Often they were nearly discovered. My husband was taken by the Gestapo for three weeks and kept in a small cell and fed only on dog's food. He lost forty-two pounds, but the Germans did not find out anything about him. So they let him go.

"It is not my story," she said, "but the story of Belgium. My two daughters and myself did what other Belgium women did. We each played our small part in the plan to help our brave allies. My husband was in charge of our zone and gave the orders. My wife told me:

"And so it went on for years. Finally, the great day came. Our men got into their uniforms and joined the fighting. I think that was the happiest day of my husband's life."

· · · · ·

In September it looked for a time as if the final German collapse was near. Towards the end of the month the Allies made a great effort to cross the lower Rhine at Arnhem and bring the war to a swift conclusion, but the Germans managed to rally on their own frontiers and to stop the Allied armies.

THE MEN OF ARNHEM

Stanley Maxted, Home Service, September 27 1944

About five kilometres to the west of Arnhem, in a space 1,500 yards by 900, on that last day, I saw the dead and the living—those who fought a good fight and kept the faith with you at home, and those who still fought magnificently on. They were the last of the few. I last saw them yesterday morning as they dribbled into Nijmegen. They had staggered and walked and waded all night from Arnhem about ten miles north, and we were busy asking each other if this or that one had been seen. Everyone wondered what the final check-up would amount to. I walked up to one young lieutenant to ask him about his sergeant— a stout lad if ever there was one—and he started to explain what had happened and then turned away. Remember all of these men had been practically ten days and ten nights under the most murderous concentrated fire I have seen in two wars. Then he turned again and said: "It's hell to be pulled out when you haven't finished your job, isn't it?" That's the way they all felt. It didn't occur to them that if they hadn't held that horde of enemy force at Arnhem, that force would have been down at Nijmegen upsetting the whole applecart.

That was yesterday morning. Late on the afternoon before we were told that the remnants of the First Airborne Division were going to pull out that night. The enemy was making it impossible for the elements of the Second Army to relieve us. We were told to destroy all our equipment with the exception of what would go into a haversack, to muffle our boots with bits of blanket, and be ready to move off at a certain time. When the various officers were told to transmit this news to that thin straggle of hard-pressed men around the pitifully small perimeter, a great silence seemed to come upon them even in the middle of the shelling-day or night the shelling and mortaring never stopped. The ones I saw just drew a deep breath and said: "Very good, sir." Then those staring eyes in the middle of black muddy masks saluted as they always would, and faded away to crawl out on their stomachs and tell their men.

Perhaps I should remind you here that these were men of no ordinary calibre. They had been nine days in that little space I mentioned being mortared and shelled, machine-gunned and sniped from all around. When a tank or a self-

Paratroopers on their way to Arnhem.

propelled eighty-eight gun broke through, two or three of them had detached themselves and somehow or another had put it out of business. For the last three days they had had no water, very little but small arms ammunition, and rations cut to one-sixth. Luckily or unluckily, it rained and they caught the water in their capes and drank that. These last items were never mentioned— they were airborne, weren't they? They were tough and knew it. All right, water and rations didn't matter. Give them some Germans to kill and even one chance in ten and they'd get along somehow.

At two minutes past ten we clambered out of our slit trenches in an absolute din of bombardment—a great deal of it our own—and formed up in a single line. Our boots were wrapped in blanket so that no noise would be made. We held the tail of the coat of the man in front. We set off like a file of nebulous ghosts from our pock-marked and tree-strewn piece of ground. Obviously, since the enemy was all round us, we had to go through him to get to the river Rhine. After about two hundred yards of silent trekking we knew we were among the enemy. It was difficult not to throw yourself flat when machine-gun tracers skimmed your head or the scream of a shell or mortar-bomb sounded very close—but the orders were to "keep going." Anybody hit was to be picked up by the man behind him. A major had reconnoitred the route earlier on with a headquarters officer and had it memorised.

The back of my neck was prickling for that whole interminable march. I couldn't see the man ahead of me—all I knew was that I had hold of a coat-tail and for the first time in my life was grateful for the downpour of rain that made a patter on the leaves and covered up any little noises we were making. At every turn of the way there was posted a sergeant glider pilot who stepped out like a shadow and then stepped back into a deeper shadow again. Several times we halted—which meant you bumped into the man ahead of you—then, when the head of our party was satisfied the turning was clear, we went on again. Once we halted because of a boy sitting on the ground with a bullet through his leg. We wanted to pick him up but he whispered: "Nark it; gimme another field-dressing and I'll be all right, I can walk."

As we came out of the trees—we had been following carefully throughout footpaths so far—I felt as naked as if I were in Piccadilly Circus in my pyjamas, because of the glow from fires across the river. The machine-gun and general bombardment had never let up. We lay down flat in the mud and rain and stayed that way for two hours till the sentry beyond the hedge on the bank of the river told us to move up over the dyke and be taken across. Mortaring started now and I was fearful for those who were already on the bank. I guessed it was pretty bad for them. After what seemed a nightmare of an age we got our turn and slithered up and over on to some mud-flats. There was the shadow of a little assault-craft with an outboard motor on it. Several of these had been rushed up by a field company of engineers. One or two of them were out of action already. I waded out into the Rhine up to my hips—it didn't matter, I was soaked through long ago—had been for days. A voice that was sheer music spoke from the stern of the boat saying: "Ye'll have to step lively boys, it ain't healthy here." It was a Canadian voice, and the engineers were Canadian engineers. We helped push the boat off into the swift Rhine current and with our heads down between our knees waited for the bump on the far side-or for what might come before. It didn't come. We clambered out and followed what had been a white tape up over a dyke. We slid down the other side on our backsides; we sloshed through mud for four miles and a half-me thinking, "Gosh! I'm alive, how did it happen?"

In a barn there was a blessed hot mug of tea with hot rum in it and a blanket over our shoulders. Then we walked again 11 night. After daylight we got to a dressing station near Nijmegen. Then we were put in trucks and that's how we reached Nijmegen. That's how the last of the few got out to go and fight in some future battle. No matter what battle that is, I know they won't let you down.

· · · · ·

On the Eastern front the Russians had been advancing at a rate hitherto unseen in military history, and at the end of July the guns of the Russian army could be heard in Warsaw. But the Russian lines of communication had been extended to their utmost limit and when the population of the Polish capital rose against the Germans the Russians were unable to strike across the river.

When at last the heroic rising of the Poles had been beaten down by the Germans, the Polish Prime Minister, Mikolaiczyk, made the following address to Warsaw.

MIKOLAICZYK'S MESSAGE TO WARSAW

European Service, October 3 1944

After sixty-three days of fighting and exertions, yesterday at 6 p.m., the last bastion of resistance in Warsaw—the centre of the City where, apart from the soldiers of the Home Army, 260,000 civilians were assembled—has fallen. It has fallen after a terrific artillery and air bombardment which the Germans concentrated during the last day on this sector, after the fall of Mokotov on the 27th, and of Zoliborzh on the 30th of September. The cessation of hostilities took place after the exhaustion of military supplies, food, medical supplies and dressings needed by thousands of wounded, dying in cellars without medical assistance. Warsaw fell after unsuccessful efforts to break through the German ring of steel, after all hope of rescue had proved in vain in view of the public statement in Moscow on September 30th that the capture of Warsaw can only take place after the encirclement of the city, as the attempts to force the Vistula directly from Praga had failed. Sixty-three days of struggle, of destruction, of hell.... Sixty-three days of hope and despair, sixty-three days of freedom, and a new serfdom for those who have survived.

Just as in March of this year in Volhynia and later in Nowogrodok, the region of Wilno, Lwow, Lublin, Rzeszow, everywhere at the sound of the approaching Soviet front, Poles rose from the underground and started open fighting against the Germans, so in the same way Warsaw surged to battle.

On July 31st, the thunder of Soviet guns approaching Warsaw shook her walls. Soviet airmen engaged the Luftwaffe in the skies over Warsaw. The German civilian population left the city. German newspapers ceased to appear. The Gestapo and the military authorities ordered a mass evacuation of civilians. From the West, German reinforcements began to arrive. Reports were coming in about the approach of the Soviet Army to a distance of 20 kilometres from Warsaw's suburbs.

On August 1st, at 3 p.m., the explosion of a mine laid under the premises of the German military headquarters, gave the signal for the rising.

Warsaw rushed into battle, to take control of the city, and to erect barricades. The greater part of the city and some centres in Praga were seized. In those days Warsaw said, "We are not afraid of anything, give us only arms."

During the days of August 5th and 6th the bridges over the Vistula, and the central railway station changed hands several times.

The Germans tied Polish women and children to their tanks. German strategy aimed at the control of the main arteries, the Poniatowski and Kierbedz bridges. They attacked with tanks and burned the adjoining houses, mopping up the terrain for the transport of reinforcements to Praga. At the same time, groups of insurgents were clearing the ground from the Germans, taking prisoners and concentrating mainly in the centre of the city, in Mokotov and the old town. In Zoliborz, the Poles, in a counter-attack, gained some ground.

On August 6th, German artillery and the Luftwaffe began the bombing of centres of. Polish resistance. Newly-brought reinforcements with tanks and flame-throwers attacked the Poles.

Sappers were digging tunnels and started to blow up house after house. All in vain. The Germans threw in armoured trains, the insurgents counter-attacked, captured some German tanks and put others out of action.

On August 10th, the Germans dropped leaflets bearing forged appeals from the Allies to cease fighting. On the 11th they presented an ultimatum which Warsaw answered by contempt and increased fighting.

The Germans brought into battle Goliath tanks, loaded with dynamite—mortars of the heaviest calibre and land-mines. They executed hostages. The Luftwaffe bombed house after house from roof-top level. From the ruins of Warsaw, life descended underground and into the sewers. Calls went out to the world for help in arms and for the bombing of German airfields and concentrations of artillery—of mortars and armoured trains. The Germans brought into action grenades with asphyxiating gases. All in vain.

The Germans, who were forced to abandon supplying Praga via Warsaw, built pontoon bridges outside the city in order to maintain the flow of transport to Praga.

On the 4th September, the electric power station and the waterworks were destroyed. The struggle went on in darkness without water and with an increasing lack of food. The help which was coming from Italy at the cost of great sacrifice on the part of the British. South African and Polish airmen could not satisfy even a fraction of the needs.

On the 9th of September the situation became very critical and on the 10th, after an interval, new help arrived from Italy.

On the 11th of September, the Soviet Air Force appeared over Warsaw, stopping further destruction of the city by the Luftwaffe. On the following day Praga was attacked and small droppings effected which were repeated during the night of September 13th-14th.

Help was still inadequate and exhaustion increased. The wounded in ever-rising numbers were in cellars without proper care. The enemy surrounded the insurgents with an ever-tightening ring. On the 18th of September, the great American relief expedition which had been delayed several days because of weather conditions, took off.

On the 20th, direct liaison with Marshal Rokossowsky was established. In the meantime, however, the German pressure was increasing. Mokotov fell, attempts to force the Vistula from Praga were frustrated.

On the 29th September, General Bor pressingly appealed to Marshal Rokossowsky for help in the form of a renewed assault, as he foresaw the inevitable catastrophe in view of German artillery's and air force's renewed bombardment which met with no opposition. The exhaustion and famine spread and there was no possibility of attending the wounded.

On the 30th of September, Zoliborz fell and it became clear that the liberation of Warsaw could only take place by an encircling movement, which required time. After the capture of Zoliborz and Mokotov, the German pressure and bombardment concentrated on the centre of the city, holding over 250,000 civilians, and finally the resistance of the insurgents was broken.

The same people, who, as "Blyskawica" radio said were free during two months, must again become slaves. The same people, who, without any exception, young men, old people and children, men and women of all classes and political convictions, have given the highest proof of sacrifice and heroism in the fight for freedom, descend into darkness at a time when the sun of freedom rises for others.

Poles, homage to the memory of those who have fallen. They rest in the ruins of Warsaw which are now deserted. Their blood and sacrifice will not be in vain. We swear on the memory of the dead that we shall not put to waste and shall not allow to diminish what they have achieved by showing the world that there is no price Poles would not pay for true freedom and independence. Every Pole, every soldier, airman and sailor will repay the Germans for what they have done to Warsaw.

The fight goes on. The end of the Germans is near, and Poland, despite the clouds on her skies must be and will be truly strong, free and independent. With clenched fists and teeth, checking the outbursts of grief and sorrow, we shall march forward to our Motherland, to our homes, to freedom which must dawn for us.

Farewell to you who have survived, farewell not for long, until the day of final freedom and independence.

CHAPTER IX

The Last Winter

October, 1944—April, 1945

In East and West the Germans had succeeded in establishing a line after the sweeping advances through the summer of the Russian and Allied armies. But in south-eastern Europe the autumn and winter of 1944 saw the liberation of new large territories.

A BBC correspondent, Kenneth Matthews, who shared the life of the partisans in Yugoslavia who had for so many years fought the German invaders, gave the following account from the mountains of Slovenia a few months before the country was set free.

WITH THE PARTISANS IN YUGOSLAVIA

Home Service, September-October, 1944

I

I have spent seven weeks at Slovene headquarters in Yugoslavia. What single impression stands out from all the others? Certainly the enthusiasm of the people. They are a people inspired. You have to be very cold-blooded if you don't want to be carried away by their vision of liberty.

The fight against the enemy is going well, if slowly, in Slovenia. But every day a new village and another area is cleared of the enemy; and there are many signs of his loosening grip. For example, the Allies landed the first jeeps in the district while I was there, and the Russians landed their first aircraft on Slovene soil.

It is a good and generous life with the Partisans, and although I saw wounds and death, it is not all hardship and fighting. I could tell you of games of chess played on the mountain side and of the highly intellectual debates that went on by candlelight till long after midnight. The Partisans were always good companions. But I wouldn't like to give even the shortest picture of Partisan life without mentioning the civilians—especially the sun-burnt women and old men and even children who worked in the fields so that life could go on.

The Slovenes are now carrying out a general mobilisation. One old man of seventy-one offered himself for service. When they told him he was too old, he made the recruiting officers laugh by saying, "Hitler would have taken me."

There are very few public clocks in Slovenia, and the best way of putting your watch right is by the BBC news. I spent three years in the European Service of the BBC, but I was never certain of the times of the transmissions in Slovene and Serbo-Croat till I went to Partisan Yugoslavia. It was the queerest sensation to hear the London news booming out of the forest in the middle of occupied Europe. Sometimes we got the news of events only twenty or so miles away— from London first. Twenty miles is six hours' walk for a courier, perhaps several days' walk if there's a railway line in the way.

Nevertheless, the news service of the Partisans is one of their most brilliant achievements. Pick up any one of the four chief Slovene newspapers and ask yourself how many free countries in the world are producing better. It is incredible that these serious, serene-looking, beautifully-printed newspapers should be produced at all; and yet each of them has a circulation of 15,000 copies in territory overrun by the enemy. The editorial offices of the "Slovene Herald," which is the official paper, are high in the forest. The printing is done in three main centres. There have to be three separate printings, because it is impracticable to carry large numbers of the printed newspaper over the Sava River or the Ljubljana-Trieste railway. So the courier slips over these heavily defended obstacles carrying only the "copy" with him.

The distribution of the newspapers, in fact of all the big Partisan publications, is organised from one centre. It is a modest little farmhouse, hidden among pear and walnut trees, and its most imposing piece of furniture is the map on the wall. This map shows 120 subsidiary distribution centres, scattered far and wide over Slovenia, from which the final local distribution is made. The idea is that no one who speaks the Slovene language, even if he lives within the old Austrian border, shall lack the chance of keeping contact with his own people and their Allies.

In May, three Slovene officers went north from headquarters to set the border country alight against the Germans. These three men, "Gashper" the Commandant, "Tairil" the Political Officer, and "Marko" the Chief of Staff, put new heart into the people. The country people fed and sheltered the Partisans, and the Partisans developed a technique for safeguarding the civilians. For example, they could remove their radio apparatus, aerial, batteries and generator in less than seven minutes and leave no trace in the house where they had been. It was a rule that they stayed in no place more than two days; they never took their boots off. It was a highly dangerous area, the very gateway to the Reich, but it was not least dangerous for the Germans.

The Germans, said my officer friend, knew pretty well where the Partisans were, and when they attacked, they could attack from four, five or six directions. The Partisans had to be like a gas, all-pervasive and mobile, giving ground to the enemy and closing round him again. They developed these tactics to such perfection that the Germans never attacked with fewer than 3,000 men. "Gashper," the Commandant, was a guerrilla fighter of superb bravado. With a battery of pistols at his belt, with his curving side whiskers and one eyebrow shot away, he looked rather like an old-style pirate. To the delight of his men, he would wilfully expose himself at the height of battle, in order to taunt the enemy. He would shout such things as "500 marks if you can hit me," and they never did. He had been, in civil life, a simple farmer.

The Allies dropped supplies by parachute. Unarmed Partisan recruits waited at the dropping ground and marched off with the arms as they fell. Many of these new Partisans had had their training in the use of arms in the German Army. If they got hold of an unfamiliar weapon. like the American Springfield, or Marlin, they would have it to pieces in half an hour and understand its mechanism.

Major R., a New Zealand surgeon, treasures a photograph of Marshal Tito inscribed in Tito's own handwriting, "To Dr R. who has done so much for the Yugoslav wounded." One morning last week, I stood beside his operating table in Slovenia. Six Partisan wounded had been brought in during the night. The doctor tied the white surgical mask over my mouth and nostrils, and as he worked, lectured me as if I had been a medical student.

Last December, Dr R. could remember a case when a Partisan girl was brought to him in Dalmatia. When he lifted the blanket from her, he found similar wounds which had been inflicted two months before and never had any dressing. He operated without anaesthetic. He offered her something to ease the pain, but she said, "Oh no! it's not necessary. I'll just sing," and sing she did until she lost consciousness.

Major R. has operated on Partisan wounded in the Dalmatian islands, in Croatia, and at Marshal Tito's headquarters. He talks now of going to work behind the Japanese lines in China.

No one in present circumstances can claim to have a first-hand knowledge of the whole of Yugoslavia. What you can see for yourself depends on where the Germans are and how far you can walk in a day. What I saw in Slovenia is not necessarily typical of other parts of Yugoslavia. The central political fact is the explosion of the popular will, which makes both leaders and people believe that all things are possible to them. One consequence of the Partisan war is a greatly heightened nationalism. But it is not likely to take a jealous or exclusive form among the Slovenes, who are proud of their place in the world alliance of nations. Britain, the Soviet Union and America—usually in that order—appear on half the proclamations and posters. The Soviet Union occupies a special place in their affections, as America does in ours: there is the strong tie of common language and brotherhood. But Partisan foreign policy requires that no favouritism is shown to any ally. A British doctor is established in a Slovene hospital; a Russian doctor is established in another one. You see more British books and papers about than Russian ones.

The cost of the Partisan war in Slovenia has been sickeningly high. I asked Colonel Luka, the Chief Medical Officer, to give me an estimate of the battle casualties. He said no one could give such an estimate. The early Partisans, of whom he was one, were kept too busy to make records. They fought to the death, anonymously. If there is any family in Slovenia which does not count its dead, I did not hear of it; and I am convinced it would be a conservative estimate to say that one out of every ten men, women and children will never see his home again.

If that is the cost, what is the gain? The immediate gain is the inspired unity of the people. In that strange and dangerous Partisan community of fighters and civilians, you get something of the family atmosphere which developed for a while during the bombardment of London.

Politically, this unity is expressed by a united front of parties called by the Slovenes the "Liberation Front." Their leaders declare that this coalition will continue into the post-war period. It includes both the Communists and the Catholics.

I came away from Slovenia feeling that they might never be able to count a material profit on the Partisan war, but that they had gained an inestimable moral power which would sustain their children and their children's children for many generations to come.

II

You have got to be for ever ready to move in Yugoslavia—to move instantly—and, like Lot in the Bible story, to cast no regretful glance behind. In spite of this handicap, it is astonishing what an edifice of solid organisation the Partisans have built up. I am sending this despatch from the nerve centre of the liberation struggle in Slovenia, and around us within a circle whose radius I will not attempt to measure, lies all the apparatus of a modern state: ministries, newspapers, schools, post, telephone and electricity services, a Slovene National Bank and the National Liberation Council. The comparative safety and stability of all these institutions are made possible by what the Partisans call "The Conspiracy."

First of all, it is a question of hiding-places. This country has been clothed by nature from head to foot in vegetation. In the valleys, maize grows tall enough to hide a man standing; the middle hill-slopes are a tangle of bushes and bracken; the mountain tops are as solemn as a cathedral nave, roofed darkly over by high trees and carpeted with beech leaves, pine cones and blooms of cyclamen. You would think you could hide anything anywhere, but it is not so easy as that. The enemy has even the smallest tracks charted, but above all he knows where the springs are. Consequently, the Partisan positions have to be removed from the springs and it is not uncommon to bring in water from two or three hours' distance.

I can illustrate how effectively the positions are concealed, from my own experience. I set off to visit an outpost with two friends who had made the journey many times before. It was supposed to be forty minutes' walk, but after nearly two hours' twisting and turning on mountain tracks both my companions admitted they were lost. One of them—an American—scratched his head and said, "I could have sworn we were not more than three hundred yards away." But there was nothing for it but for one of us to go back to the nearest Partisan post and ask for a guide. It turned out that in fact we were as near as the American had supposed. A wooden shack suddenly came into sight among the wild raspberry bushes and it seemed incredible that we could have missed it. An American boy received us in the cabin, which was hung with trophies, including an automatic rifle and a picture of Tito.

He told us that during the war the enemy had three times come up the main trail without discovering the position.

The Germans call us bandits. They conduct frantic operations against what they describe as bandit hordes; and "the bandits' nest" is the name by which they dignify the headquarters where I am writing this. It has often occurred to me that the term banditry must have a very wide meaning in German to include such things as the delicate art of Miss Simchicheva, who has come to us from the Ljubljana National Theatre, or the solid learning of Professor Zwitter, who is the head of the Research Institute. It might be a good idea if I were to introduce you to some of these bandits; for example, Major Natasha. I saw her first on the night of my arrival. She was moving about on an airfield among the Partisan wounded, moving so unobtrusively I should never have guessed that she was in charge of their evacuation. I was surprised to see the gold bars of her rank on her sleeve, and I was considerably more surprised the next day when I learnt that this was the heroine of Louis Adamic's American best-seller "My Native Land," the girl medical student who stood with her lover on the Slovene mountain (this was before the war began), talking of the brave new world they would build together in Yugoslavia. This girl was reported by the Italians during the war to have killed herself when they discovered the cave hospital in which she was nursing wounded Partisans. I said to her "So you are not dead after all?" "No," she answered, and laughed at the joke. "I'm not dead yet." In three years those small hands of hers have performed some of the heaviest operations known to surgery. On one day of horror last year the hospital had been overrun by the German offensive and she had heard the wounded crying out helplessly as the killers came in. Major Natasha is now in charge of another hospital, which I believe no German will ever discover; but for all that she sleeps with a loaded automatic rifle at her bedside.

Then there was the mayor whom I met by accident. I called for a drink at his house, a solid-looking farmhouse standing among orchards. The mayor is sixty-nine years old—a tough patriarchal old farmer with enormous moustaches. He was already mayor in the far-off days of the Austro-Hungarian Empire. Now he has been elected chairman of the local Partisan committee. Over mugs of cider, I asked him how he and his household had come to support the Partisans. He replied, "At first there were only three or four of them—young boys. We knew them; we gave them food secretly. Perhaps we thought they could never pull it off. Afterwards, when the Italians gave up and you British came, we knew they had succeeded." He went on, " We had to do what we could to keep our Slovene language spoken in Europe." This old farmer with his caution, his honesty and his patriotism seemed to me to be representative of all those thousands of country people who have supported this national movement without complaint through every hardship.

Bozhidar Yakats is an artist, known internationally. You may have seen his portrait of Tito. He showed the original drawn in red crayon. All his possessions, all his pre-war paintings, have been confiscated by the enemy in Ljubljana. In their place he treasures the public proclamation issued by the Quisling authorities denouncing him as a traitor. Now he lives in a cottage shaded by pear and walnut trees and he draws his fellow Partisans at the same fee as they take for fighting—that is, nothing. His album is a sort of national biography. He has drawn the leaders, and he has drawn many of the Partisan rank and file, some with a quality of haunting beauty which must have captured the artist's imagination, others with round, simple peasant faces. Yakats' album will be one of the great memorials of the Partisan movement when the war is over.

My own portrait gallery would be far too long if I went on talking, but I must find room for Mitska, whom I visited on a mountain top. It was not the best situation for her week-old baby, but Mitska was a well-known Partisan, in spite of her child-like face, and no place in the valley would have been safe from the Germans. She had fallen in love with a friend fighting in the same brigade; a political officer had married them at the battlefront. Then one desperate day in a rear-guard action with the enemy, her husband was killed and she herself was wounded. She went back to find her husband's body and she dug his grave herself in the forest. Now she was lying with an infected thigh wound in as wild and strange a maternity ward as could be imagined. The baby, perfectly healthy, slept under a coverlet of pink parachute silk, and young fawns from the hills strayed in and out and occasionally nuzzled at the tiny pinewood cot. In all that I have seen of war I have not seen one sight that touched me more deeply. I am quite satisfied to be a bandit in such company.

. . . . .

The first German city to be conquered fell to the American armies. It was Aachen, the ancient city of the German emperors. A Czech mar correspondent who entered the city immediately after it had been taken, gave the following description.

THE FALL OF AACHEN

George Mucha, Home Service, October 17 1944

I have just returned to Brussels after four days of street fighting in Aachen. I have seen the city of German Emperors being wiped out after it had refused the offer of honourable surrender, and I found its people crushed to desperation by a double misery, by our onslaught and by the cruelties of their Nazi masters. When I first approached Aachen, the town was burning. From an American observation post just above the city I could see immense columns of smoke rising to the sky where some sixty allied dive-bombers were freely forming up for attack and diving unmolested on their objective. As the bombs came down, red jets of flame spouted up among the houses which stood there silent without a sign of life. It was an eerie sight, no enemy guns, no movements in the streets, only the incessant rumbling of explosions. And then we went in. On both sides of the deserted streets stood empty carcasses of burnt-out houses; glass, debris and tree branches were strewn on the pavements, and almost in every street a building was burning like a huge torch.

We arrived at a huge concrete surface shelter. These shelters are ugly, gloomy constructions with many floors above and below the ground, where hundreds of civilians were hiding for the last five weeks in darkness and stench. Army officers and the police had the entrance blocked, and no one was allowed to leave the place. In the meantime, Gestapo and soldiers were looting the town, grabbing in mad lust the property of their own people, although they had no hope to carry it away. The Army refused to open the shelter. For several hours it was besieged by American soldiers, then a German officer offered to surrender, if he was allowed to take away all his things, plus his batman.

Lieutenant Walker, a young Company Commander, made no effort to accept such a ridiculous offer and threatened to use flame throwers. That helped. The doors opened and out came the drabbest, filthiest inhabitants of the underworld I have ever seen, as people came stumbling out into the light, dazed, then catching a breath of fresh air, and finally starting to jabber, push, scream and curse. Some precipitated themselves to me, brandishing their fists. Where have you been so long, they shouted. Why didn't you deliver us sooner from those devils. It was a stunning sight. These were the people of the first German town occupied by the allies. And they were weeping with hysterical

A Tommy with prisoners.

joy amidst the smouldering ruins of their homes. We have been praying every day for you to come, said a woman with a pale, thin face. You can't imagine what we have had to suffer from them. And then came the insults. Bloodhound, bandit, gangster. All this was the beloved Fuehrer. There is no one who can hate and curse so thoroughly as the Germans, and these people were all green with hate of the Nazis. It was no trick. I certainly would not be cheated.

It was the breakdown of a nation after having played for five years on the wrong cards. Maybe it was the rage of a gangster, let down by his gang-leader, but it was a hatred you find only in civil wars. The people were brought into a big German barracks on the outskirts of the town.

We made our way towards the heart of the city where the dark dome of the cathedral still stands over the grave of Charlemagne.

. . . . .

Further south the re-born French Army forced the Belfort Gap and liberated Alsace. A British correspondent who followed with the advancing French forces, paid this tribute to the French Army.

SALUTE TO THE FRENCH ARMY

Vaughan Thomas, December 1 1944

There are few moments in this dirty, inhuman, soul-destroying business of modern war on which I shall ever want to look back with pride. But I have just lived through one of them—I've been with the re-born French Army during the days of its triumph its justification. The days of the forcing of the Belfort Gap and the freeing of Alsace. There were occasions, I'll admit, during the last few weeks especially, when I was being driven by a French chauffeur, who had one hand on the wheel and the other enthusiastically waving as he turned his back on the traffic to explain what he would do with the "sales boches," when I wished myself anywhere but with our gallant allies. But now—veteran of a hundred traffic fights—I can sit back and see the new French Army as it really is. One of the fastest moving, best handled and most picturesque armies facing the Germans today. It is certainly fast moving. Speed is the first impression you get when you are out with the French. No one seems to travel less than sixty miles per hour and my memory of a French convoy is of a mile-long pandemonium—lorries coming bumper to bumper one way—lorries meeting them head-on coming from the other way—jeeps weaving in and out. And everyone hand-waving, tying themselves into knots and backing into each other's vehicles with the greatest goodwill in the world. A famous cartoon in the American Service paper, "Stars and Stripes" sums it up. It shows a line of disconsolate American lorry drivers being addressed by their Lieutenant before departure. "Men," says the Lieutenant, "Some of you may never come back. There's a French convoy on the road." But somehow or other the French convoys do get down the roads, and the French front advances with a dash and an "élan" that has got impressive results during the last few days. I sometimes think that the reason it goes ahead is that I've never heard any French officer issue any other order except "En Avant"—"Forward." No French Command Post seems to be anywhere except slightly ahead of the front line. When a French Colonel invites you to visit the front—he means the Front. And the first thing you know is a sudden shower of shells as the gallant officer points to the farmhouse a hundred yards away. "Les Boches?" you ask nervously. "Ah! there they are les Salauds," he says. And you prepare immediately to take off rapidly to the rear. For you know exactly what the next order will be: "Forward—en avant." And forward they do go against the toughest resistance.

This new army of France has got something to revenge—something which makes it dare the impossible. It has got nothing in common with the disillusioned armies that went down to defeat in 1940. It has got, as its basis, the armies of Africa with the colonial troops and a corps of officers, who have the traditional skill of the French in the business of war. But it has now got armoured divisions of Frenchmen from France—shock battalions of patriot volunteers—and the French Forces of the Interior, fighting side by side with the veterans of North

Africa and Italy. And above all, it has thrown up new generals—new leaders! These new generals are exciting, vivid personalities. English generals—and today there are none better—sometimes give the impression that they are a bit apologetic about making war. American generals feel that they are expected to be tough 'he-men.' But the French generals—ah! they are generals in the grand manner. Until you have seen General de Montsabert decorating an officer with a double-barrelled embrace on both cheeks, or General de Lattré de Tassigny explaining his plans at a press conference—you haven't seen a general. Such clarity—such eloquence—such Napoleonic orders of the day, and out of it all such a resounding, invigorating success as the forcing of the Belfort Gap.

Yes, I am proud of the memorable days I spent with the new armies of France, and I can look back on them with more pleasure now that I've got an American driver who drives at twenty-five miles an hour on the right side of the road.

· · · · ·

In December, the Germans launched a strong offensive through the Ardennes in order to upset the allied plans and reach Antwerp. They very nearly succeeded, but were stopped by the Allies transferring powerful armoured forces to the threatened sector, and through the efforts—in spite of the winter weather—of the RAF and the American Air Force.

In January, the Chief of the Eighth American Air Force, General Doolittle, gave an account of the origin of his Force and of the remarkable collaboration between the Americans and the British.

GENERAL DOOLITTLE ON THE EIGHTH AMERICAN AIR FORCE

Home Service, January 28 1945

Three years ago today, in an armoury in Savannah, Georgia, the Eighth Air Force was activated for service in England. Three days later, General Ira Eaker and a staff of six officers were ordered here as an advance echelon.

By March 7, there were in England 19 American Air Force officers. But the strength of the Eighth Air Force in England was not 19. The strength of the Eighth in England was many thousands—for the 19 officers were quartered with RAF Bomber Command, who placed at their disposal the experience, resources and personnel of that huge Air Force which even then could send a thousand bombers over Europe.

The diary kept in our early days contains hardly an entry that does not, in some way, refer to the help of the RAF The headquarters for the new air force was located in close proximity to Bomber Command headquarters. British enlisted personnel was assigned to our headquarters until American personnel could be brought over; the first aeroplane that the Eighth Air Force had in England was a Harvard trainer assigned to it by the RAF.

On paper, the Eighth was a completely new air force without a single day of operational experience, but in reality, it was an old experienced air force—for it had put at its disposal every bit of knowledge gained by the Royal Air Force in two years of war.

The Eighth was the first major unit of the United States forces to arrive in England. Since then, literally millions of American soldiers have passed through here on their way to the war fronts. And now the Eighth is the last major American unit to be based in England.

You who have seen us grow and helped us grow are entitled to a report of our accomplishments. But it is difficult to list the results of strategic bombing in figures.

We can tell you that we have dispatched approximately half a million aircraft in the past three years. We can tell you that we have dropped over half a million tons of bombs on the enemy, and have destroyed over 12,000 of his aircraft. We can now send as many as 3,000 aircraft over Germany on a single mission. We must also tell you that over 5,000 of our own aeroplanes have failed to return and some 40,000 of our men have been killed or missing.

But this does not tell the story of our accomplishments. We have worked as a team with RAF Bomber Command, and the round-the-clock bombing has cut deeply into the enemy's ability to produce material necessary to wage war. Just how much we have accomplished can best be told by the German High Command. We know that it is considerable.

Infantry units of Great Britain and the United States, fighting side by side on the eastern front, will remember each other with mutual admiration. Members of the British and American Fleets operating together throughout the world are learning each to respect the seamanship and valour of the other.

But I do not believe that among all the far-flung fronts of this war there is an example of more closely-knit co-operation between forces than exists here in England between the Eighth and the Royal Air Force.

We are more than Allies. We are one.

One force, doing one job. And with God's help, we will accomplish our purpose and aid in bringing about the one peace for which we all pray-the peace that will last for all time.

. . . . .

America's immense contribution to the war an Europe was made at the same time as the American forces—assisted by the Australians—carried out a growing offensive against the Japanese in the Pacific.

The following is an account by Captain Frank Owen of the British Fourteenth Army and its advance on the Burma Front.

THE BURMA FRONT

Home Service, December 12 1944

You are sitting in a forest. The nearest city to you is five hundred miles away. Apart from a large village and a small market town, the whole of the way from that far forest back to that nearest city is jungle. If you're lucky, your home up there is a bamboo hut with an earthen floor. It keeps out most of the rain, some of the heat, and none of the insects. If you're unlucky you're squatting in a foxhole under Japanese mortar fire, waiting to assault a Japanese machine-gun nest, and it is probably still raining.

This is the Burma Front. A quarter of a million British soldiers live there, fight there, march, patrol and stick it out. Some have been on duty there for three years, guarding the gates to India. Now they are deep into Burma, driving the enemy down the road to Mandalay, down the long, long road to Singapore where sixty thousand of our comrades, prisoners of war in the hands of the Japanese, are waiting for us to come and set them free. There's a way back from the front, but it doesn't run direct between your outpost and that first big city at the base. It was built, a miracle of skill and daring by our Army engineers, shearing its path through a wilderness, clinging to the face of a precipice, winding its way up into the clouds eight thousand feet high, and above the clouds.

Along this road every day must flow the food for the great army forward. It is the largest single army in the world. For besides the British, up there are Indian soldiers, even more numerous than the British; and we have Ghurkas, West Africans and East Africans, Chinese, Burmese, and the warrior hill tribes of the jungle, the Nagas, the Chins, Kachins, Karens—altogether six hundred thousand troops are fighting in the Fourteenth Army, and all must eat. So, every twenty-four hours two thousand tons of food go rattling up that single-track mountain railway, and along those military roads. Motor-trucks, jeeps, ox-wagons, mules, donkeys and elephants carry it up to the front. Though landslides block the railway or the highway and floods sweep away the bridges, the goods will get there.

War in the jungle is really first and foremost the art of keeping that road open; if you don't you may die. And secondly, it is the art of cutting the road behind the enemy; then he will die. The Japanese forgot that first law of the jungle. But the men of the Fourteenth Army, warriors from the cities and little country towns of Britain, they learned it so well that in this year's battle along the Burma Front they have killed seventy thousand Japanese.

The Fourteenth Army and the airmen of the Eastern Air Command, have beaten the Japanese at something else, how to improvise a new line of supply when the existing one is broken. For on a front such as ours, twenty thousand square miles of the wildest country in the whole world, it must always be possible for a party of daring raiders to penetrate your zone and cut your roads. But today, when the Jap does this, our troops simply stand fast where they are and our aircraft feed them from the sky, dropping them their rations every day by parachute, with ammunition, weapons, medical supplies, cigarettes and even newspapers. In Arakan we had an entire division completely cut off for twenty-three days, until they were ready to break out and smash the surrounding enemy.

In the great siege of Imphal we had an entire Army Corps encircled and every road cut. The Air Force—British and Yank—poured in supplies through the roof of the jungle. They brought into that battle by air, two and a half divisions of reinforcements, with all their guns, wagons, jeeps and mules. They brought in bulldozers and even steamrollers to make new landing-strips for the planes. And most wonderful, they took out safely, thirty-thousand wounded to the great hospitals in India. They flew blind those pilots, through the black monsoon mists, over those terrible mountains, without a single casualty. The soldiers will never forget the air force for that. At a single stroke they cut in half the sufferings of the jungle war.

It is morning and you are two thousand feet up on a gun-site in Arakan. The gunners are stripped to the belt, bronzed almost as black as their Indian and African comrades. And the horseflies are eating their lunch off them. At sunset will come the mosquitoes, eating their supper, and bringing malaria too if you don't look out. When night steals up out of the plain, it will be as cold as December over here.

It is blazing noon and you belong to the eternal, indomitable infantry-the unsung heroes of the County Regiments. For example, the Dorsets, Devons, Durhams, the Lincolns, Yorks. and Lancs., the Scots and Welsh Border regiments. You're slogging your way along a jungle river-bed or slashing a path foot by foot through a bamboo forest so thick that it resembles a hedge of thorns an acre deep. You've got your pack on your back and your rifle slung on your shoulder, and five days' rations, and a few hand grenades to cart along with you, and the slope ahead is a gradient of one in two—and it is your turn to carry the bren-gun, chum!

It is night and you're on patrol. For a week you've been moving through an uncharted forest, of trees a hundred feet high with long, trailing vines, in a green darkness where curious beasts and birds and insects live. The moon makes shadows on the walls of the trees. There is an eerie sharp crackle of the bamboo branches high above you in the windless night... what was that? Or the leaves falling softly like a footfall. You hear birds calling to one another. They might be Japs! Signalling to one another! There's a sudden mocking laugh. It is to provoke you to laugh. Be dead silent and don't move or a stream of bullets will whip through the trees. But if you are silent the Jap will try again, and he will betray his position.

And the jungle? It has its own strange beauty, but it is evil. It is a place of treachery, and, for those who don't know it, of terror. The Fourteenth Army soldiers had to beat the jungle before they beat the Japanese. Is the jungle the terrible, un-tameable, savage enemy that the legend says? No, it is just a bully relying on man's fear of the unknown. In this murky, shadowy war, if a soldier is brave, few even of his comrades see it. If he quits, perhaps nobody will see it. All then depends on the soldier himself, on his loyalty to his comrades, to his regiment, to the army. All depends on what each man feels in his own heart. Every soldier has to conquer himself, and this also has been done.

They are the masters of the jungle now. And anyone who crosses the broad Brahmaputra River and enters the territory of the Fourteenth Army will feel at once the sure, high, confident spirit of that great army. No braver, no finer, prouder or more devoted soldiers walk this earth. The Fourteenth Army will do their duty to the end, to the final battle, and with the last enemy.

. . . . .

In February, 1945, Winston Churchill, President Roosevelt and Marshal Stalin met for conference at Yalta in the Crimea. Agreement was reached about military plans for the final defeat of Germany. It was decided that the British, American, Russian and French forces would each occupy a separate zone of Germany. A Central Control Commission consisting of the supreme commanders of the four powers would have headquarters in Berlin.

"We are determined," said the communiqué, signed by the heads of the three Governments, "to disarm and disband all German armed forces; to break up for all time the German General Staff; remove or destroy all German military equipment; eliminate or control all German industry that could be used for military production; bring all war criminals to justice and swift punishment and exact reparation in kind."

The final defeat of Germany was drawing near. But where the Germans withdrew they left misery, poverty and starvation behind. Here are two descriptions from February, 1945; one from Greece, which was liberated in October, 1944, but afterwards torn by a bitter civil war; the other front Holland, largely still under German domination, and probably the country in Europe that suffered most under the Nazis in the final stage of the war. This description from Holland was written by the Editor of Radio Oranje, Louis de Jong.

LIFE IN GREECE

Kenneth Matthews, February 2 1945

There are two zones in Greece; and two propagandas. There is a city life and there is a mountain life. There are those who have lived for four years with

Germans because they had to; and there are those who scarcely saw a German all the time. As you might expect, the mountaineer is liable to call the city dweller a collaborationist. Or sometimes he uses another word—Greeks have some fine shadings in words of political abuse: he calls him an "Antidrastic." And of course, if your opponent is antidrastic you feel justified in being rather drastic in return.

It will take more than signatures on a document to get these two worlds together. If any single thing could do it, I would say it would be to rebuild the three hundred odd railway bridges which the Germans blew up behind them. People must travel and mix again. Ideas must circulate, for ideas are as important as food.

In and around Athens, life is creeping back to the standard it reached before the Civil War. But unemployment is still at a high figure. Although destitute persons receive basic food rations, these must be the lowest of any liberated capital in Europe. Athens is beginning to recover. But outside Athens it is a different story. I went into the mining town of Lavrion the other day behind the first British patrol. Lead and silver were mined here from early antiquity, but it is now a depressed area. Eighty-five people are at work in Lavrion's factories, while five thousand five hundred draw rations from the Red Cross, a third of whom are unable to pay even the nominal Red Cross prices. Bread, beans and boiled grasses are what keep the people of Lavrion alive.

The children stood in eager groups in doorways watching my car pass— desolate waifs most of them, bare-footed in a bitter north wind and with rags for clothes. Nobody has thought of children's shoes, but there are forty million garments on the programme for Greece this year, and that should make a difference in Lavrion.

The villages in farming areas are probably the best provided homes in Greece today; but other villages may be in the abyss of misery. Some are quite inaccessible. Red Cross teams are marching on foot, drawing sledges laden with supplies behind them, but still there are places they cannot reach. In E.L.A.S. territory the Red Cross is working where it can; but the British Army is precluded by the terms of the truce from taking supplies in. In short, the rescue of Greece has hardly begun. If food and work are the basis of society, then Greece is living on the bare bread of charity. Going about among people these last few days I have often thought of the curses which were sent to test the faithfulness of job.

Let me give you one example: let me tell you about the old chemist of Koropi. I first went to Koropi in October, just after a German reprisal squad had dusted the whole town with incendiary powder and sent it up in flames. I was the first Englishman to be seen there. Among the smoking ruins of people's homes I was cheered, smothered with flowers and kissed on both cheeks by the chemist, Lambrou, who carried me off to drink a toast at his shop, accompanied by practically all of the town's nine thousand inhabitants. When I left, old Mrs Lambrou pressed two pomegranates into my hands with the traditional Greek wish: "May your life be as full as these pomegranates."

I saw Koropi again yesterday. We happened to be passing through, two friends and myself, and we called in the chemist's shop. But we intruded on a tragedy. The house was full of mourners. The old wife was rocking herself to and fro on the bed lamenting as Greek women do with piercing cries of grief. The old man bowed over in a chair, tears running down his unshaven face. The only unconcerned person was their baby granddaughter, Antonia, smiling happily out of her cradle in a corner.

What had happened to these people who had seen their town burnt over their heads without losing heart? Their second son, Apostolis, had been murdered. He had been fighting beside the British Eighth Army in Italy, but he was not killed in battle: he was shot in the back by a friend from his own town. Apostolis had been assigned by the British to guard a camp of E.L.A.S. prisoners of whom this friend was one. His friend begged Apostolis to let him out; "You know I'm not a Communist," he said. So Apostolis let him go. Two days later his friend came back to thank him, and when Apostolis turned away after their conversation he shot him with a revolver. The whole scene took place on an RAF airfield and the murderer was arrested.

This is the last curse which has fallen upon Koropi—after being burnt down by the Germans to have her sons killing one another. This is vendetta—which had been all but stamped out of civilised Europe till the war came, blew on the smouldering embers and scattered them far and wide. You discover this thing as soon as you get anywhere beneath the surface of Greek social life. British officers are up against it in the mountain districts where people are threatened with death or worse if they help in billeting the homeless or distributing food. Reconstruction will not get very far till this problem has been radically settled. The Greeks themselves cannot explain it. They say it is "ungreek"; they blame foreign influences. I remember an eighteen-year-old girl who was standing twisting her handkerchief at one of those dreadful exhumation grounds outside Athens.

They had turned up the bodies of her father and brother there. Dry-eyed and stolid in her grief, she showed me their photographs. Then she fumbled for something else and brought out a dirty newspaper cutting. The newspaper said that these atrocities were the work of the Bulgarians. She was Greek to the core, that girl, she couldn't bear to think of the evils she saw there as being the work of her own fellow-countrymen.

And she was right in a sense. For the crimes of the Greek Civil War were hatched on that black day when Hitler started gang law in Europe and turned it to his own political use. They have nothing to do with the civilisation which we share with Greece, and which takes half its inspiration from the Parthenon.

NAZI POLICY IN OCCUPIED HOLLAND

Louis de Jong, Home Service, February, 1945

The other day a man came to see us in our London office, who had recently left Rotterdam. He told us about life in occupied Holland, about the hunger and the cold, about the shootings and the man-hunts, and about the underground papers that still come out and the resistance that is being kept up. He talked for hours, as all people talk who come from an occupied country. And as he talked it got dark. "I suppose," he said, "that a good many people over there are lying in bed. What else should they do? They can't sit on the floor all the evening."

"Why do they sit on the floor?" one of us asked. And the man replied, "They have burned all their furniture as fuel; the chairs and the tables and the covers. And in the houses of many working people the rooms are empty, just empty."

Since the autumn of last year there has been far more suffering in occupied Holland than ever. And there had been plenty of suffering before. More than twenty thousand of our best men had died in prisons and concentration camps. More than a hundred thousand of our Jewish citizens had been deported and gassed somewhere in Poland. People were undernourished. Children were walking on bare feet. Nearly half a million men and boys had been sent to German war factories. But compared to what has happened since the autumn of last year, all the years before were like a holiday.

You remember the allied airborne landings in the middle of September last year? The news of Monday, September 18, announced that the Dutch Government "after consultation with the Allied High Command deems that the moment has come to give the instruction for a general strike of all the railway workers." This announcement was broadcast to the people of Holland at a quarter to seven on Sunday evening, September 17. That same night the Dutch railways stopped. Not an engine was running, not a man was working. Every station, every railway office was deserted. The strike affected about thirty thousand people. It was nation-wide. It was total. The signalmen went on strike. So did the engineers. So did the directors. Occupied Europe had never seen anything like it. The Germans were hit very hard. If in that critical second half of September they could have made use of the Dutch railways for the transport of men and weapons, the Second Army might have been stuck at Nijmegen before the broad river Waal, and many of those who were able to return to our lines after that magnificent stand at Arnhem would be in German prisoner-of-war camps today. I suppose that if the Dutch railways had been kept in running order, many more German V-bombs would have fallen in southern England. But the Dutch railway strike has continued. It has continued now for five months. For five months, thirty-thousand railway men, who knew they would be shot if the Germans got hold of them, have been living in hiding, with their own families in other people's homes. They are still living there now.

Now what did the Germans do? The Germans have always been trying hard to pose as the friends of the Dutch. "The Dutch," they said, "are a nation of Germanic brothers." I suppose for that reason we in Holland got a German civil administration which was far more total and far more inquisitive, which made life far more difficult, than the German military administration in France and Belgium. Right from the beginning there has been much resistance in Holland: material resistance, sabotage and the blowing up of factories and railways; and spiritual resistance on the part of the churches, the schools, the universities, the medical profession, and that splendid Dutch underground press. But the railway strike was different. Then the Germans realised that they had lost the game, definitely lost it. And their professed love for Holland turned into a very ugly hate. They had been thrown out of France and thrown out of Belgium. They took their revenge on Holland.

First of all they started a campaign of destruction and looting, which is hard to beat for its scope and methods. The big ports of Rotterdam and Amsterdam were largely destroyed. Most of the factories were closed; their machinery was, as the Germans put it, "exported to Germany." Every office was looted till there was not a typewriter left. All this, of course, was done in the interest of the defence of Europe against bolshevism. The highest German authority in Holland, the Reich Commissar, Dr Arthur Seyss-Inquart, said a few weeks ago: "If people in Germany need sewing machines, and if there are sewing machines in Holland, we take them." And they took them. There are very few sewing, machines, very few prams and very few bicycles left in Holland today. They have all been exported. Some German soldiers have even been seen exporting their exports on flat doors with roller skates under them. Next the Germans increased the areas of inundations. Perhaps a quarter of the total arable part of Holland is under water today, much of it salt water. You can imagine what this means in lost houses, lost crops, lost cattle—and lost happiness.

In the third place the Germans started to deport all our men between seventeen and forty years old. Terrible man-hunts were organised in all the towns, big and small. One day in November the Germans arrested fifty thousand men in Rotterdam. Most of them were forced to walk to Utrecht, a distance of forty miles, without food and without sleep. They left Rotterdam on a Saturday afternoon; they arrived in Utrecht on Sunday evening. I have talked to a man who saw them arrive. They dragged themselves along the streets, deadly pale, completely exhausted. Those who had dropped by the roadside were carried in wheelbarrows, one on top of the other. These man-hunts, of course, forced the Germans to use quite a number of police and army troops. So at Christmas they issued a decree which ordered all our men between seventeen and forty to report at the Labour Offices. By Christmastime there was famine in western Holland. People were living on one or two slices of bread and a few potatoes a day. It was freezing and there was no fuel, no gas, no electricity, no coal. The Germans sent loudspeaker cars through the streets announcing that those who did report for work in Germany would be decently treated. They would get a warm meal in a warm room—after reporting. Ninety per cent refused. I told you there was famine in western Holland. You may ask who was responsible for it. The Germans said the railway strikers were. They did not say that only a very small part of the food used to be carried to the towns by means of the railways. Most of it came in barges and in trucks. After the railway strike started, however, the Germans stole most of the remaining food stocks, they confiscated all trucks and most of the barges. All that was part of a deliberate policy of mass starvation. It is the deliberate policy of the Germans to starve the Dutch nation to death or to surrender. The result has been that in the weeks gone by, hundreds of thousands of people in western Holland, where three-and-a-half million people are living, have been leaving the towns and roaming the country, desperately looking for food.

One of our underground papers, *Het Parool*, wrote, "There is an unending stream of people, old men, women and even children, who for days, sometimes even for weeks, wander around. Many of them have already met death by the roadside as a result of their exhaustion and hunger. Countless numbers do not complete a journey, they turn back halfway, they are ill, with empty hands. In the evening, the wanderers, who are tired and cold, and generally without a dry thread to their bodies, must find some sort of accommodation for the night, in the villages, in an empty school or in the straw at some farmer's place. Then off again next morning over the wet and muddy roads and few reach their homes again without reverses and accidents."

The Dutch resistance movement recently declared to the world that we are not asking for pity because we know what we are fighting for. But we cry out to the free world: a people of ancient culture is threatened with extinction by Hitler's barbarians. Let the free nations raise their voices so that every German who has not lost his reason may pause to think, and the others may abandon their devilish aim for fear of retribution. We in occupied Holland stand fast.

. . . . .

Late in March the British forces crossed the Rhine; the Americans followed after with a break-through of powerful armoured forces into the heart of Germany, while the Russians struck, first on the Danube and then against Berlin.

The co-ordination of the attacks closely followed the military agreements of the Crimea Conference. But one of the three great Allied leaders did not live to see the final victory. Franklin Roosevelt died on 12 April.

Germany was near its end. Like an enormous tree it had overshadowed all smaller growths around it, and its fall showed how rotten it had been.

Here is an account of one of the German concentration camps which was liberated by the advancing Allied armies.

BUCHENWALD CONCENTRATION CAMP

Edward Murrow, Home Service, April, 1945

I propose to tell you of Buchenwald. It is on a small hill about four miles outside Weimar. It was one of the largest concentration camps in Germany, and it was built to last. As we approached it we saw about a hundred men in civilian clothes, with rifles, advancing in open order across a field. There were a few shots; we stopped to enquire. We were told that some of the prisoners had a couple of S.S. men cornered in there. We drove on. We reached the main gate. The prisoners crowded up behind the wire. We entered.

And now let me tell this in the first person, for I was the least important person there, as you shall hear. There surged around me an evil-smelling horde, men and boys reached out to touch me. They were in rags and the remnants of uniform. Death had already marked many of them, but they were smiling with their eyes. I looked out over that mass of men to the green fields beyond where well-fed Germans were ploughing. A German, Fritz Kersheimer, came up and said: "May I show you round the camp? I've been here ten years." An Englishman stood to attention saying: "May I introduce myself? Delighted to see you, and can you tell me when some of our blokes will be along?" I told him "soon," and asked to see one of the barracks. It happened to be occupied by the Czechoslovakians. When I entered men crowded round; tried to lift me to their shoulders. They were too weak; many of them could not get out of bed. I was told that this building had once stabled eighty horses; there were twelve hundred men in it, five to a bunk. The stink was beyond all description.

When I reached the centre of the barracks a man came up and said: "You remember me. I'm Peter Zenkl, one-time Mayor of Prague." I remembered him, but did *not* recognise him. He asked about Benes and Jan Masaryk. I asked how many men had died in that building during the last month. They called the doctor; we inspected his record. There were only names in the little black book, nothing more. Nothing of who these men were, what they had done, or hoped. Beside the names of those who had died there was a cross. I counted them; they totalled two hundred and forty-two. Two hundred and forty-two out of twelve hundred in one month. As I walked down to the end of the barracks there was applause from the men too weak to get out of bed. It sounded like the hand-clapping of babies; they were so weak. The doctor's name was Paul Heller; he had been there since 1938. As we walked out into the courtyard a man fell dead. Two others—they must have been over sixty—were crawling towards the latrine. I saw it, but will not describe it.

In another part of the camp they showed me the children, hundreds of them; some were only six. One rolled up his sleeve and showed me his number: it was tattooed on his arm. B.6030 it was. The others showed me their numbers; they will carry them till they die. An elderly man standing beside me said:

"The children—enemies—of the State." I could see their ribs through their thin shirts. The old man said: "I am Professor Charles Richer of the Sorbonne." The children clung to my hands and stared. We crossed to the courtyard. Men kept coming up to speak to me and to touch me: professors from Poland, doctors from Vienna; men from all over Europe.

We went to the hospital. It was full. The doctor told me that two hundred had died the day before. I asked the cause of death. He shrugged and said: "Tuberculosis, starvation, fatigue, and there are many who have no desire to live. It is very difficult." Doctor Heller pulled back the blankets from a man's feet to show me how swollen they were. The man was dead. Most of the patients could not move. As we left the hospital I drew out a leather bill-fold, hoping that I had some money which would help those who lived to get home. Professor Richer from the Sorbonne said: " I should be careful of my wallet if I were you. You know there are criminals in this camp, too." A small man tottered up saying: "May I feel the leather, please? You see, I used to make good things of leather in Vienna." Another man said: "My name is Walther Roeder. For many years I lived in Joliette. Came back to Germany for a visit and Hitler grabbed me."

I asked to see the kitchen: it was clean. The German in charge had been a Communist, had been at Buchenwald for nine years, had a picture of his daughter in Hamburg—hadn't seen her for almost twelve years; and if I got to Hamburg would I look her up? He showed me the daily ration—one piece of brown bread about as thick as your thumb, on top of it a piece of margarine as big as three sticks of chewing-gum. That, and a little stew, was what they received every twenty-four hours. He had a chart on the wall; very complicated it was. There were little red tabs scattered through it. He said that was to indicate each ten men who died. He had to account for the rations and he added: "We are very efficient here."

We went again into the courtyard, and as we walked we talked. The two doctors, the Frenchman and the Czech, agreed that about six thousand had died during March. Kersheimer, the German, added that back in the winter of 1939 when the Poles had begun to arrive without winter clothing, they died at the rate of approximately nine hundred a day. Five different men asserted that Buchenwald was the best concentration camp in Germany; they had some experience of the others.

Dr Heller, the Czech, asked me if I would care to see the crematorium. He said it would not be very interesting because the Germans had run out of coke some days ago and had taken to dumping the bodies into a great hole nearby. Professor Richer said perhaps I would care to see the small courtyard? I said: "Yes." He turned and told the children to stay behind. As we walked across the square I noticed that the Professor had a hole in his left shoe and a toe sticking out of the right one. He followed my eyes and said: "I regret that I am so little presentable, but what can we do?" At that point another Frenchman came up to announce that three of his fellow-countrymen outside had killed three S.S. men and taken one prisoner. We proceeded to the small courtyard. The wall was about eight feet high; it adjoined what had been a stable or garage. We entered. It was floored with concrete. There were two rows of bodies stacked up like cordwood. They were thin and very white. Some of these bodies were terribly bruised, though there seemed to be little flesh to bruise. Some had been shot through the head, but they bled but little. All except two were naked. I tried to count them as best I could, and arrived at the conclusion that all that was mortal of more than five hundred men and boys lay there in two neat piles.

There was a German trailer which must have contained another fifty, but it was not possible to count them. The clothing was piled in a heap against the wall. It appeared that most of the men and boys had died of starvation; they had not been executed. But the manner of death seemed unimportant. Murder had been done at Buchenwald. God alone knows how many men and boys have died there during the last twelve years. On Thursday I was told that there were more than twenty thousand in the camp. There had been as many as sixty thousand. Where are they now? As I left that camp a Frenchman, who used to work for Havas in Paris, came up to me and said: "You will write something about this perhaps?" And he added: "To write about this you must have been here at least two years—and after that you don't want to write any more."

. . . . .

On 25 April 1945 the American and Russian armies met at Torgau on the Elbe. The BBC correspondent, Frank Gillard, described the visit made by the American General Bradley, Commander of the 12th Army Group, to Marshal Koniev after the link-up.

THE LINK-UP OF THE AMERICAN AND RUSSIAN ARMIES

European Service, April, 1945

We drove first along roads guarded by American troops, then into a village occupied by both Americans and Russians, and then on eastward deep into the territory held by the Russians. The Russian troops were gathered in large groups in the villages and hamlets, and they came running out of the woods and the lonely wayside cottages to see our column pass. They saluted, they grinned, and they waved and very often they cheered. At each crossroad the crowd was held back by a stalwart-looking girl military policeman, with rifle slung across her shoulders, who directed the traffic.

The Red flags were flying in the villages, often clusters of flags, the Red Flag, the Union Jack and the Old Glory. Here and there were large red banners with gold lettering reading in Russian: "Long live the Russian, American and British Military Alliance."

Everywhere along the roads we kept running into columns of motorcycles and sidecars. A motor cycle and sidecar seems to be the jeep of the Red Army, and, I may add, the way the Russians load them up they carry just as many people. The Russian motor transport reminded me very much of the 8th Army's transport at the end of the North African campaign after it had been driven 2,000 miles across the Western Desert. It looked, in fact, rather ancient and rather worn-out. We saw a certain number of American six-wheeled trucks and these still looked good, but for the rest, it was an odd collection of vehicles, Russian, some German, very many German, large numbers of them obviously picked up on the way during the long journey from Russia. It's not to be expected that the Russian Army should be as highly mechanised as our own; all the more credit to the Red soldiers for their great victories.

Marshal Koniev's headquarters was at a pleasant country house. Three enormous rooms on the first floor of the house, opening one into the other, had been laid out for a banquet, at the end of which toasts were drunk. Toasts from the high table where Marshal Koniev, a pleasant smiling chairman, sat with General Bradley and their respective staffs, and toasts at the individual tables to fill in the interval. The Russians praised the Americans and the British in high terms and General Bradley spoke equally warmly of the Russians. Each side lauded the other's military achievements; they drank to continued co-operation and lasting friendship. The Russians thought of everybody's comfort, and, of course, our drivers, who had a banquet all to themselves, and were waited on by Russian officers.

During the afternoon the two Commanders had a private conversation on future developments, and they exchanged gifts. Bradley gave Koniev a jeep, a 12th Army Group Standard and an American Carbine. Koniev presented Bradley with a fine horse and a Russian revolver. On the lower level, too, there was much swopping of souvenirs and giving of keepsakes and mementoes; yes, it was a grand occasion.

. . . . .

The last great battle of the war was fought in the ruins of Berlin, finally conquered by the Red Army. On 1 May the German radio announced the death of Hitler and added that Admiral Doenitz had been appointed as his successor. A few days later the German army had ceased to exist.

CHAPTER X

Victory

May—August, 1945

Germany's unconditional surrender was made in four stages. The surrender of the German Southern Army of a million men to Field-Marshal Alexander was signed at Caserta on April 29, 1945 (to take place from 2 May).

Next, all German forces in North-West Germany, Holland and Denmark surrendered on 4 May to Field-Marshal Montgomery at Luneburg Heath.

The final complete and unconditional surrender of Germany to Britain, Russia and the United States was signed at Reims on 7 May 1945, and was ratified in Berlin on the following day.

A BBC correspondent gave a description of the surrender to Field-Marshal Montgomery on 4 May.

GERMAN SURRENDER

Chester Wilmot, Home Service, May 4 1945

This afternoon at six-thirty, British Double Summer Time, at Field-Marshal Montgomery's Tactical Headquarters, German plenipotentiaries signed the document which will end war in Europe for the 21st Army Group at eight o'clock tomorrow morning. The Germans agreed to surrender unconditionally all the forces in Holland, in north-west Germany, including the islands off the coast, in Schleswig-Holstein and Denmark and all the ships in these areas. That means the surrender of all the Germans facing the 2nd British Army and the 1st Canadian Army—the surrender of at least a million troops. The formal act of surrender was carried out in a tent at Montgomery's headquarters on a wooded hill near the Elbe. In this tent Field-Marshal Montgomery and the German plenipotentiaries sat at two tables covered with ordinary grey army blankets. After Field-Marshal Montgomery had read out the detailed terms of surrender, the Germans signed in turn. First, the Commander-in-Chief of the German Navy, General-Admiral Von Friedeburg, then General Kinsel, Chief of

The surrender to Field-Marshal Montgomery.

Staff to Field-Marshal Busch, who is Commander-in-Chief, North-West, put his signature on the deed and three lesser representatives followed.

The German representatives originally came to Montgomery's headquarters yesterday, but then they were not empowered to surrender unconditionally. They offered at first to surrender on behalf of Field-Marshal Busch, the armies on Montgomery's right. That is the armies that were being driven back into our lines by the Russian advance. Montgomery's reply was short and to the point. "Those armies are fighting the Russians," he said, "they must surrender to the Red Army and not to me." Montgomery then asked the Germans if they would surrender all the forces on his left flank—in Holland, Denmark and north-west Germany. The Germans replied that they had no power to do so. They were then asked if they knew the real battle situation and they were shown a map which revealed to them for the first time the full extent of our break-through to the Baltic. When the chief of their delegation, Admiral Von Friedeburg, saw it, he broke down and wept. It was quite clear that he had had no idea how bad the situation was.

When the Germans had digested the position, Field-Marshal Montgomery said to them that if they wanted to surrender at all, they must surrender unconditionally. Only after they'd done this, would he discuss details of occupation and the feeding of civilians. Otherwise, he said to them, he would carry on his attack without respite. Von Friedeburg then said that he would go back and see Busch and return today with the answer. He left with one staff officer and Busch's chief of staff and the other staff officer remained at Montgomery's headquarters as guarantor of good faith. Today Von Friedeburg came back with full power to surrender unconditionally. His preliminary conversation with Field-Marshal Montgomery this afternoon lasted only five and a half minutes. Then he walked over to the tent where the instrument of surrender was signed. Another five minutes and the deed was done.

The last capital in Europe to be liberated from the Germans was Prague.

THE LIBERATION OF PRAGUE

V. Duckworth-Barker, European Service, May, 1945

It is fitting that the end of the European war should be associated with Prague, which was the stage on which the curtain-raiser to the international tragedy was presented. Never in modern times has the name of Prague been on so many lips as during the ominous negotiations at Munich and the still more ominous march in by Hitler in the spring of 1939.

Prague has endured the presence of the Germans longer than any other Allied capital. It has known more than six years of humiliation and suffering. They are years which will recall to many the struggle of the last war and their culmination in Masaryk's triumph. Many who welcome President Benes on his return after a second period of exile will remember the little, scholarly, white-bearded figure of Masaryk riding past his beloved fellow-countrymen in December, 1918. Masaryk and Benes together had made possible the creation of a genuinely independent State, backed by the goodwill of the Western Allies. For 20 years, Czechoslovakia was to be an island of enlightened democracy in the Central European area. By bold and quite independent political thinking, Masaryk went a long way towards restoring to his people the glory they once achieved under the Bohemian kings. The epithet Golden, so often applied to Prague, was not an idle one. Amidst fascinating historical monuments like the Hradcany Palace, the University, for long the greatest in Central Europe, and the wonderful 600 year old bridge across the Vltava, the citizens set out to win for their ancient city a place of honour in new spheres.

It is too early to say what differences there will be between Masaryk's Czechoslovakia and the new one which will emerge from the collapse of the Third Reich. Present indications are that the Soviet Union, with which President Benes has signed a very close treaty of alliance, will have a considerable influence on the rebuilding of Czechoslovak institutions. If French political thought was to some extent behind the first emergence of Czechoslovakia, the characteristic Russian ideology seems destined to play an important part in the second.

The liberation of Prague means that both a city with a magnificent spiritual record and a profoundly democratic people have emerged from the darkness.

. . . . .

Field Marshal Wilhelm Keitel signing the ratified surrender terms for the German military in Berlin, 8 May 1945. Although the military had surrendered earlier, Stalin demanded this further document.

On 8 May Churchill announced the end of the war in Europe to the British people.

CHURCHILL'S ANNOUNCEMENT OF END OF WAR IN EUROPE

Home Service, May 8 1945

Yesterday morning at 2.41 a.m., at General Eisenhower's headquarters, General Jodl, the representative of the German High Command, and Grand Admiral Doenitz, the designated head of the German State, signed the act of unconditional surrender of all German land, sea, and air forces in Europe to the Allied Expeditionary Force, and simultaneously to the Soviet High Command.

General Bedell Smith, Chief of Staff of the Allied Expeditionary Army, and General Francois Sevez, signed the document on behalf of the Supreme Commander of the Allied Expeditionary Force, and General Suslapatov signed on behalf of the Russian High Command.

Today this agreement will be ratified and confirmed at Berlin, where Air Chief Marshal Tedder, Deputy Supreme Commander of the Allied Expeditionary Force,

Winston Churchill on the balcony of the Ministry of Health in Whitehall, 8 May 1945.

and General de Lattre de Tassigny will sign on behalf of General Eisenhower. Marshal Zhukov will sign on behalf of the Soviet High Command.

The German representatives will be Field-Marshall Keitel, Chief of the High Command, and the Commanders-in-Chief of the German Army, Navy, and Air Forces. Hostilities will end officially at one minute after midnight tonight, Tuesday, May 8 ...

The German war is therefore at an end.

. . . . .

The scene of surrender in Berlin was described by the well-known Canadian war correspondent, Matthew Halton.

GERMAN UNCONDITIONAL SURRENDER IN BERLIN

Matthew Halton, European Service, May 9 1945

In Berlin, at ten minutes past twelve midnight this morning, Air Chief Marshal Sir Arthur Tedder, Deputy Supreme Commander of the Allied Expeditionary Force rose from his seat beside Marshal Keitel, the German delegate. "Have you received the document of unconditional surrender?" he asked. "Are you prepared to sign it and execute its provisions?" Keitel, the Junker of Junkers, fixed his monocle in his left eye. He held up the document impatiently to show he'd received it and he said, "Yes, it's in order. I am prepared to sign." At fifteen minutes past twelve Keitel took the glove off his right hand and signed the document which ratified the unconditional surrender of the German power already given at Reims twenty-three hours before. And this time it was in the ruins of Berlin.

Perhaps it's because some of we observers of these solemn events have hardly slept a wink in three days and three nights, that we feel bemused and as in a dream. But really, is all this true? We were in Berlin. We had heard "God Save the King" played on the Tempelhof aerodrome. We'd seen the fourth largest city in the world in utter ruin—ruin too appalling and frightening to gloat over. With the fires still burning and the smoke pall hanging over the dead city; and the few wretched German civilians sitting, like scarecrows in their heaps of rubble, to watch the American, British and Russian flags go by.

We had been at Alamein and Stalingrad; and now in Berlin we heard on the radio the voice of Winston Churchill saying the German war was over. There were no more than twenty-five of us in the four Dakota aircraft which carried the Allied delegation to Berlin. We left Reims early on Tuesday morning: we landed at Stendal aerodrome on the west bank of the Elbe to wait for the German delegation coming from Flensburg on the Danish-German frontier. And for the Russian fighter aircraft which were to escort us to Berlin. The Germans arrived first. Then there was a roaring in the sky. And the Russian fighter escort arrived and we took off for Berlin.

For 20 minutes we watched the Red Star fighters dipping, soaring and circling. And we strained our eyes for Berlin. Many thousands of British and American aircraft had come this way during the last five years, running into a tempest of steel that has cost us many of our finest lives. And now, we came in luxuriously-equipped passenger planes, in perfect safety, to watch the last scene in the long ghastly drama of the war.

The RAF and the RCAF have dropped a total of 45,000 tons of bombs on Berlin; and the American Air Forces have dropped about 20,000. Now, we saw the result, and what we saw is the most staggering sight in the world.

As we flew over the wooded lake lands west of Berlin I recognised the great Olympic Stadium. But I recognised nothing else. Even from the air we could see that Berlin was gone. Air ChiefMarshal Tedder was received on Tempelhof aerodrome by General Malinin, Zhukov's Chief of Staff. The flags of Britain, Russia and the United States held by three Russian officers, floated infront of the guard of honour. There was a silence for a few seconds. The band struck up; and there on Tempelhof aerodrome we heard the strains of "God Save the King." It was followed by "The Star Spangled Banner," and then the Russian National Anthem. The Guard of Honour, consisting of three companies of

Russian Guards, marched past Tedder and his delegation in magnificent if melodramatic style.

Field-Marshal Keitel, Admiral Von Friedeburg and their aides watched a scene that was unforgettable for us and doom for them and the things they stood for.

A procession of 40 cars now left Tempelhof for Marshal Zhukov's headquarters.

We drove north, towards the heart of Berlin. We saw the fourth city of the world in such complete and overwhelming ruin that I really doubt that it can ever be rebuilt. Multiply by five hundred times the obliterated sections of London's East End, or the area around St. Paul's, as they were the morning after they were destroyed, still burning and smoking with nothing but jagged edges of brick and stone against the lurid sky, and you have Berlin.

The eight-mile route to Zhukov's headquarters in the suburb of Karlshorst was lined by Red Army Guards and by Russian women soldiers. One of these handsome radiant women stood at each corner with signal flags. We passed buildings still burning, and a number of German "Tiger" tanks, and several Russian tanks wrecked in the ferocious 11-day battle in the streets of Berlin.

To see Berlin you know at once that the last stand of the Nazis in their capital was a suicidal and mystic frenzy. There was nothing here to fight for but chaos and the body of Goebbels.

I shall long remember the German civilians; old men, children and women whom we passed on the way; a few did lift their heads in interest when they saw the British and American flags with the Russian. But most of them were indifferent scarecrows.

We reached the end of our journey, and Marshal Zhukov came out of his headquarters to greet Air Chief-Marshal Tedder, Deputy Supreme Commander of the A.E.F.

On one hand Tedder—that strong and brilliant but charming and unpretentious figure in the blue uniform of the RAF; it was fitting that an officer in that uniform should be in Berlin at this hour; and on the other hand, Marshal Zhukov, one of the greatest soldiers of the world; to look at, here was no flashing Napoleonic figure. Zhukov is thickset with a large head and strong heavy features. Except for his uniform he looked more a politician than a soldier, yet this man has proved himself one of the most bold and imaginative captains of history. Now, in a schoolhouse in Berlin, the largest city ever to be taken by storm, he received the Western Allies and sat down with them to take the unconditional surrender of Germany.

Today I heard from a man, who certainly should know, an estimate of what it cost the Russians to reach the end, and come to this triumph in Berlin. Between twelve and fifteen million dead at least; of whom about half were soldiers and half civilians. There were times, said a Russian general, when we had to lose half-a-million men at a time to save the Army itself; to keep the Army in being.

Marshal Zhukov was the master of ceremonies at the banquet which marked the victory and the end. The banqueting and the toasts went on all night; in one of his many speeches the Marshal said: "Our ally Great Britain has suffered much and fought gallantly. During that fight she has produced some famous war leaders. I lift my glass now to the great Air Marshal Tedder, aide to the great General Eisenhower. Look round Berlin and you'll agree with me that the Germans will remember for a long time his technical and operational skill. Let's drink to him and to continued success for the British nation. And to the continuing friendship between Great Britain and the Soviet Union. That friendship is necessary for the future of mankind"; Marshal Zhukov said that with warmth and with the most evident sincerity. All round us, in a hundred square miles of utter and appalling ruin, was the warning that friendship between East and West was no luxury but the bare necessity for the continued life of civilisation.

. . . . .

General Dwight D.
Eisenhower with
Winston Churchill.

At the end of the war three striking surveys of the British war effort were given in the Home Service of the BBC. One was a picture of the results of the RAF and USAAF bombing offensive against Germany, the second about the achievements of the British worker and the third a talk on the battle of the Atlantic.

THE RESULTS OF THE ALLIED BOMBING OFFENSIVE

Wing-Commander John Strachey, Home Service, May 9 1945

I want to give you a report on what some of our main objectives in Germany look like today. Within a minute or so of flying over the German frontier you see Cologne. I cannot hope to convey to you the impact of that first sight of a ruined city. We had flown out over London and looked carefully at the patches of bomb damage as we passed; but the moment we saw Cologne we realised that we had never yet seen devastation. One's first sight is of the six long bridges. all down-some destroyed by bombing, others destroyed by the retreating Germans, with the Rhine washing white in foam against the wreckage. As the aircraft drops lower you see that the bombs have ploughed into the railway centres and cut the lines as well as crashed through the factory roofs. And then there is nothing but acre after acre of roofless, gutted, crumbled buildings, passing slowly under you as the aircraft circles.

Next, Krupps was beneath us. One by one the great square workshops of Europe's largest munition plant went by. Not one had its roof on and in many the walls had crumbled down upon the rows of machine tools Over the expanse of dull red rust of these ruined plants, there shone and glittered little points of light. I think it was the shattered glass thrown about like confetti by the bomb-bursts. We flew on up the Ruhr, that valley which rang and trembled with flak barrage and the bomb-bursts. Now it lay silent and dead in the sunshine. We passed the places where the two Gelsenkirchen oil plants had stood, and then the shell of Dortmund. We turned left along the broad thread of the Dort-mund-Ems Canal. After a few miles the canal ran dry and empty, and then the neat, clear outline of the embankment, which carried the water some twenty feet above the surrounding country at this point, was abruptly swallowed up into what looked like a morass. The yellow subsoil had been spread over the countryside, covering an area of perhaps a square mile. Four violent attacks on this one point had obliterated one of the greatest of the inland waterways of Europe.

How well I remember the time when we first began to consider the problem of how to cut the water and rail communications of the Ruhr; of how to breach the Dortmund-Ems Canal and break the massive spans of the Bielefeld railway viaduct. Neither the techniques of bombing nor all the appropriate weapons were then in existence. The four-track trunk railway crosses the valley at Bielefeld on two long viaducts, several yards apart. Two-thirds of the way across the valley seven piers are now missing from each of the viaducts. They are neither damaged nor broken. They have simply gone. The railway tracks droop and sag over the gaps, like iron hammocks slung between the remaining piers. What happened was that in one of the attacks, a special squadron of Bomber Command put one of the new ten-ton deep penetration bombs exactly between the two viaducts. The bomb drove deep into the earth, as it was designed to do, and uprooted the piers of both viaducts. The ten-ton bomb is a weapon the uses of which are only beginning to be explored.

From Bielefeld we flew on east past devastated Hanover and Brunswick, and then turned south for Cassel. Of Cassel and its industries, one can only say simply that they have been destroyed. I saw some houses which were habitable in the suburbs, but in the city proper I did not see one in which people could live, at any rate above-ground. But people are living there, no doubt in cellars, for one sees them in the streets. Moreover, I must report a remarkable fact about these people. Amidst these heaps of rubble they appear neat, well-dressed and healthy. It is true they are mostly women, young children and old men, but they do not look in the least like the shattered or ragged survivors of a catastrophe. The bomber offensive was not, of course, designed to kill or wound civilians but to destroy the enemy's centres of production; at Cassel it certainly did that.

Next morning we set course north-east for Leuna. After about an hour's flying, the biggest industrial plant I have ever seen in my life loomed up under our port wing. As we circled Leuna, nearly three miles long by a mile wide, with the labour camp built beside it so that thousands of workers could be rushed in to repair after every bombing, we realised that what we were looking at was one of the main battlefields of this war. Leuna lies hundreds of miles from the Normandy beaches, the Siegfried Line or the Eastern Front. Nevertheless, this was the scene of one of the great victories of the Allies in this war.

We looked down on this new kind of battlefield, and saw the debris of battle-wrecks of our own aircraft which had been shot down, as well as shattered chimneys and gas-holders. For the advantage in this battle of Leuna had swayed first one way and then another: it had not swayed backwards and forwards as a land battle does, but rather up and down, for this was a ground to air battle on the vertical plane; the defence and the repair squads on the ground now gaining the advantage, then the attacking bombers coming down from above to inflict another wound. Do not let us forget these air battlefields of the Second World War—Cassel, Leuna, Yolitz, Brux, Hamburg, the Ruhr and Berlin. Here the air crews fought savage battles to shatter the main supports on which the structure of German war economy rested. As, one by one, those supports were shattered, the German war effort sagged and drooped, much as I saw the railway lines sag and droop over the gap in the Bielefeld viaduct. It was thus that the Allied armies were able to win their magnificent and indispensable victories without suffering the terrible casualties of the last war.

From Leuna we began to fly back south-west towards the cities of the Upper Rhineland. But on the way we found something for which we were not looking—we found a hollow hill. It was a short, steep ridge or hill—a hogsback, as we should call it in this country. But there was something peculiar about this hill. Even at first glance we saw that the top of it had been sliced off to make a runway for the take-off of aircraft. We went down to investigate: —we saw workings all round the hill. Shafts ran into it at half-a-dozen points. There was no doubt about it. The hill was hollow. Inside, the Germans had been building one of their new underground aircraft plants. Rocket or jet fighters were no doubt to be assembled in that hill, raised on lifts to the runway and flown off the top. Some of these underground plants were already working this spring. One of our party had the opportunity of examining perhaps the largest of them, a place called Niedersachswerfen. Here, twenty thousand foreign slave workers, driven by five hundred German foremen, were only last month turning out V2 rockets in the underground galleries. Now the slave workers are camping in the huge tail sections of the rockets while they wait till they can get back to their homes. Such is the crack-up of the final Nazi plan to win the war by fantastic new weapons. It brought home to us all that the devastation done by our bombers, far from being too much, might well have been too little and too late had we slackened or paused in our air attack for a single week.

Frankfurt, Darmstadt, Pforzheim, Stuttgart, Karlsruhe, Saarbruecken were merely further examples of devastation in varying degrees of completeness. The destruction of the industrial area at Bremen is a completed job. One section of Hamburg, lying away from the docks and factories, is relatively undamaged, but all the rest has gone.

From Kiel we set course for home: but we had one more call to pay. We crossed Holland, and below us lay the countryside on which the Dutch cities depend for food, sodden and flooded by the dykes which the Germans had broken. Our pilot was a Dutchman, one of the highly-skilled men of the KLM Air Lines, who have flown with us throughout the war. We were passing over Amsterdam, looking down with relief on an undamaged city, when once again, and this time unexpectedly, we felt the aircraft losing height and beginning to circle. We passed low over a house on the outskirts of the city, turned, passed over it again, a third time, and then a fourth time. On that fourth circuit a woman and boy ran out of the door of the house; it was the pilot's wife and son whom he had not seen for five years. Worse, he had not had any word from them since last November; and that meant that he did not even know what had happened to them in these last months of famine which the Dutch people suffered under the German occupation.

If all the ruins we had seen had made any one of us feel that our bombing of Germany had been too ruthless, that incident at Amsterdam would have served to remind us why we had to destroy Nazi Germany. It would have been an unpardonable crime to withhold a single bomb, the bursting of which on Germany could shorten the Nazi tyranny over Europe by an hour. The punishment which fell upon the German people was severe indeed, but that punishment was inflicted, inevitably but incidentally, in the course of the combined bomber offensive. In the words of the Prime Minister's message to Sir Arthur Harris, the purpose of that offensive was, to make "a decisive contribution to Germany's final defeat." And that purpose was accomplished.

· · · · ·

THE BRITISH WORKER

Wilfred Pickles, European Service, May, 1945

Behind the story of every one of the battles that mark the long and uphill struggle from Dunkirk to the capitulation of the German armed forces lies another story—the story of five years of strenuous effort, of courage and self-sacrifice on the part of the workers of Britain's bombed and blacked-out factories who produced the weapons that outfought the enemy, of her railway and dock and road transport workers who saw them through to their destinations, of the men and women on the farms who grew the food that fed their fellows and released the ships to bring first the raw materials and finally the troops and war material from our Allies overseas, with whose massive aid we finished the job.

The real effort of all these workers began seriously in 1940, when the whole nation, with its 45 millions of population to set against Hitler's 80 millions, settled down in the beleaguered fortress of Great Britain, in the island that was to be, at the same time, battlefield, arsenal and offensive base, to the job of staving off defeat and going on, alone if need be, to beat the enemy. The first task was mobilisation of manpower. A few days after Mr Churchill took office, while the Deputy Prime Minister was introducing the Emergency Power Act, the Minister of Labour was explaining the Act to employers and Trade Unions, who immediately agreed to relax their rules in order to bring millions of unskilled men into the depleted and inadequate ranks of their skilled workers. And then the great drive began. Thousands of engineering workers, at their own urgent request, worked a 74-hour week for months on end—and with the rest of the country working only a little less hard, they kept it up through the heat of that 1940 summer in factories blacked-out by day and night, under air-raids and in bomb-damaged buildings and towns, until the worst of the immediate crisis was past. By then, many new factories were built or building and workers had been found and trained to man them. Whole industries were closed down, or nearly so, and their staff and premises turned over to war work. Millions of men and women were sent to new jobs and new homes or to part-time work nearer home and 3½ millions were added to the country's total labour force. There are 33 million people in Great Britain between the ages of 14 and 65. Of these, 23 million—nearly 70 per cent—were either in the Forces or in industry in whole or part-time work by the middle of 1943, and a year later the figure had risen still further. Among women alone, the total number employed in industry reached nearly eight millions—of whom nearly three millions were married—while at least another million were doing voluntary work—this, of course, in addition to the half a million odd in the Forces and Civil Defence Services. All this vast mobilisation on a scale never imagined by the Nazis even in their wildest totalitarian dreams was achieved with a minimum of friction, and with the active co-operation of the workers themselves, both as individuals and through their Trade Unions. The same active co-operation was forthcoming within the factories, where thousands of ingenious inventions submitted by workers through their joint production committees helped to increase or to speed up or to cheapen production.

By the middle of last year, Britain's enormous and highly organised labour force had tremendous achievements to its credit. It had produced over 100,000 aircraft (of which over 10,000 were heavy bombers), nearly 6,000 naval vessels (including 700 of major size), nearly four million machine—or sub-machine—guns, over two million rifles, 25,000 tanks, nearly a million other service vehicles, about 35,000 ground artillery equipments, 50,000 naval guns, 900,000 sea-mines and depth charges, over 20,000 torpedoes, besides hundreds of millions of shells, thousands of millions of cartridges and engineers' stores, signal equipment, and army clothing in astronomic quantities. While all this was going on the necessary minimum of civilian production had continued, our shipyard workers had built nearly five million gross tons of shipping and our diminished agricultural labour force had increased its production of essential foodstuffs by more than 70 per cent.

These are just a few of the figures. What they all amount to is this: that in war-time conditions, with over six million men and women in the Forces, with a monotonous diet and reduced leisure, with rations and queues and coupons and shortages of every kind of household article, with all the demands of home defence and civil defence to be satisfied, British workers have reached a level of production per head of population greater than that of any other country at any time.

We have not forgotten the achievements, either of our Allies or of our enemies, but we have not forgotten the differences either. The Nazis achieved their war production by long years of preliminary preparation and by enslaving first their own people and then those of the occupied lands. The United States have re-oriented their machinery in the briefest time and achieved a war production on an immense scale, to which the British worker is the first to pay tribute—but they did it at a distance of 3,000 miles from the nearest enemy base, and with

Ernest Bevin visits No.
11 Royal Ordnance
Factory, Newport,
Monmouthshire, 1943.

rather more warning than we had. Even our Russian Allies had the advantage
of vast spaces, remote from enemy action, and of inexhaustible raw material
resources available within their own frontiers. No one has followed the
stupendous effort of both our great Allies with more excited admiration than
the British workers—but we persist in believing, with what we hope is legitimate
pride, that our own effort, in very different circumstances, will be counted by
historians as one of the greatest achievements of this war.

. . . . .

THE BATTLE ON THE ATLANTIC

Rear-Admiral R. K. Dickson, Chief of Naval Information,
Home Service, July 1945

One night in January, 1942, I stood with Admiral Sir Percy Noble in the War
Room at Liverpool. We were looking at the great map which showed the
situation in the Atlantic as it changed hour by hour—on and above the surface
of the sea. The German armies had conquered Europe and were in the heart
of Russia. The City of London and Liverpool itself had been partly destroyed,
we had suffered sudden disaster in the East, and in the year just ended we

had lost three million tons of British merchant shipping. Before that we'd lost another three millions and in the year then beginning we were destined to lose far more. I said to Admiral Noble: "When you wake up in the morning and remember once again that you're Commander-in-Chief, Western Approaches, don't you sometimes wonder where you will find strength to carry on through another day?" And he answered: "Yes, I do. I just don't know how we're going to win this war, *but I'm absolutely certain that we shall*! " It was the loyalty of thousands, whose names we shall never know, which pulled us through the longest and most crucial battle of the war. But their loyalty would have availed them nothing, had not this blind faith in the destiny of our country and Empire inspired our leaders at times when they had little else in which to put their trust.

Hitler began where the Kaiser left off, with an all-out attack on the British Merchant Navy. Once in the last war the submarines brought us within six weeks of starvation and total defeat, but we had forgotten that. The Germans hadn't. They knew that Britain had far fewer merchant ships than in 1914, and they knew she would still have to depend on merchant ships alone to carry her armies overseas, and to bring in the food and raw materials she needed from all over the world. Besides, control of the air would be a vital factor in every phase of *this* war, and the Germans knew that without seaborne petrol no aircraft could leave the ground in Great Britain.

The Battle of the Atlantic is a vague term, meaning the defence of Allied merchant ships against all forms of German attack everywhere. This world-wide story was an Anglo-American story. But the battle in distant seas never compared in scale and ferocity with the long fight against the weather and the U-boats on the ocean routes from the United Kingdom to America and Gibraltar, and on the Arctic passage to North Russia. I can't define what was at stake except by saving it was fundamental. As this battle ebbed and flowed it governed what we could do with our ration books. But it did far more than that. The parts which could be played by all arms of all the Services of all the Allies, operating from this island springboard of the United Nations, were dictated by the fortunes of the war at sea. This the Germans foresaw; and so, even before Poland was invaded, Hitler sent out his submarines to wait. On the first day of the war the *Athenia* was sunk in the Atlantic, and on the last day ships were sunk in the Firth of Forth. In all those years the battle never stopped for one day or one night.

We began by directing it from Plymouth, where so many of our naval enterprises have started. But soon the fall of France left the Channel untenable and the magnetic mines closed our East Coast ports to deep draught ships. We were faced with the sheer necessity of supplying this country through the bottlenecks of the Clyde, the Mersey and the Bristol Channel. Naval command had to be transferred to Liverpool. Maintenance and training bases for large fleets of destroyers, frigates, corvettes and other small ships had to be created from nothing at places like Londonderry and Tobermory; and the RAF had to build a chain of airfields stretching in a great semi-circle from Iceland to Cornwall. So it was that the Western Approaches Command was established in February, 1941. Two months later the Government placed Coastal Command of the RAF under Admiralty operational control; and then for four long years our surface and air forces trained and fought together to protect our convoys at sea.

Admiral Noble was transferred to Washington in November, 1942, after two years in command; and that famous submarine officer, Admiral Sir Max Horton, relieved him in the Western Approaches. He inherited an organisation which had discovered how to do the job but lacked the means. Many of his escort vessels had been withdrawn for the North African operation, and he was short of long-range aircraft. But it was now clear to everyone that the prospect of invading the Continent would depend absolutely on the outcome of the Battle of the Atlantic, and so the Combined Chiefs of Staff directed that it should have over-riding priority. It reached its great climax in March, 1943, when the enemy had 100 U-boats at sea, and when they sank more than half a million tons of Allied shipping. Next month the sinkings were halved, then they became less and less. We had won, though we didn't know it for certain till months afterwards. But, as after Trafalgar, our armies were now able to pass to the final offensive. Two more years of bitter fighting still lay before us in the Atlantic; but the surety of our sea control was never again in doubt, even when the appearance of the Schnorkel transformed the whole science of submarine warfare and caused the battle to flare up again near the English coast. It was then too late for the Germans to recover. Besides, their U-boat crews could no longer take it. Their spirit had failed them.

Now here's something I want to say, because I feel it very much. *Everyone* in Britain played some part in the sea affair, because everyone is born within eighty miles of the sea and is therefore sea-minded, although perhaps unconsciously. That's why the Salvage Campaign worked—when the need for saving shipping space was explained to the people. That's why "Dig for Victory" worked. That's why public opinion always frowned on the petrol black market. And so on. All this may have been instinctive, but it was there as it could never have been in a continental country.

But, of course, the brunt of the battle fell on the Navy and Air Force. Behind the distant shield of the Home Fleet the little ships had the duties of close escort round the convoys and of hunting the U-boats to death with depth charges wherever they could he found. The aircraft were killers, too—indeed a high proportion of the total bag of U-boats fell to shore-based aircraft alone. But the job which only aircraft could do was to range far ahead of the convoys, keeping the submarines down and therefore blind by day, and so lessening their chances of being in the right position to attack the merchant ships at night. All the British Dominions and all our Allies had their share in this world-wide undertaking; especially the Canadians, who eventually took over not only the bulk of the close escort work in the whole Atlantic but shared full control with the Americans in the Western Ocean.

Now if I try, however feebly, to speak of the bravery and endurance of the men who fought this battle, I do it as a sailor and I speak of sailors. But one doesn't need to have spent one's life at sea, as I have, to realise that much of what I say applies also to those who fly over the sea.

It's a wonderful thing that six out of every eight of the naval officers and men who fought this greatest of our sea battles were amateur seamen; for that is what they were, though in six years they made themselves equal to the very best of the regular Navy, both on the Lower Deck and on the bridges of small ships.

What makes professional seamen a race apart is the fact that their whole lives are spent in dealing with an element which is stronger, more capricious and more sinister than anything known to landsmen, and which is more destructive than any instrument of war. Do you remember this, which a sailor wrote once of the sea: "Its most amazing wonder is its unfathomable cruelty"? That's Joseph Conrad, and no Act of Parliament can guard a seaman from that cruelty.

It's not without reason, taking peace and war together, that we place the enemy last when we pray for protection against "rock and tempest, fire and foe." We lost more merchant ships in this war by the hazards of the sea than by aircraft attack or any other cause except the U-boat. Experience of the sea teaches those who live by it to take its ways for granted, but these men came to us with no experience and at once they were thrown into work which might have daunted the oldest sailor.

Many of them hated it. Many of them in their hearts were often terribly frightened by it, and no wonder. It is a terrible thing to be lying torpedoed in mid-Atlantic, waiting for the next and final torpedo. But it's hardly less of a trial to find yourself in a small corvette, starting off from the bleak north-west corner of Ireland in a westerly gale, when "the deep moans round with many voices." And it takes a seaman to handle naval aircraft on the reeling deck of an escort carrier, in the Arctic darkness and in the sort of cold which people in England have never felt. I tell you that when a man has spent a few years at sea, he finds that Hitler and all his works—and much else—fall into their proper place in the scheme of things in a way they never do on shore. We asked much of our young seamen; and each year, when autumn turned again to winter, it would not have been surprising if their soul had melted away because of the trouble. But it never did. The Navy's a tough Service. It has to be, and young men are not encouraged to unburden their souls. But let me say here in words of one syllable that they won through by sheer guts. They are still fighting on the other side of the world, but the Battle of the Atlantic is over. The supreme responsibility for it, to the people of the British Empire, was carried under the Government by the Board of Admiralty, for the Royal Navy remains the senior partner in the whole majestic exercise of modern Sea Power. But it was not won by the Navy, or the Air Force, or the Merchant Service, or the dockyards alone. It was won, as the withdrawal from Dunkirk was won, by the native genius of a seafaring people, backed first by the goodwill and then by the vast resources and fighting spirit of the United States.

Only those who have been concerned in the higher direction of the war can really understand what was involved in this great tale of the sea. But there's one thing at least which every housewife will remember—and it's this—that alone among the warring rations of Europe, this country was never rationed for bread. The debt which is owed to the men—and the women—who served in the Battle of the Atlantic is immeasurable.

. . . . .

The end of the war in Europe was marked by two great speeches to the people of Britain: His Majesty's broadcast on 8 May and Winston Churchill's survey of the war.

THE KING'S BROADCAST TO HIS PEOPLE

Home Service, May 8 1945

Today we give thanks to God for a great deliverance.

Speaking from our Empire's oldest capital city, war-battered but never for one moment daunted or dismayed—speaking from London. I ask you to join with me in that act of thanksgiving.

Germany, the enemy who drove all Europe into war, has been finally overcome. In the Far East we have yet to deal with the Japanese, a determined and cruel foe. To this we shall turn with the utmost resolve and with all our resources.

But at this hour, when the dreadful shadow of war has passed from our hearths and homes in these islands, we may at last make one pause for thanksgiving, and then turn our thoughts to the tasks all over the world which peace in Europe brings with it.

Let us remember those who will not come back; their constancy and courage in battle, their sacrifice and endurance in the face of a merciless enemy: let us remember the men in all the Services, and the women in all the Services, who have laid down their lives. We have come to the end of our tribulation, and they are not with us at the moment of our rejoicing.

Then let us salute in proud gratitude the great host of the living who have brought us to victory. I cannot praise them to the measure of each one's service, for in a total war the efforts of all rise to the same noble height and all are devoted to the common purpose. Armed or unarmed, men and women, you have fought and striven and endured to your utmost. No one knows that better than I do; and as your King I thank with a full heart those who bore arms so valiantly on land and sea, or in the air; and all civilians who, shouldering their many burdens, have carried them unflinchingly and without complaint.

With those memories in our minds, let us think what it was that has upheld us through nearly six years of suffering and peril. The knowledge that everything was at stake—our freedom, our independence, our very existence as a people—but the knowledge also that in defending ourselves we were defending the liberties of the whole world: that our cause was the cause not of this nation only, not of this Empire and Commonwealth only, but of every land where freedom is cherished and law and liberty go in hand.

In the darkest hours we knew that the enslaved and isolated peoples of Europe looked to us: their hopes were our hopes; their confidence confirmed our faith. We knew that if we failed the last remaining barrier against a world-wide tyranny would have fallen in ruins. But we did not fail. We kept faith with ourselves and with one another: we kept faith and unity with our great Allies.

That faith, that unity, have carried us to victory through dangers which at times seemed overwhelming.

So let us resolve to bring to the tasks which lie ahead the same high confidence in our mission. Much hard work awaits us, both in the restoration of our country after the ravages of war and in helping to restore peace and sanity to a shattered world.

This comes upon us at a time when we have all given of our best. For five long years and more, heart and brain, nerve and muscle have been directed upon the overthrow of Nazi tyranny. Now we turn, fortified by success, to deal with our last remaining foe. The Queen and I know the ordeals which you have endured throughout the Commonwealth and Empire. We are proud to have shared some of those ordeals with you, and we know also that together we shall face the future with stern resolve and prove that our reserves of will-power and vitality are inexhaustible.

There is great comfort in the thought that the years of darkness and danger in which the children of our country have grown up are over—and, please God, for ever. We shall have failed, and the blood of our dearest will have flowed in vain, if the victory which they died to win does not lead to a lasting peace, founded on justice and goodwill. To that, then, let us turn our thoughts, on this day of just triumph and proud sorrow; and then take up our work again, resolved as a people to do nothing unworthy of those who died for us, and to make the world such a world as they would have desired for their children and for ours.

This is the task to which now honour binds us. In the hour of danger we humbly committed our cause into the Hand of God, and he has been our Strength and Shield. Let us thank Him for his Mercies, and in this hour of

King George VI with
Winston Churchill.

victory commit ourselves and our new task to the guidance of that same strong
Hand.

WINSTON CHURCHILL'S SURVEY OF THE WAR

Home Service, May 13 1945

It was five years ago on Thursday last that His Majesty the King commissioned
me to form a National Government of all parties to carry on our affairs. Five
years is a long time in human life, especially when there is no remission for good
conduct. However, this National Government was sustained by Parliament and
by the entire British nation at home and by all our fighting men abroad, and
by the unswerving co-operation of the Dominions far across the oceans and of
our Empire in every quarter of the globe. After various episodes had occurred it
became clear last week that so far things have worked out pretty well and that
the British Commonwealth and Empire stands more united and more effectively
powerful than at any time in its long romantic history. Certainly we are—this is
what may well, I think, be admitted by any fair-minded person—in a far better

state to cope with the problems and perils of the future than we were five years ago.

For a while our prime enemy, our mighty enemy, Germany, overran almost all Europe. France, who bore such a frightful strain in the last great war, was beaten to the ground and took some time to recover. The Low Countries, fighting to the best of their strength, were subjugated. Norway was overrun. Mussolini's Italy stabbed us in the back when we were, as he thought, at our last gasp. But for ourselves—our lot, I mean—the British Commonwealth and Empire, we were absolutely alone.

In July, August and September, 1940, forty or fifty squadrons of British fighter aircraft in the Battle of Britain broke the teeth of the German air fleet at odds of seven or eight to one. May I repeat again the words I used at that momentous hour: "Never in the field of human conflict was so much owed by so many to so few." The name of Air Chief Marshal Lord Dowding will always be linked with this splendid event. But conjoined with the Royal Air Force Jay the Royal Navy, ever ready to tear to pieces the barges, gathered from the canals of Holland and Belgium, in which a German invading army could alone have been transported. I was never one to believe that the invasion of Britain, with the tackle that the enemy had at that time, was a very easy task to accomplish. With the autumn storms, the immediate danger of invasion in 1940 passed.

Then began the blitz, when Hitler said he would "rub out our cities." That's what he said, "rub out our cities." This blitz was borne without a word of complaint or the slightest sign of flinching, while a very large number of people—honour to them all—proved that London could "take it," and so could our other ravaged centres. But the dawn of 1941 revealed us still in jeopardy. The hostile aircraft could fly across the approaches to our island, where forty-six millions of people had to import their daily bread and all the materials they needed for peace or war: these hostile aircraft could fly across the approaches from Brest to Norway in a single flight and back again. They could observe all the movements of our shipping in and out of the Clyde and Mersey and could direct upon our convoys the large and increasing numbers of U-boats with which the enemy bespattered the Atlantic—the survivors or successors of which U-boats are now being collected in British harbours.

The sense of envelopment, which might at any moment turn to strangulation, lay heavy upon us. We had only the north-western approach between Ulster and Scotland through which to bring in the means of life and to send out the forces of war. Owing to the action of Mr de Valera, so much at variance with the temper and instinct of thousands of Southern Irishmen who hastened to the battle-front to prove their ancient valour, the approaches which the Southern Irish ports and airfields could so easily have guarded were closed by the hostile aircraft and U-boats. This was indeed a deadly moment in our life, and if it had not been for the loyalty and friendship of Northern Ireland we should have been forced to come to close quarters with Mr de Valera or perish for ever from

Winston Churchill with
his 'V for Victory' sign.

the earth. However, with a restraint and poise to which, I say, history will find
few parallels, His Majesty's Government never laid a violent hand upon them,
though at times it would have been quite easy and quite natural, and we left the
de Valera Government to frolic with the Germans and later with the Japanese
representatives to their heart's content.

When I think of these days I think also of other episodes and personalities. I
think of Lieutenant-Commander Esmond, V.C., of Lance-Corporal Kenneally,
V.C., and Captain Fegen, V.C., and other Irish heroes that I could easily recite,
and then I must confess that bitterness by Britain against the Irish race dies
in my heart. I can only pray that in years which I shall not see, the shame will
be forgotten and the glories will endure, and that the peoples of the British
Isles as of the British Commonwealth of Nations will walk together in mutual
comprehension and forgiveness.

My friends, when our minds turn to the north-western approaches, we will
not forget the devotion of our merchant seamen, and our minesweepers out
every night, and so rarely mentioned in the headlines. Nor will we forget the
vast, inventive, adaptive, all-embracing and, in the end, all-controlling power

of the Royal Navy, with its ever more potent new ally, the air. These have kept the life-line open. We were able to breathe; we were able to live; we were able to strike. Dire deeds we had to do. We had to destroy or capture the French Fleet which, had it ever passed undamaged into German hands would, together with the Italian Fleet, have perhaps enabled the German Navy to face us on the high seas. This we did. We had to make the dispatch to General Wavell all round the Cape at our darkest hour, of the tanks—practically all we had in the island—and this enabled us as far back as November, 1940, to defend Egypt against invasion and hurl back with the lass of a quarter of a million captives and a heavy slaughter the Italian armies, at whose tail Mussolini had already planned to ride into Cairo or Alexandria.

Great anxiety was felt by President Roosevelt, and indeed by thinking men throughout the United States, about what would happen to us in the early part of 1941. The President felt to the depths of his being that the destruction of Britain would not only he an event fearful in itself, but that it would expose to mortal danger the vast and as yet largely unarmed potentialities and the future destiny of the United States. He feared greatly that we should be invaded in that spring of 1941, and no doubt he had behind him military advice as good as any that is known in the world, and he sent his recent Presidential opponent, the late Mr Wendell Willkie, to me with a letter in which he had written in his own hand the famous lines of Longfellow, which I quoted in the House of Commons the other day:

> Sail on, O Ship of State!
> Sail on, O Union, strong and great!
> Humanity, with all its fears,
> With all the hopes of future years.
> Is hanging breathless on thy fate!

We were, however, in a fairly tough condition by the early months of 1941, and felt very much better about ourselves than in those months immediately after the collapse of France. Our Dunkirk army and field force troops in Britain, almost a million strong, were nearly all equipped or re-equipped. We had ferried over the Atlantic a million rifles and a thousand cannon from the United States, with all their ammunition, since the previous June. In our munition works, which were becoming very powerful, men and women had worked at their machines till they dropped senseless from fatigue. Nearly one million of men, growing to two millions at the peak, although working all day, had been formed into the Home Guard. They were armed at least with rifles and armed also with the spirit "Conquer or die."

Later in 1941, when we were still alone, we sacrificed unwillingly, to some extent unwittingly, our conquests of the winter in Cyrenaica and Libya in order to stand by Greece; and Greece will never forget how much we gave, albeit unavailingly, of the little we had. We did this for honour. We repressed the German-instigated rising in Iraq. We defended Palestine. With the assistance of General De Gaulle's indomitable Free French we cleared Syria and the Lebanon of Vichyites and of German aviators and intriguers. And then in June, 1941, another tremendous world event occurred.

You have no doubt noticed in your reading of British history—and I hope you will take pains to read it, for it is only from the past that one can judge the future, and it is only from reading the story of the British nation, of the British Empire, that you can feel a well-grounded sense of pride to dwell in these islands—you have sometimes noticed in your reading of British history that we have had to hold out from time to time all alone, or to be the mainspring of coalitions, against a Continental tyrant or dictator, and we have had to hold out for quite a long time: against the Spanish Armada, against the might of Louis XIV, when we led Europe for nearly twenty-five years under William III and Marlborough, and a hundred and fifty years ago, when Nelson, Pitt and Wellington broke Napoleon, not without assistance from the heroic Russians of 1812. In all these world wars our island kept the lead of Europe or else held out alone.

And if you hold out alone long enough there always comes a time when the tyrant makes some ghastly mistake which alters the whole balance of the struggle. On 22 June 1942, Hitler, master as he thought himself of all Europe—nay, indeed, soon to be master of the world, so he thought—treacherously, without warning, without the slightest provocation, hurled himself on Russia and came face to face with Marshal Stalin and the numberless millions of the Russian people. And then at the end of the year Japan struck a felon blow at the United States at Pearl Harbour, and at the same time attacked us in Malaya and Singapore. Thereupon Hitler and Mussolini declared war on the Republic of the United States.

Years have passed since then. Indeed every year seems to me almost a decade. But never since the United States entered the war have I had the slightest doubt but that we should be saved and that we only had to do our duty in order to win. We have played our part in all this process by which the evildoers have been overthrown, and I hope I do not speak vain or boastful words, but from Alamein in October, 1942, through the Anglo-American invasion of North Africa, of Sicily, of Italy, with the capture of Rome, we marched many miles and never knew defeat. And then last year, after two years' patient preparation and marvellous devices of amphibious warfare—and mark you our scientists are not surpassed in any nation in the world, especially when their thought is applied to naval matters—last year on June 6 we seized a carefully selected little toe of German—occupied France and poured millions in from this island and from across the Atlantic, until the Seine, the Somme and the Rhine all fell behind the advancing Anglo-American spearheads. France was liberated. She produced a fine army of gallant men to aid her own liberation. Germany lay open.

Now from the other side the mighty military achievements of the Russian people, always holding many more German troops on their front than we could do, rolled forward to meet us in the heart and centre of Germany. At the same time, in Italy, Field-Marshal Alexander's army of so many nations, the largest part of which was British or British Empire, struck their final blow and compelled more than a million troops to surrender. This Fifteenth Army Group, as we call it, British and American joined together in almost equal numbers, are now deep in Austria, joining their right hand with the Russians and their left with the United States armies of General Eisenhower's command. It happened, as you may remember—but memories are short—that in the space of three days we received the news of the unlamented departures of Mussolini and Hitler, and in three days also surrenders were made to Field-Marshal Alexander and Field-Marshal Montgomery of over two million five hundred thousand soldiers of this terrible warlike German army.

I shall make it clear at this moment that we have never failed to recognise the immense superiority of the power used by the United States in the rescue of France and the defeat of Germany. For our part, British and Canadians, we had had about one-third as many men over there as the Americans, but we have taken our full share of the fighting, as the scale of our losses shows. Our Navy has borne incomparably the heaviest burden in the Atlantic Ocean, in the narrow seas and the Arctic convoys to Russia, while the United States Navy has had to use its immense strength mainly against Japan. We made a fair division of the labour, and we can each report that our work is either done or going to be done. It is right and natural that we should extol the virtues and glorious services of our own most famous commanders, Alexander and Montgomery, neither of whom was ever defeated since they began together at Alamein. Both of them have conducted in Africa, in Italy, in Normandy and in Germany, battles of the first magnitude and of decisive consequence. At the same time we know how great is our debt to the combining and unifying commands and high strategic direction of General Eisenhower.

And here is the moment when I must pay my personal tribute to the British Chiefs of Staff with whom I worked in the closest intimacy throughout these heavy, stormy years. There have been very few changes in this small, powerful and capable body of men who, sinking all Service differences and judging the problems of the war as a whole, have worked together in perfect harmony with each other. In Field-Marshal Brooke, in Admiral Pound, succeeded after his death by Admiral Andrew Cunningham, and in Marshal of the Air, Portal, a team was formed who deserved the highest honour in the direction of the whole British war strategy and its relations with that of our Allies.

It may well be said that our strategy was conducted so that the best combinations, the closest concert, were imparted into the operations by the combined staffs of Britain and the United States, with whom, from Teheran onwards, the war leaders of Russia were joined. And it may also be said that never have the forces of two nations fought side by side and intermingled in the lines of battle with so much unity, comradeship and brotherhood as in the great Anglo-American armies. Some people say: Well, what would you expect, if both nations speak the same language, have the same laws. have a great part of their history in common, and have very much the same outlook upon life with all its hope and glory. Isn't it just the sort of thing that would happen? And others may say: It would be an ill day for all the world and for the pair of them if they did not go on working together and marching together and sailing together and flying together, whenever something has to be done for the sake of freedom and fair play all over the world. That is the great hope of the future.

There was one final danger from which the collapse of Germany has saved us. In London and the south-eastern counties we have suffered for a year from various forms of flying bombs—perhaps you have heard about this—and rockets, and our Air Force and our ack-ack batteries have done wonders against them. In particular the Air Force, turned on in good time on what then seemed very slight and doubtful evidence, hampered and vastly delayed all German preparations. But it was only when our armies cleaned up the coast and overran all the points of discharge, and when the Americans captured vast stores of rockets of all kinds near Leipzig, which added to our information we had only the other day, and when all the preparations being made on the coasts of France and Holland could be examined in detail, in scientific detail, that we knew how grave had been the peril, not only from rockets and flying-bombs but from multiple long-range artillery which was being prepared against London. Only just in time did the Allied armies blast the viper in his nest. Otherwise the autumn of 1944, to say nothing of 1945, night well have seen London as shattered as Berlin.

For the same period the Germans had prepared a new U-boat fleet and novel tactics which, though we should have eventually destroyed them, might well have carried anti-U-boat warfare back to the high peak days of 1942. Therefore we must rejoice and give thanks not only for our preservation when we were all alone but for our timely deliverance from new suffering, new perils not easily to be measured.

I wish I could tell you tonight that all our toils and troubles were over. Then indeed I could end my five years' service happily, and if you thought that you had had enough of me and that I ought to be put out to grass, I tell you I would take it with the best of grace. But, on the contrary, I must warn you, as I did when I began this five years' task—and no one knew then that it would last so long—that there is still a lot to do, and that you must be prepared for further efforts of mind and body and further sacrifices to great causes if you are not to fall back into the rut of inertia, the confusion of aim, and the craven fear of being great. You must not weaken in any way in your alert and vigilant frame of mind. Though holiday rejoicing is necessary to the human spirit, yet it must add to the strength and resilience with which every man and woman turns again to the work they have to do, and also to the outlook and watch they have to keep on public affairs.

On the Continent of Europe we have yet to make sure that the simple and honourable purposes for which we entered the war are not brushed aside or overlooked in the months following our success, and that the words "freedom," "democracy," and "liberation" are not distorted from their true meaning as we have understood them. There would be little use in punishing the Hitlerites for their crimes if law and justice did not rule, and if totalitarian or police governments were to take the place of the German invaders. We seek nothing for ourselves. But we must make sure that those causes which we fought for find recognition at the peace table in facts as well as words, and above all we must labour that the world organisation which the United Nations are creating at San Francisco does not become an idle name, does not become a shield for the strong and a mockery for the weak. It is the victors who must search their hearts in their glowing hours and be worthy by their nobility of the immense forces that they wield.

We must never forget that beyond all lurks Japan, harassed and failing but still a people of a hundred millions, for whose warriors death has few terrors. I cannot tell you tonight how much time or what exertions will be required to compel the Japanese to make amends for their odious treachery and cruelty. We—like China, so long undaunted—have received horrible injuries from them ourselves, and we are bound by the ties of honour and fraternal loyalty to the United States to fight this great war at the other end of the world at their side without flagging or failing. We must remember that Australia and New Zealand and Canada were and are all directly menaced by this evil Power. They came to our aid in our dark times, and we must not leave unfinished any task which concerns their safety and their future. I told you hard things at the beginning of these last five years; you did not shrink, and I should be unworthy of your confidence and generosity if I did not still cry: Forward, unflinching, unswerving, indomitable, till the whole task is done and the whole world is safe and clean.

. . . . .

On 15 June the long Parliament was dissolved and on 5 July the General Election took place. At the middle of the month, Churchill, Truman and Stalin met for conference at Potsdam. The result of the election was announced on 26 July and was a great victory for the Labour Party. The Labour Party got 12 million votes and the Conservatives about 9 million, the Liberals 2 million and the Communists somewhat over 100,000 votes. Labour got 393 candidates in, the Conservatives 198.

The new Premier, Clement Attlee, and the new Foreign Secretary, Ernest Bevin, replaced Churchill and Eden at the Potsdam Conference.

Sir Alexander Cadogan (left), Group Captain D. M. Somerville (centre), and Ernest Bevin, Minister for Foreign Affairs, talk together after arriving at Gatow Airport in Berlin, Germany to attend the Potsdam Conference, 28 July 1945.

The war which from the very beginning had been one long series of surprises held one more terrible surprise.

On 6 August the first atomic bomb was dropped on Hiroshima in Japan. This terrible new weapon, whose secret—as Churchill said—"had long been mercifully withheld from mankind," put an end to the Second World War, but remains a warning that a new war would mean the destruction of civilisation.

A British scientist who had taken part in the production of the atomic bomb told, in the BBC, how the bomb was tried out before it was used in the war against Japan.

TRYING OUT THE ATOMIC BOMB

Sir Geoffrey Taylor, Home Service, August, 1945

I was one of the group of British scientific men who worked at Los Alamos in New Mexico, where most of the recent experimental work on atomic bombs was carried out, and I saw the first bomb explode. Before I tell you about this,

I ought to say that I have witnessed many ordinary bomb trials. In such trials the kind of result to be expected is always known beforehand, and the trial is designed to find out just how much damage the bomb will do. The first atomic bomb test had to be approached with a totally different outlook because it was not possible to make any previous experiment on a smaller scale. None of us knew whether we were going to witness an epoch-making experiment or a complete failure. The physicists had predicted that a self-propagating reaction involving neutrons was possible and that this would lead to an explosion. The mathematicians had calculated what mechanical results were to be expected. Engineers and physicists had set up an apparatus rather like that used in testing ordinary bombs, to measure the efficiency of the explosion. But no one knew whether this apparatus would be needed, simply because nobody knew whether the bomb would go off.

Our uncertainty was reflected in the bets which were made at Los Alamos on the amount of energy to be released. These ranged from zero to the equivalent of eighty thousand tons of T.N.T. Those of us who were to witness the test assembled during a late afternoon in July at Los Alamos for the two-hundred-and-thirty-mile drive to the uninhabited and desolate region where the test was to be made. We arrived about three o'clock in the morning at a spot twenty miles from the hundred-foot tower on which the bomb was mounted. Here we were met by a car containing a radio receiver. Round this we assembled, listening for the signal from the firing point which would tell us when to expect the explosion. We were provided with a strip of very dark glass to protect our eyes. This glass is so dark that at mid-day it makes the sun look like a little undeveloped dull green potato. Through this glass I was unable to see the light which was set on the tower to show us where to look. Remember, it was still dark. I therefore fixed my eyes on this light ten seconds before the explosion was due to occur. Then I raised the dark glass to my eyes two seconds before, keeping them fixed on the spot where I had last seen the light. At exactly the expected moment, I saw, through the dark glass, a brilliant ball of fire which was far brighter than the sun. In a second or two it died down to a brightness which seemed to be about that of the sun, so, realising that it must be lighting up the countryside, I looked behind me and saw the scrub-covered hills, twenty-two miles from the bomb, lighted up as though by a midday sun. Then I turned round and looked directly at the ball of fire. I saw it expand slowly, and begin to rise, growing fainter as it rose. Later it developed into a huge mushroom-shaped cloud, and soon reached a height of forty-thousand feet.

Though the sequence of events was exactly what we had calculated beforehand in our more optimistic moments, the whole effect was so staggering that I found it difficult to believe my eyes, and judging by the strong ejaculations from my fellow-watchers other people felt the same reaction. So far we had heard no noise. Sound takes over one and a half minutes to travel twenty miles, so we next had to prepare to receive the blast wave. We had been advised to lie on the ground to receive the shock of the wave, but few people did so, perhaps owing to the fact that it was still dark, and rattle-snakes and tarantulas were fairly common in the district. When it came, it was not very loud, and sounded like the crack of a shell passing overhead rather than a distant high-explosive bomb. Rumbling followed and continued for some time. On returning to Los Alamos, I found that one of my friends there had been lying awake in bed and had seen the light of the explosion reflected on the ceiling of his bedroom, though the source of it was over a hundred and sixty miles away in a straight line.

. . . . .

On 8 August Russia declared war on Japan, and Soviet forces broke over a broad front into Manchuria, where thirteen years ago Japan had started her war of aggression.

On 9 August the second atomic bomb was dropped over Nagasaki.

The second atomic bomb, Nagasaki, 9 August 1945.

Finally in the midnight bulletin of the BBC on 14 August England's new Premier announced the unconditional surrender of Japan.

It was followed on Victory Day, 15 August 1945, by the King's second victory speech.

MR. ATTLEE'S ANNOUNCEMENT ON JAPAN'S SURRENDER

Home Service, Midnight, August 14 1945

Japan has today surrendered. The last of our enemies is laid low. Here is the text of the Japanese reply to the Allied Command: "With reference to the announcement of August 10 regarding the acceptance of the provisions of the Potsdam Declaration and the reply of the Governments of the United States, Great Britain, the Soviet Union and China sent by Secretary of State Byrnes on the date of August 11, the Japanese Government has the honour to reply to the Governments of the four Powers as follows:

1. His Majesty the Emperor has issued an Imperial rescript regarding Japan's acceptance of the provisions of the Potsdam Declaration.
2. His Majesty the Emperor is prepared to authorise and insure the signature by his Government and the Imperial H.Q. of the necessary terms for carrying out the provisions of the Potsdam Declaration.
3. His Majesty is also prepared to issue his command to all military, naval and air authorities of Japan and all the forces under their control wherever located to cease active resistance and to surrender arms, and to issue such other orders as may be required by the Supreme Commander of the Allied Forces for the execution of the above-mentioned terms.—Signed, Togo.

Let us recall, that on December 7, 1941, Japan, whose onslaught China had already resisted for over four years, fell upon the United States, who were then not at war, and upon ourselves, who were sore pressed in our death struggles with Germany and Italy, taking full advantage of surprise and treachery.

The Japanese forces quickly overran the territories of ourselves and our Allies in the Far East, and at one time it appeared as though these invaders would reach the mainland of Australia and advance into India. But the tide turned.

With ever-increasing speed the mighty forces of the United States and the British Commonwealth and Empire and other Allies were brought to bear.

Their resistance has now everywhere been broken.

At this time we should pay tribute to the men from this country, from the Dominions, from India and the Colonies, to our Fleets, Armies and Air Forces that have fought so well in the campaign against Japan.

Clement Atlee as Prime Minister.

Our gratitude goes out to all our splendid Allies; above all to the United States, without whose prodigious efforts this war in the East would still have many years to run.

We also think especially at this time of the prisoners in Japanese hands, of our friends in the Dominions, Australia and New Zealand, in India and Burma, and in those Colonial territories upon whom the brunt of the Japanese attack fell.

We rejoice that these territories will soon be purged of the Japanese invader.

Here at home you have earned rest from the unceasing efforts you have all borne without complaint through so many dark years.

When we return to work on Friday morning we must turn again to the great tasks before us. But for the moment let all who can relax and enjoy themselves in the knowledge of work well done.

Peace has once again come to the world. Let us thank God for this great deliverance and His mercy. Long live the King.

. . . . .

THE KING'S VICTORY SPEECH

BBC, August 15 1945

Three months have passed since I asked you to join with me in an act of thanksgiving for the defeat of Germany.

We then rejoiced that peace had returned to Europe, but we knew that a strong and relentless enemy still remained to be conquered in Asia. None could then tell how long or how heavy would prove the struggle that still awaited us.

Japan has surrendered, so let us join in thanking Almighty God that war has ended throughout the world, and that in every country men may now turn their industry, skill and science to repairing its frightful devastation and to building prosperity and happiness.

Our sense of deliverance is overpowering, and with it all, we have a right to feel that we have done our duty.

I ask you again at this solemn hour to remember all who have laid down their lives, and all who have endured the loss of those they love. Remember, too, the sufferings of those who fell into the hands of the enemy, whether as prisoners of war or because their homes had been overrun. They have been in our thoughts all through these dark years, and let us pray that one result of the defeat of Japan may be many happy reunions of those who have been long separated from each other.

The campaign in the Far East will be famous in history for many reasons. There is one feature of them which is a special source of pride to me, and also to you, the citizens of our British Commonwealth and Empire to whom I speak. In those campaigns there have fought, side by side with our allies, representatives of almost every unit in our great community—men from the Old Country, men from the Dominions, from India and the Colonies. They fought in brotherhood; through their courage and endurance they conquered. To all of them and to the women who shared with them the hardships and dangers of war I send my proud and grateful thanks.

The war is over. You know, I think, that those four words have for the Queen and myself the same significance, simple yet immense, that they have for you. Our hearts are full to overflowing, as are your own. Yet there is not one of us who has experienced this terrible war who does not realise that we shall feel its inevitable consequences long after we have all forgotten our rejoicings of today.

But that relief from past dangers must not blind us to the demands of the future. The British people here at home have added lustre to the true fame of our Islands, and we stand today with our whole Empire in the forefront of the victorious United Nations. Great, therefore, is our responsibility to make sure by the actions of every man and every woman here and throughout the Empire and Commonwealth that the peace gained amid measureless trials and suffering shall not be cast away.

In many anxious times in our long history the unconquerable spirit of our peoples has served us well, bringing us to safety out of great peril. Yet I doubt if anything in all that has gone before has matched the enduring courage and the quiet determination which you have shown during these last six years. It is of this unconquerable spirit that I would speak to you tonight. For great as are the deeds that you have done, there must be no falling off from this high endeavour. We have spent freely of all that we had: now we shall have to work hard to restore what has been lost, and to establish peace on the unshakable foundations, not alone of material strength, but also of moral authority. Then, indeed, the curse of war may be lifted from the world, and States and peoples, great and small, may dwell together through long periods of tranquility in brighter and better days than we ourselves have known.

The world has come to look for certain things, for certain qualities from the peoples of the Commonwealth and Empire. We have our part to play in restoring the shattered fabric of civilisation. It is a proud and difficult part, and if you carry on in the years to come as you have done so splendidly in the war, you and your children can look forward to the future, not with fear, but with high hopes, of a surer happiness for all. It is to this great task that I call you now, and I know that I shall not call in vain.

In the meantime, from the bottom of my heart, I thank my peoples for all they have done, not only for themselves but for mankind.

THE END

Epilogue

As early as the autumn of 1939 it struck me, when listening to the BBC, how much of actual historical value was to be found in the great broadcast talks. From this early stage and for nearly six years I collected material for this "broadcast history" of the war: speeches by the leading Allied statesmen in Britain during the war, such as Winston Churchill, General de Gaulle and General Smuts; outstanding eye-witness accounts from the battle fronts; the authentic descriptions by RAF pilots in the Battle of Britain; pictures from London under the Blitz; the commando describing the raid on St Nazaire; the saboteurs being trained in Britain before they were dropped over the Continent; the naval officer in Mediterranean waters; a Polish courier telling of the under-ground army in Poland; the soldier in the jungle of Burma; and the parachutist jumping into action on D-Day. But also Russia and America were to be represented together with accounts from all occupied countries of Europe. It became a question of selecting, out of perhaps ten thousand broadcasts, about a hundred so as to cover all the main phases of the war, and to link them together in such a way as to form a continuous narrative.

Many excellent broadcasters and famous commentators are not represented in this book. It is primarily a book of great speeches and first-hand accounts, but not of comment. I have tried to leave out "propaganda," and to retain what is historically true and humanly valuable.

Invariably something very vital is lost by these "talks" being read. But perhaps these pages will help the reader to re-live such great moments as when Churchill spoke on the Invasion of Russia, or when we listened to Guy Byam's breathless description of his parachuting into France on D-Day. I also believe that even to people who did not hear them, some of the descriptions from the greatest years in British history will retain their value.

On leaving Britain to settle in my own country, Denmark, after seven years, I want to express my gratitude to the British Broadcasting Corporation, that great institution where I had the privilege of working during the war.

In all occupied Europe the BBC gave hope during the years of tyranny and strengthened resistance to the common enemy. It also gave expression to that common sense, tolerance and humanity which constitute the only hope of the future of mankind.

HENNING KRABBE
London, July, 1946.